RENAISSA
ARCHITEC TURE

Critics ◆ Patrons ◆ Luxury

For
AMY, age 5
and
FRASER, age 2,

without whose loving attentions
this book would have been
written in half the time
but with half the pleasure.

RENAISSANCE ARCHITECTURE

Critics ◆ Patrons ◆ Luxury

David Thomson

Manchester University Press

Manchester and New York

Distributed exclusively in the Usa and Canada by St. Martin's Press

Copyright © David Thomson 1993

Published by Manchester University Press
Oxford Road, Manchester M13 9PL, UK
and Room 400, 175 Fifth Avenue, New York, NY 10010, USA

Distributed exclusively in the USA and Canada
by St. Martin's Press, Inc., 175 Fifth Avenue, New York,
NY 10010, USA

British Library Cataloguing-in-Publication Data
A catalogue record for this book is available from the British Library

Library of Congress Cataloging-in-Publication Data
Thomson, David. 1951–
Renaissance architecture : patrons, critics, and luxury / by David
Thomson.
p. cm.
ISBN 0–7190–3922–3. — ISBN 0–7190–3963–0 (paper)
1. Architecture, Renaissance. 2. Architects and patrons.
3. Architecture and society — History — 16th century. I. Title.
NA510.T56 1993
724′.12—dc20 93–16088

ISBN 0 7190 3922 3 *hardback*
ISBN 0 7190 3963 0 *paperback*

Typeset in Hong Kong
by Graphicraft Typesetters Ltd
Printed in Great Britain
by Bell & Bain Ltd, Glasgow

CONTENTS

LIST OF FIGURES

Preface

BOWERBIRDS AND ARCHITECTURE

New Guinea and Australia may seem a strange part of the world in which to open a highly selective, critical account of some aspects of Renaissance architecture in Europe. However, there are solid reasons for detecting common behavioural sim-ilarities between antipodean bowerbirds and builders who built to impress in Renaissance Europe. A French writer, François de la Noue, whom we quote at length in our first chapter, makes the avian connexion in the 1580s. An over-ambitious and feather-brained nobleman declares 'This cage is too small for so beautiful a bird [i.e. himself], it must have a more stately one.'

The displays of male bowerbirds are the most elaborate in the avian world, and involve building specialised structures. These serve no function other than as a setting for display, and are entirely distinct from the nest, which is built after mat-ing by the female in a tree where she alone cares for the young ones. The Satin Bowerbird (Ptilonorhynchus) clears a space in his habitat of dense scrub to build a structure of twigs planted in the ground, consisting of two parallel walls some fifteen cm apart, twice as high as wide and ninety or more cm in length. This gallery-like structure with its inward-arching walls is always accurately aligned on a north-south axis. The males of some species paint the twigs of their bower with berry juices, and they fastidiously maintain the freshness of their colour scheme when it comes to be damaged or washed off by rainfall. On the ground around the structure are laid out a variety of carefully chosen brightly coloured objects such as fragments of beetle elytra, shells, feathers, berries of brilliant hues, flowers and young green leaves. The Satin Bowerbird especially favours blue objects. Display bowers are 'luxury architecture' in precisely the terms discussed here.

Gardener Bowerbirds (Amblyornes) build more complex bowers. They select the trunk of a sapling or young tree and pile interlaced branches around it to form a central pillar, onto which are propped long sticks. These bowers might be one metre high and one and a half metres in diameter, and they are found in two basic forms. The Vogelkop Gardener Bowerbird builds a conical theatre, whereas MacGregor's Gardener Bowerbird makes his in a saucer shape. These artfully designed and built bowers with their rich collection of decorative baubles belong to the male in a full proprietorial sense. They are tended daily for at least six months in the year. Courtship and sexual display involves not only parading and ritualised dances and advances; the male can also be seen stopping to pick up decorative objects for the female to admire. Where the bowers are close to human habitation, bits of pottery, glass, paper and such special refinements as ring-pulls from beer cans are incorporated into the stock of the male's wealth of possessions. That an aesthetic process is involved in the choice and arrangement of objects is seen most clearly in the behaviour of the Satin Bowerbird, which has a strong preference for blue objects. These treasured finds are constantly rearranged, when bits are added as well as thrown away.

Bowerbird-like behaviour did exist in Renaissance Europe. The dynamics which propelled princes, grandees or merchants to build in ways calculated to impress and overawe would be called sexual only for the sake of an amusing and diverting argument. Compulsion to display and to compete in properties and possessions is a parallel between wealthy Renaissance builders and Bowerbirds, but there the analogy must stop.

Great builder-kings such as Francis I or Henry VIII expressed their wealth and their artistic and political pretensions in their palaces. Their motives were always complex, constantly changing and never had anything to do with attracting a mate. The archives of the proud Gonzaga of Mantua or of the Este of Ferrara are full of accounts dealing with new spaces, refurbished apartments and sometimes entirely new wings, to be created for the reception of a new bride. Lower down the social scale, there may exist some evidence somewhere in an archive of a young Hanseatic merchant, a Spanish hidalgo or an English squire building a fine house to impress the girl he would wed (or her father), but all the choice examples known show that building took place after marriage.

The role-playing of courtship is a matter for consideration in a much wider study of human luxury, which would include clothes, food and a wide range of ephemeral pleasures. Luxury and architecture as subjects are not traditional bedfellows, but the samples and examples described in these pages are an attempt to revise and dispel some of the values and assumptions about Renaissance architecture which have evolved in the nineteenth and twentieth centuries. Tourism and scholarship are equally to blame for much passive admiration of and interest in buildings whose vulgarity or controversial qualities would impress or offend contemporaries but fails to do so now. This surely must be counted as a loss. I have derived much pleasure from trying, in a small way and in a limited area of research, to redress the balance.

The architecture of the male bowerbird is a necessity, not a luxury. The aberrations and accidents of evolution have made this specialised activity needed. This context of survival does not apply to men. This is how luxury becomes an issue.

The Italian for 'bowerbird' is *Uccello di raso*; the French, *Fauvette des réseaux*; the German, *Laubenvogel*.

The standard work on bowerbirds is A.J. Marshall : *Bower-Birds*, Oxford 1954.

Acknowledgements

Much my greatest debt of gratitude is to long-suffering friends and colleagues who have sacrificed their valuable time to bring order to a disorderly typescript: Rosalys Coope, Adrian Forty, Keith Grasby, Ed Lilley and Nigel Llewellyn. All the surviving awkwardnesses and illiteracies are mine alone.

For criticisms, ideas, references and conversation, I would like to thank David Akerman, Ian Campbell, Richard Cocke, Jean Guillaume, Sandy Heslop, Neil McWilliam, Jean Michel Massing, John and Victoria Mitchell, John and Elizabeth Onians, Cesare Poppi, Alex Potts and Veronica Sekules.

Without the emotional and technological support of my wife, Juliet, these essays could never have become a book.

Katharine Reeve of Manchester University Press has never wavered in her enthusiasm and determination to get this text into print. I am deeply indebted to her.

Wymondham
March 1992

1

LUXURY AND BUILDING: THE LONG LIFE OF AN ISSUE

From Genesis to Perpendicular England

Two social ideals have been at war in Western thought for over two thousand years. They are whether private property on the grand scale is a natural right and trust, or an evil which has evolved as men and women have become more inclined to luxury.[1] If we see every developed society as by definition a hierarchy, an inevitable consequence must be dissension between the 'haves', the 'have-some' and the 'have-nots'. Amongst issues concerning the ethics of wealth luxury becomes a key to thought. It involves justification, legalisation or damnation of a society's material status-seekers. Luxury is desirable, but luxury is always dangerous.

Luxury as a term of commendation is a recent development in Western European languages and cultures. Talk of luxury hotels and travel or 'de luxe' goods of all sorts is simply understood as innocuous terms of inducement. Comfort or superior quality are luxury or luxurious in the modern market. 'Luxury toilet tissues' are so labelled in supermarkets as a feeble blandishment. The alternative is 'budget', 'economy' or even 'recycled', which will appeal according to the shopper's means and sense of self-righteousness. Luxury is a bonus; it is a consequence of prosperity with no tinge of corruption. From the time of ancient Greeks to about the period of the Napoleonic Wars, opposition to luxury was not an attempt to prevent the accumulation of material wealth, but rather to regulate it. The language of controversy has changed, and the closest modern equivalent is political debate about taxation, in which issues of privilege, justice and even justifiable envy are never far from the surface. Luxury has lost its symbolic and ethical bite as social contention.

The simplest and most enduringly popular definition of luxury in the West comes from Genesis II–III. There, luxury is identified as 'anything unneeded'. In the books of Samuel and Kings luxury is presented as the material state which propels the nation of Israel into calamitous decline. The meaning of luxury is amplified to 'anything to which one has no right or title'. With this the claims of the 'haves' are accommodated. As the Old Testament progresses the justification of right to land based on historical, racial and caste precedence becomes fully integrated into an ethos in which inequality is God's design and will. The rift between advocates and critics of luxury in the early Judaeo-Christian world usually centred on the assessment and definition of the 'needed', rather than on an attempt to deny the existence and allure of luxury. Luxury has been a subject for controversy from the earliest civilised times, with political and ethical thinkers drawing and redrawing the bounds of the appropriate social and material benefits due to the rich and to others.

To describe luxury not in terms of its being straightforwardly corruptive, but as a force within human psychological nature, is to say it is impossible for men to be long content with the simple life of honest earned comfort. In attacking luxury both Plato and Aristotle were warning of a fatal flaw in the universal norms of nature, which ought to make possible natural harmony amongst unequals. The ideal of natural harmony was blown apart in Aristotle's often quoted proposition in the *Politics* that 'From the hour of their birth some are marked out for subjection, others for rule.' This means there has to be a conflict of interests amongst the people of any small or large group, where subjects serve to enrich the few or many who rule. The tenacity of Aristotle's maxim has been demonstrated on innumerable occasions. It was reiterated and adapted in political and historical writing from the Roman imperial era to the ethical texts of the Middle Ages, the most famous of which is Saint Thomas Aquinas' widely circulated *Summa Theologica,* written in the years before 1273.

In the *Nicomachean Ethics* Aristotle propounded notions of the moral virtues which should attach to wealth. These informed and inspired all courtier literature from the heyday of Augustan Rome to the Renaissance in the West. To Aristotle '. . . great expenditure is becoming to those who have suitable means to start with, acquired by their own efforts or from ancestors or from connections, and to people of high birth and reputation, and so on; for all these things bring with them greatness and prestige'. Here are all the seeds for the growth of later controversies involving matters of architecture and building.

A Roman moralistic tradition stretching from Cato the elder (234–149 BC) through Marcus Terentius Varro and Cornelius Nepos to Pliny the Elder (AD 23–79) and beyond classed great expenditure on private housing as *luxuria*, a social malaise that involved the squandering of patrimonial substance on worthless and ruinous show.[2] The application of the word 'luxuria' to describe a social problem is highly significant, for 'luxus' can be translated as sensuality, splendour or pomp, whilst its derivative 'luxuria' is harsher, meaning riot, excess, extravagance. The first century AD saw a developing disaffection, amongst agronomes and philosophers alike, towards builders with sufficient wealth, who built purely for pleasure. Varro and Seneca looked on their own times as a watershed. Industry, courage and thrift were the qualities of their ancestors, who had built and made Rome great. Now, damage to the public good was being done by the unproductive luxury of the modern generation. Seneca idealised earlier generations, pointing to great men such as Scipio, who worked his own land and lived frugally in his fortified villa. There was nothing new about old men complaining of younger generations being sybaritic; however there is a growing body of historical and archaeological evidence pointing to a proliferation of villas dating from the first century AD, which were built exclusively as places for relaxation and entertainment.[3]

Having the means and, possibly, rank to build splendidly was not an entitlement to do so. For Varro (116–27 BC), Seneca (AD 4–65) or Pliny the Elder (AD 23–79), having the means to build in an established, peaceful society had proved an irresistible inducement to luxury. The antidote to such pessimism is found in the outlook of Pliny the Younger (c.AD 61–113). The famous descriptions in his letters of his enormous Laurentine and Tuscan villas might have been written with the strictures of Varro, Seneca or of his uncle in mind. He could never be accused of being corrupted or made indolent by his very considerable wealth. He describes his villas as 'ample enough for my needs, but not extravagant to manage'. Given their considerable size this was an understatement. The mind and the body thrive in such settings of buildings and landscape as those described by Pliny with charm and calculated persuasiveness. His letters describe how a man should be reinvigorated by the pleasures of freedom and sociability afforded by luxury in choice surroundings. Aristotle is be vindicated, when men of rank and means can excuse their exceptional material advantages by sustaining an active role in the maintenance of the social and political order. The life of Pliny the Younger cannot be bettered in Roman times, as an exemple of how luxury and splendid building should accord perfectly with the public career of a patrician.

Aristotle's advocacy of the greatness and prestige to be derived from great expenditure can be made to serve the case both for and against luxury architecture. Few dared to attack lavish spending by emperors on *res publica*, but the real divergence of opinion centres on the influence and effect of such activity by citizens on *res privata*. According to modern research the Athens of Aristotle was striking in the modesty of its domestic architecture, in sharp contrast to the splendour of the city's public buildings.[4] Educated Romans of the Imperial Age, part of whose intellectual formation took place in Athens, would not have taken Aristotle's meaning as sanctioning a proliferation of competitive private building. It was Cicero (106–43 BC) in his *De Officiis*, who first sought to reconcile his personal ideal of simplicity with the *luxuria* endemic in a rich society in which there was a fair degree of social mobility. Reclusive, indolent comfort is not a vice of the active and ambitious; to Cicero a house ought to reflect precisely the *dignitas* of men. It must be just as great as they and no greater. He defends 'new men', who might be accused of vain ostentation. He reasons that overbuilding would be counter-productive. An over-large house would draw attention by its empty spaces and lack of visitors. Those adept at building as a part of their personal, social or political strategy would calculate what was needed to receive the various ranks of their 'clientèle' and their friends. Social standing in Republican Rome in part depended on and was measured in terms of volume of social activity. With such provisos Cicero did not hesitate to admonish specific individuals who had succumbed to *luxuria* in their building. An insurmountable problem is that we know much about luxury in the abstract from Roman writers such as Cicero, and almost nothing about its practical influence on people's lives.[5]

This is a little easier to grasp in the medieval period. In western thought the most widely read of the ascetics who attacked luxury, art and building was the founder of the Cistercian Order, Saint Bernard of Clairvaux (1090–1153).[6] When churchmen made general points about over-expenditure on building, the relevance and value of their comments extends to the secular. Many of Saint Bernard's lengthy tirades, heavily laced with quotations from Roman satires, make him the most useful and eloquent source for bridging the silence of the 'Dark Ages'. He is an outright, uncompromising anti-Aristotelian. He asks 'what has gold to do with holiness?' Why, he continues, is it necessary to 'arouse the devotion of fleshy people with adornments, seeing they [the bishops and monks] cannot do so with things of the spirit?' The fabulous objects of *ars sacra* whose 'beauty is more admired than sanctity revered' are 'not more vain than insane'. The effect on the common people and on the priesthood and aristocracy is profoundly deleterious. 'The eyes of the rich are gladdened at the expense of the needy. The curious find matter for pleasure where the wretched do not even find sustenance . . .'[7] The cloisters where monks were supposed to meditate on the law of God were enriched with carvings of filthy monkeys, savage lions, monstrous centaurs, half men, spotted tigers, soldiers fighting, huntsmen, fish with animal heads, and many other bizarre convolutions of nature. 'In the name of God', he exclaims, 'if one is not ashamed of these absurdities, why not feel sorrow at the cost?' The Cistercians led the monastic renewal, which a number of modern historians label 'The Twelfth-century Renaissance', but this can be a misleading title if it suggests a renewal of interest in antique art or architecture. The churches the Cistercians built and the services they held were shorn of anything they deemed to be superfluous. Beauty and truth were to be seen most clearly and felt most deeply in austere surroundings.

Saint Bernard's rebukes led others to launch attacks on lavish building, especially members of the international community of scholars and theologians which made up the Schools of Paris. The best known of these were written by the Englishman Alexander Neckham (1157–1217) and Pierre Le Chantre (d.1197).[8] Unlike any Roman writer these men's sense of values was primarily offended by the deepening of the misery of the poor by concentration of wealth on luxuries and building. Neckham is appalled by roofs richly adorned with painting and carving, when all that is needed is something to keep the bad weather out. Luxury, Neckham is in no doubt, is the destroyer of wealth, a yoke which consigns most men to slavery. The products of luxury he counts as 'unlawful inventions', that is to say that such things specifically contradict the Commandments. 'Behold the superfluous and vain contrivances connected with buildings, clothing, food, trappings, furniture, and finally various adornments, and rightly you will be able to say: O vanity! O superfluity!' Pierre Le Chantre makes many points similar to those of Neckham, including comments such as '. . . this lust for building is testified by the palaces of princes, reared from the tears and the money wrung from the poor'. And he goes further when he develops the 'unlawful' nature of luxury building further by saying that 'Men sin even in building churches.' The significance of this startling statement is to do with men's hypocritical motive of self-gratification in building, which he characterises as 'morbus aedificandi'. Money is no use in heaven. Investing in vain architecture could never be appreciated by God. In stark contrast to the Roman tradition, lavish expenditure on shrines and sacred buildings is not exempt from accusations of either *luxus* or of *luxuria*. These Schools Latinists could not have used these terms about the churches and palaces which surrounded them without clearly understanding the gravity of their accusations against their superiors in church and state. These sermons from junior scholars are not known to have inhibited or touched the conscience of any cathedral, palace or tomb-builder.

It is a small step from such rhetoric to anti-clerical polemics. In the fourteenth century the satires of Boccaccio, Chaucer, Langland and others point out a wide range of abuses by the clergy, merchants and usurers, but none take up the theme of building as a vice or folly. Descriptions of the settings for stories are cursory, for the morality of the tales is portrayed by manners and behaviour. Petrarch's intense dislike of the modern world ought to have produced some comments on the architecture and building of his times. Surprisingly his perception of architecture developed no further than mundane considerations on the dates of ancient monuments in Rome.[9] It is possible that his obsession with the illustrious Roman past persuaded him that recent or modern building was unworthy of comment. His silence may be significant, but it is unhelpful. The fourteenth century is a fallow period for building and architecture as matters of controversy.

In the next century we know of a most unusual and revealing case of a caution on the undesirability of immodest building. It came from high up the social scale in England. The contract of 1440 for the masonry for the Divinity Schools in

Oxford (figure 1) provides unambiguous evidence of a reasoned reaction against richly decorated buildings instigated

... by numerous of the realm and other knowledgeable [*sapientes*] men, who do not approve, but reprehend, the over curiosity of the said work already begun [at the Divinity Schools], therefore the said University wishes the said Thomas [Elkyn] to continue, as he has already begun, to restrain the superfluous curiosity of the said work, as in niches for statues, bowtels, casements and fillets, and in other foolish curiosities, which do not concern the work, but cause too great and extravagent expenses by the University, and undue delay of the said work.[10]

The Oxford Divinity Schools were a bastion of theological orthodoxy. However well-endowed they could not indulge in 'foolish' or 'superfluous curiosities' of a kind which Saint Bernard had derided. As the building appears on the outside, it would seem that the ground floor, built by Richard Winchcombe between 1424 and 1439, represents the flamboyance shunned by the fellows of the University in the wording of the 1440 contract. The expansive and expensive glazed lights of the ground floor recede into much meaner or less 'curious' double lancets on the first floor. There is no trace of the niches and other fripperies listed in the memorandum, which would suggest that the authorities were taking a preventative measure.

Also in 1440 the young and pious Henry VI founded Eton College and King's College, Cambridge (figures 2–3). State papers make it clear that Henry saw these ambitious building initiatives partly as traditional statecraft, to commemorate the reign and his House, and partly as a genuine act of gratitude to the Creator who inspired the schemes. The history of Henry's long reign is one of accelerating deterioration towards the civil 'Wars of the Roses', which made the question of how his kingship was to be remembered in the best possible light the more poignant and urgent for him. His prayers for political salvation were never answered. The *morbus aedificandi* in Henry grew as things got worse. From his Will and Intent of 1448 it can be calculated that Eton College Chapel was to be comparable to any English cathedral, with a nave as long as Lincoln, and a width which would have been exceeded only by York.[11] Reading of the early construction history and troubled times of Eton and King's College Chapels shows that there seems to have been a growing reliance on the buildings as symbols of hope for deliverance. The Will and Intent of 1448 describes one stage of a revised and more ambitious plan to extend the scale of the structures. This Henry was never able to do before his downfall in 1461. In fifteenth-century northern Europe there are few better examples in the domain of architecture of the fulfilment of Aristotle's dictum, that great expenditure brings greatness and prestige. The author of the most scholarly modern biography of Henry boldly concludes that his foundations of Eton and King's 'were the only great achievements of his reign'.[12] It is ironic that within King's College Chapel the memory of the founder was usurped by the profusion

1   Oxford. The Divinity Schools. Begun *c.*1420, completed 1490.

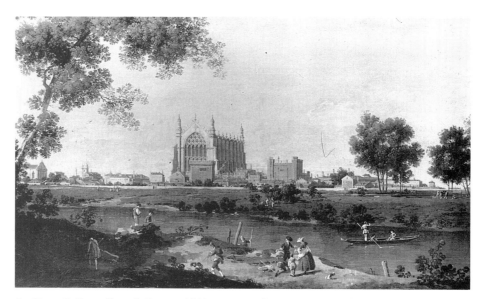

2 Eton College Chapel. Begun 1449, continued up to *c*.1460, then in-building *c*.1469–
c.1475, antechapel added *c*.1479–*c*.1482.

3 Cambridge. King's College Chapel. Begun
1446, completed 1515.

of Tudor roses set wherever convenient in order to claim all credit for Henry VII or Henry VIII.[13]

Renaissance Italy

At the same time the most enthusiastic exponents of the Aristotelian legacy were Florentine. An invaluable tract was written between 1454 and 1456 by an Augustinian, Timoteo Maffei, in defence and in praise of the public and private building programmes of Cosimo de' Medici (1389–1464). Maffei provides a distilled argument specifically in favour of grandiose building.[14] Cosimo's building is portrayed as guided by pure Christian charity. The text is in the form of a dialogue with much of the substance lifted from Saint Thomas Aquinas' discussion of magnificence. Maffei shifts the central point of the argument away from the accommodation of the sin of usury and the value to society of private wealth, which resulted in Saint Thomas' equivocal conclusions. Maffei's thesis emphasises the abstract status of magnificence as a virtue. Cosimo's buildings for the church or himself are portrayed as an incentive for others to attain greater things. The selflessness which Maffei spuriously describes as guiding Cosimo reaches a near comic level in his commentary on the Palazzo Medici, which had been begun a decade before in 1444 (figure 4). We are told:

> ... And in his house he has not thought about what Cosimo wanted, but what was consistent with such a great city as Florence, in that he thought that if he was not going to look ungrateful, it was necessary that he should appear more fully equipped and more distinguished than the other people in the town, in the same proportion that he received benefits from it greater than theirs.

Maffei's text reads as if it was formulated as a retort to criticism of Cosimo's drive to outdo all others in the scale and opulence of his palace. Unfortunately no record of the case against him has been found, but any attack or reproach must have been prompted by a grievance, that Cosimo under the constitution of the Florentine Republic was a citizen and commoner, however rich. He risked being seen as aping the behaviour of despised kings and tyrants.

Antagonisms provoked by ostentatious building were familiar to Alberti (1404–72) during the early 1450s, when he was composing his ten books, the *De re aedificatoria*. His profound knowledge of Greek and Latin authors gave him a freedom to comment on a wide range of social and ethical matters which had a bearing on architecture. He used ancient authors as if he were calling a series of unprejudiced witnesses to help resolve modern problems. The first chapter of the ninth book consists of a seemingly random sample of cases from antiquity of reaction to extravagance in private building and ornament. Significantly Alberti

4   Florence. Palazzo Medici. Built 1444–64. Architect Michelozzo.

never made a comment or passed judgement on any secular building of his own times. He was undoubtedly aware of the topical significance of his subject. The specifics of contentions in Alberti's times have been lost; however, much in his writing preserves the flavour and substance of real debates about the ethics of public and private building. He might well have had the Palazzo Medici in mind when he wrote '. . . if you want my advice, I would rather the private houses of the wealthy were wanting in things that might contribute to their ornament, than have the more modest and thrifty accuse them of luxury in any way'. Luxury is Alberti's favourite term for excess, which no man could admire or defend. However, he adheres to ancient and modern theories of magnificence and seems to echo Maffei's clumsy reasoning with the opinion that 'we decorate our property as much to distinguish family and country as for any personal display (and who would deny this to be the responsibility of a good citizen?)'. This is not to condone or criticise exceptional builders like Cosimo de' Medici. Alberti in a conciliatory tone goes on to suggest that 'any person of sense' would want to have a house which is much like 'those of others', meaning people of their own class. To outdo one's peers can be counter-productive and generate envy. The background of dynastic and factional rivalry in the richest Italian city-states proved ideal for the urgent and detailed formulation of the socially acceptable and unacceptable in matters architectural.

It was a Florentine banker who gave Alberti the commission to design his palace, where we would expect to see the application of his principles of architectural decorum, innocent of the reviled weakness of luxury. Giovanni Rucellai's palazzo was begun about 1446, at the time when feelings for and against Cosimo's giant enterprise must have been a highlight of the talk of the town (figure 5). Rucellai (1403–81) wanted and got the first Roman-looking facade seen in the city. It was novel in Florence with its three orders of pilasters, which obediently echo the 'Colosseum principle' with Doric, then Ionic, and Corinthian for the top floor. Rucellai had firsthand benefit of Alberti's scholarship, and he felt bold enough to confound any would-be critics; his compulsion to record and justify his building was set out twenty years later in his *zibaldone*, an autobiographical memoir.[15] Alberti's social opinions and view of the full and good life were most influenced by Cicero's bedside manual for the ambitious, the *De officis* or 'On duties'. Measured architectural self-glorification, when transformed from a vanity to a duty, was too important an issue for Rucellai to pass by. He needed to explain why and how he had got it right. The banker took to heart and paraphrased Cicero's report of how Gnaeus Octavius justified his lavish palace on the Palatine Hill. It had been built to impress as part of his strategy to advance his political career in the consular elections. If it was sage for a Roman to express his personal consequence and measured ambition in a building, it was right and proper for the successful Florentine Rucellai to do the same.

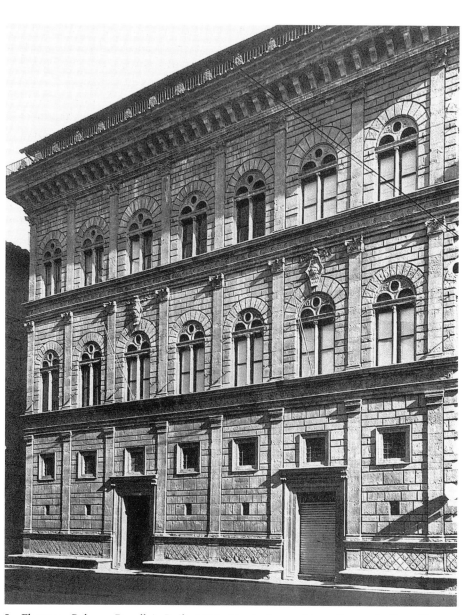

5 Florence. Palazzo Rucellai. Built 1446–51. Acting architect Bernardo Rossellino, to Alberti's designs.

Several architectural features of Rucellai's facade were derived from the Palazzo Medici, such as the form of the windows and the rustication. Alberti advised that it was be prudent to imitate, but not exceed the works of superiors. The facade of the Palazzo Rucellai falls foul of the definition of luxury in Genesis as 'anything unneeded'. It was neither planned nor built in conjunction with the interior. This is in accord with Alberti who, in book IX, chapter 8, asserts that a building should be 'constructed naked and clothed later'. The theme of this part of his treatise is that patrons should see to the essentials within their means, before embarking on work that lends dignity to the whole. In the terms of Samuel and Kings, Rucellai had all the rights, titles and social standing for the facade of his palace to be deemed appropriate and creditable. It was justifiable luxury. It is noteworthy that Alberti never quotes from or paraphrases the Bible, and thus his selective use of a mass of ancient writing is not fettered by nor embroiled with Christian ethics. The 'ancestors' whom he repeatedly praises for their frugality were virtuous Greeks or Romans, not Jews. Likewise his patron Rucellai was not satisfied exclusively with Christian solutions to moral problems. One of the most startling comments in his *zibaldone*, which would have horrified his merchant ancestors, encapsulates his independent spirit. He wrote 'I think I have done myself more honour by having spent money than in having earned it. Spending gave me a deeper satisfaction above all in regard to the building I have done.' On the frieze under the pediment of Santa Maria Novella he had his name inscribed in giant letters so that posterity could never ignore his largesse and love of spending (figure 6).

Having satisfied himself that all his spending on benefactions, his family and palace amounted to a balanced public and private legacy, Rucellai rested content on his vast fortune for the rest of his days. He could not be accused of luxury. None of his intentions were excessive or out of keeping with his actual status. Although much may be lost, no one is known to have taken Rucellai to task. Looking backwards to the fourteenth century and the annals of Giovanni Villani and other eyewitnesses, the special sensitivity of Florentine patricians about the reception of their buildings can be clearly understood. They report large-scale destruction of houses caused equally by natural disasters of fire and flood and by the mob. Most poignant are the accounts of the sack of the houses of those whose political fortunes had gone awry. In ways peculiarly Florentine, during the fifteenth century the palacebuilders sought both to distance themselves from as well as to commend themselves to the common people. It is the proof of the success of the established families, who built magnificently, that none of these palaces was attacked or destroyed in times of adverse political fortune, not even the Palazzo of the Medici during their periodic banishments. These buildings came to be valued and prized as assets for the whole city, which was precisely the social objective of the propaganda and public relations of the builders. The volatile palace-burning-classes had been mollified. Money spent on the building and the luxury trades meant widespread economic benefits.

6 Florence. Santa Maria Novella, frieze, 1470. Architect Alberti.

However much or little indignation was stirred by Cosimo's palace, the Medici cleared the way for emulators and inevitably, in a city of factions, spurred competitors to outdo them. Any conventions and legislation which sought to impose moderation were shown to be impotent with the building of the Palazzo Strozzi (figure 7).[16] The dynamic entrepreneur Filippo Strozzi (1428–91) wanted it known that all he wished for was 'a comfortable, everyday house', but none could have taken him seriously. Since the death of Cosimo in 1464 the Medici bank had been in steady decline. By the time of the ostentatious stage-managed foundation ceremony for the Palazzo Strozzi on 6 August 1489, a political tide was running against the Medici, which culminated in their second period of exile starting in 1494. Strozzi's transparently insincere disclaimers could never disguise the fact of his intention to build the largest private palace yet seen in the city, whose main purpose was to surpass the Palazzo Medici. All contemporaries understood this. However, it would be a serious misunderstanding to see the Palazzo Strozzi as a brash and provocative challenge to the Medici. Filippo's son Lorenzo recorded that his father had subtly manoeuvered Lorenzo de' Medici ('the Magnificent') into giving more than mere moral support to the project. Lorenzo was a keen amateur architect, and he seems to have made a number of suggestions for the design. Little could have been more sweetly satisfying, than making the most considerable potential opponent an accomplice in Strozzi's scheme of self-aggrandisement. Filippo Strozzi died in 1491, but he had made full provision for the finance and materials for the fifteen-year building campaign to have the fabric of the palace completed. In all that has been written about the Palazzo Strozzi, there is nothing which berates it as luxurious. It is remarkable that Filippo Strozzi generated widespread popular interest and excitement about his building plans, which served to deflect any accusations of vanity and egotism others had endured. Fifty years after occupying the palace Lorenzo and his family were rattling around in it with most of the largest and grandest rooms empty and unused. Cicero's warning not to build over-large houses with visitorless empty spaces was not heard, but despite this emptiness the *dignitas* of the Strozzi seems to have been untarnished.

As an early exercise in public relations the launch of the Palazzo Strozzi is a novel feature in the history of architecture. Everything we know about Filippo Strozzi's behaviour in public and private life forms a picture of a man excelling others and keenly aware that his achievements risked being spoilt if he could not persuade the patriciate and people of his *virtù*. In this his triumph was more complete than any. With the one possible shortcoming of not being as well-read as Rucellai, he represented much of Alberti's ideal of a patron. He sought and got all the best advice. The administration of the finances and the building work was nearly faultless, and did not falter at his demise.

Strozzi's boldness tempered by perspicacity attracted intense interest around the Courts of the peninsula. The eminent Ercole d'Este, Duke of Ferrara, wanted at an

7 Florence. Palazzo Strozzi. Begun 1489, largely complete by 1523. Architect Benedetto da Maiano.

8 Ferrara. Palazzo dei Diamanti. Begun 1493, stopped 1504, completed 1567. Architect
Biagio Rossetti.

early stage to know all the details of Strozzi's scheme. He was a prince embarking
on the most ambitious programme of urban planning of late fifteenth-century
Europe.[17] The *Addizione Erculea* more than doubled the built-up area within the
city walls, and its purpose was to create a giant borough for the rich graced with
palaces on long, wide and straight boulevards. The Duke's policy for his city had
many facets, including a campaign to encourage Jews to settle, but the most
remarkable initiative from the social and economic point of view is the batch of
palaces for which he paid directly and indirectly. Building palaces out of the
public purse for the wealthy as a first priority is strongly reminiscent of Constantine
and his new city of Constantinople. There, once top people were provided for the
middle and artisan classes were expected to follow.[18] For his brother Sigismondo
the Duke had built the wonderful Palazzo dei Diamanti, whose name is a key to
the content and intention of the panegyrics which heralded and publicised the
grandiose plan (figure 8).

In 1497 a Bolognese humanist, Giovanni Sabadino degli Arienti penned a lengthy
Plutarchian panegyric, in which Ercole d'Este was conventionally compared to the

Emperor Augustus. The writer revelled in the costly or luxurious materials which adorned the new buildings.

Just as Augustus found Rome in brick and left it in marble, so too will your celsitude, by virtue of your magnificence, be recognised by posterity with very great glory. For you found a Ferrara of painted brick, and you have left it . . . carved in adamite marble, as a result of which one can already make this judgement: that this your city, gleaming more than oriental lapillo, will be among the most wondrous cities of the World.

An abundance of white marble columns with portrait busts of Roman emperors mounted on top was singled out as a special beautification of the city. The new buildings dazzled with their costliness, and the Palazzo dei Diamanti, the grandest of all, might as well have been built of diamonds. The aim of the panegyric was to create a legend, a reputation for the *Addizione Erculea* based on extravagant admiration for expensive materials. In this Sabadino perfectly mirrors a trait often found amongst the major patrons of architecture in Renaissance Italy, and we only have to look again at Giovanni Rucellai's *zibaldone* to see such values and outlook. Rucellai's account of his visit to Rome reveals no interest in the forms or history of the ancient monuments, but he was impressed by the sumptuousness of standing rows of columns and especially by the rich marble decorations in medieval churches. The marble of Rome, not the bricks, was the fascination, as he imagined what it had all cost.

Up to the end of the fifteenth century advocates and apologists for grandiose secular building reiterated Aristotle's views usually from a second-hand source. The resort to Greek or Roman sources must have been a necessity, for there was no succour to be found in the New Testament or the writings of the Early Christian Fathers. Florentine bankers succeeded in absolving themselves from any politically fatal accusation of luxury, for they were building as a trust for the future of their families and for the glory of their city. A great prince of northern Italy could add that his ambitions in public and private building works were based on natural right, whose beneficiaries would not just be counted as their individual selves. Believe any of it or not, the overt and covert propaganda of a Rucellai, Strozzi or Duke of Ferrara always reads as a response to critical opinion. The historical interest of the case for the defence of magnificent secular building in Florence or Ferrara would be far greater if we knew who mounted attacks, and the weapons and ammunition used. Dissent could spoil hopes of eternal grace invested in building, and builders in quattrocento Italy succeeded, by accident or design, in burying the opposition without trace.

After 1500

The first quarter of the sixteenth century should have produced an avalanche of polemic against luxury and architecture. The Reformation as it spread in the 1520s

9 Rome. Agostino Chigi's villa, the so-called 'Farnesina'. Built 1508–11, passed to the Farnese family in 1580. Architect Baldassare Peruzzi.

generated plenty of invective casting Rome as Babylon.[19] Now the metaphors for waste and corruption are biblical and not from Greek or Roman sources. The welter of broadsheets, pamphlets and latterly books from north of the Alps, in which the worldliness and venality of the Roman Church was deplored, missed some excellent true stories of unseemly excess. A Rome correspondent could have provided excellent copy for mockery or vilification. A choice example should have been the Roman villa and the epicurean, pagan frolics staged there by the fabulously wealthy papal banker Agostino Chigi (1465–1520) (figure 9). The spearhead of the Reformers' devastatingly effective attack was directed at Rome, but the attack amounted to an abstraction. There are good reasons for believing that the righteousness of Luther or Calvin deliberately avoided seriously questioning the Aristotelian tradition. Luxury in the public domain of the Church was damnable, but private extravagance was a matter which would be judged after this life.

Panegyrics written to celebrate the opening of Agostino Chigi's pleasure house on the banks of the Tiber make unedifying reading.[20] The Farnesina, as it is now known after its next owners, was a showcase of art and a place for sumptuous entertainments. Chigi's villa was begun in 1509 and finished in 1511. A key feature of the Aristotelian justification of very great personal riches asserts that without exceptional wealth great men would be incapable of the virtue of out-standing generosity. The early heydays at the villa witnessed plenty of the kind of open-handed hospitality to gratify Chigi's considerable social, political and literary 'clientèle'. Amongst the latter group was found a Neapolitan humanist, Girolamo Borgia, who composed a couple of sycophantic stanzas to celebrate the opening of the house, with Chigi cast in the inevitable role of Augustus:

In others, Augustus, wealth produces their shining splendour. You, on the other hand, are a light, a great glory to wealth. For you with regal expense renew the gigantic construction of Rome; thus you recall Ancus's primordial name And you prevent the loss of so many outstanding spirits, So many grand examples of genius, in our generation, Further, you foster the best in all things at your genial table teaching us what the genuine gifts of kings should be.

After illustrious Rome fell prey to barbarian furies, All the Gods withdrew, and the city collapsed. But where Agostino Chigi founded his kingly palace, And restored [thereby] a [truly] ancient splendour, Gods and their consorts at once descended again from the heavens, vying amongst themselves to favour this one blessed house. Finally Bacchus and Love, the Graces, golden Venus and Pallas vowed in a pact to inhabit just this place. Augustus, a man is blessed when benevolent Gods love his dwelling; Men too compete to praise it with admiring words.[21]

This turgid verse is significant in this context in its utter rejection of any of the constraints anticipated by earlier major private builders. Chigi did not build a house of awe-inspiring proportions, and given the size of his fortune it might have seemed modest. What makes this building remarkable is that it was neither a villa in the terms described by Alberti, nor was it an urban *domus*, palazzo or household according to any ancient or modern conventions. If contemporary writings refer-ring to Chigi's house are to be taken at face value, it was a place for first-rate cookery and fifth-rate poetry. Its fame was and is based on its architecture by Peruzzi and the frescoes of the loggia executed by Raphael and his best pupils. However, the social milieu which rejoiced in these surroundings seems to have been thick with spongers. From Biagio Pallai in 1512, who was known in Rome's humanist circles by his Latinised name of Blosio Palladio, we have deathless lines, which give a crude image of what Borgia calls Chigi's 'genial table, teaching us what the genuine gifts of kings should be'. Part of his inane eulogy to Chigi's hospitality shows the expectations of free fun amongst his parasitic guests.

While you lead us around your villa's dining rooms, And stroll through all the gardens, my dear Chigi, the time goes by and my guts are shuddering from starvation. Don't dare think that my stomach feeds on painting, Noble though it may be: come on, get on with it. Leave admiration until we are drunk; It's no use till I'm plastered. Then by all means let Blosius sing his poetry, thus your villa's esteem will grow, but the villa will proclaim your name more brilliantly to the future.[22]

Chigi's famous trick of throwing all his valuable plate into the river after a banquet, whence it was all retrieved later from hidden nets, leaves no doubt that these events were boisterous. The pagan character of the staged entertainments was geared to ritualised excess of consumption. Martin Luther's visit to Rome of 1510–11 was a catalyst of enormous historical importance, but his contempt did not extend to calling seriously for Rome to be treated like Sodom and Gomorrah. A couple of years earlier Luther had delivered lectures on Aristotle's *Ethics* at Wittenberg. There is nothing at any point in his intellectual development to suggest that he refuted the main arguments of a text which had long been venerated by his Order, the Augustinians. It is not known if Luther had any direct or indirect knowledge of Chigi. He was himself a considerable eater and drinker, and would have been little inclined to be outraged simply by the gluttony of some of Chigi's guests.

German pamphlets and woodcuts of the 1520s attacked papal Rome to desanctify the city as a place of outrageous corruption and as the home of the Devil himself, but there were no reports of the antics of real people (apart from the Pope) or of actual places where decadent rituals were acted out. This astonishingly modern propaganda campaign of words and images savaged most aspects of the mythical reputation of Rome as a sacred city. Prominent in the welter of abuse is paganism, seen as a symptom of depravity and evil. Nothing about the trappings of Renaissance villa life, architecture, painting and statues of gods and goddesses, could have been condoned, but unfortunately for us there is nothing in this mass of material which focuses on the great artistic developments. Indeed, with the exception of the fringe Anabaptists, the leading scribes and thinkers of the Reformation in Germany or France were defenders of established secular privileges and rights of property. There is a strange silence on the matter of luxury.[23]

Chigi's villa within the city was a private place for festivities. This was neither a true residence nor a place of work. To a businessman of Chigi's ability the expenditure on prestige and entertainments instead of loans and investments had to offer some level of return. In the context of early sixteenth-century Roman society it would be foolish to regard Chigi's villa as a vain luxury. He was investing in influence by popularity. Again the Reformers missed a solid piece of evidence of the decadence of Rome. A villa to Pliny or Cosimo de' Medici was a retreat from the cares of the city, where a man should think, read and meditate on how to lead a better life.[24] In Rome before the Sack of 1527 such commendable policies for patrician self-improvement were rarely mentioned.[25]

The Reformation: Fun in Protestant Basle, insecurity in Catholic Vienna

The onslaught of the Reformation brought into question an immense range of issues of public morality, but private architecture as a luxury got lost in the melée. The impact of the social tumult on bourgeois architecture seems to have been negligible. For example, the tradition of painted town houses in the most prosperous towns in any of the newly Protestant German-speaking lands were immodest celebrations of the owner's affluence, morality and ethics. At Basle and Lucerne, Holbein the Younger received two lucrative commissions for complex exterior decorations showing architecture and figures, especially the *Hauses zum Tanz* in Basle of about 1520 (figure 10).[26] The stage set fantasy of classical architecture and the friezes of gyrating dancers were there to entertain, delight and amaze. Painted houses cheered up the appearance of a street and were often seen as expressions of civic pride. They were public expressions of prosperity and conviviality, which is quite distinct from competitive, private luxury. The *Hauses zum Tanz* had to have been taken as innocent of any Roman depravity in the course of the following turbulent decades, above all in Switzerland.

The most startling example of painted decoration being used for an opposite, admonitory effect was the so-called *Hasenhaus* in Catholic Vienna (figure 11). It was built and decorated on the orders of the Emperor Maximilian I probably shortly after 1509, but it all looks like a remodelled group of buildings of the first quarter of the sixteenth century.[27] The *Hasenhaus* could have added colour but not the slightest cheer to the street. Here the world is turned upside down, with hares hunting, persecuting and devouring men. The tormented have become the tormentors. As the *Hasenhaus* was the seat of the administration for the Imperial Hunt, the iconography is ironic, black humour at the very least. A reworking of all of this ominous savagery is to be found in a Nuremberg broadsheet of 1534–5, and reprinted in 1550 with admonitory verses added at the bottom (figure 12). Irrational fears, terrifying omens and unnatural deeds were the stock tools of the Nuremberg polemicists' satirical and diabolical imagery.[28] If the *Hasenhaus* at Vienna was a fine joke, the Nuremberg broadsheet recasts the folk tale into an indictment of the oppression of the rich. Horrors, atrocities and rebellion are inevitable.

The *Hasenhaus* was a gigantic billboard of threats and reassurances. The hares were the victors, who had thrown off a yoke of oppression. The passer-by had to side with the hares out of fear. The *Hasenhaus* became a private dwelling after 1521, and later owners left this fearsome, moral comic strip from the Reformation exposed for Salomon Kleiner to record it in the mid-eighteenth century. It cannot be too much of a stretch of the imagination to see these murals as a disclaimer of the luxury of tyrants. The oppressed would inevitably take revenge.

Venice: Architecture as luxury confronted

In early and mid-sixteenth century Europe Venice was unique, as a cosmopolitan centre of religious tolerance where the large colony of Protestant northerners were

10 *left* Basle. *Hauses zum Tanz*. The house of
the goldsmith Balthasar Angeloroth. Built *c*.1520,
demolished 1909. Murals attributed to Hans
Holbein the Younger.

11 *below* Vienna. The *Hasenhaus*. Decorated after
1509, demolished 1749.

23

Ein yeder trag sein joch dise seit/ Vnd vberwinde sein vbel mit gedult.

Eins morgens gieng ich durch ein Wald/ Ob sie möchten den Jeger fellen.   Ich wölt euch drucken wie ich wolt/
Es het geschneit vnd war grimm Kalt/ In dem hört ich ein Boten schellen.   Das ir mich alzeit fliehen solt
Neben der straffen hort ich wispern   Vnd auch jauchtze der Hunde hauffe. Nach aller Hasen natur vnd art.
Etwas hind einem gestreuß laut zispern/ Anfiengen die Hasen zu lauffen   Jetz so ir haltet widerpart
Ich gugt hin durch/sah das da sassen   Hinab gen thal dem Jeger zu/   Vnd ir mein Meister worden seit/
Etwas in die zwey hundert Hasen/   Ich stund ein weil/ vnd in ein nu   Erkenn ich erst mein groß torheit.

12 Georg Pencz. *Rabbits catching the Hunters.*

wholly at ease in a Catholic state. Venice's economic interests required such pragmatism, but the interests of the state and the established order did not foster real
free speech in domestic matters. Elsewhere on the Italian peninsula internal dissen-
sions involving building and architecture survive only as the case for ambitious
building rather than against it. Official censorship or unofficial intimidation must
account for the imbalance. In Venice the suppression of dissent was well established, but with the relative freedom which allowed printing presses to flourish, one
precious attack on Venetian architectural prestige slipped through. At issue was
overspending, maladministration and miscellaneous abuses in the building of the
Scuole Grandi (figures 13–14).

The 'Myth of Venice' was built on the appearance and records of harmony and
order in official circles. It was a veil of secrecy of amazing efficiency towards the
outside world.[29] Discord is a much more exciting quarry for research, when trying
to make sense of Venetian social history and politics.[30] Many hopes of salvation
from dreaded plague were invested in a flood of cash from rich and not-so-rich
into the building of the Scuola Grande di San Rocco, patron saint of plague
sufferers. The attack on its builders is the *Sogno da Caravia* by a leading jeweller,

24

Alessandro Caravia (1503–68), published in 1541. It contains a highly courageous attack by an individual on those in positions of office and trust in the *Scuole Grandi*. Their function was to help the poor, but now the wealth of these foundations was being channelled into vainglorious, if not corrupt, pursuits such as banquets, ceremonies, honours and building. The Heads of the Council of Ten granted permission for the book to be printed. This is in itself amazing, for in waspishly satirising the behaviour and aspirations of a key sector of the citizenry, Caravia was questioning institutions and values of prestige dear to most Venetians. Some in the Council wanted it suppressed, but they were overruled, as the matter was deemed one of general public concern.[31] Caravia's targets are all but named in writing:

I wish to tell you of the many errors of some of proud habits, although I do not tell you their names. Some follow the saint of the plague and these are they who have produced such fine works with foliage, harpies and all those fine heads, fantastic columns in new styles, for each wants to prove himself a master mason. The truth is that every time there is a new chapter, everyone wants to prove himself a great deviser of schemes, changing now this staircase and now the other, doing away with former doors and windows, all quarrelling with one another, saying: Such and such a man did not know how to do things.

Alluding to the Scuola Grande di San Giovanni Evangelista he writes that the governors 'having found their purses overheavy', have built a new hospice 'where one could hold a ball if necessary'. Caravia's social outlook was much influenced by Erasmus, and probably by some of the principles of the Reform which attracted the attentions of the Tribunal of the Inquisition to him in 1557. He survived persecution on the grounds that his purpose was to publicise the degeneration of *scuole grandi*, and that his claims were not made 'in mockery of religion'. The archives of the *scuole grandi* provide ample support for Caravia's claims about quarrelling, waste on changing schemes and unnecessary alterations and additions to their meeting houses. We can still see the consequences in the hybrid character of the facades of the Scuola Grande di San Marco and especially that of San Rocco. Here the columns were an enrichment added to the original programmes by a change in the governors, who then by custom changed the architect (figure 13).[32] Each new board of trustees bid to make the public face of their buildings more monumental architecturally than that attempted by any of their rivals. At San Rocco they clearly succeeded, as well as disposing of a good part of their embarrassment of riches. Caravia was a brave man to publish such a tract independently, and as far as we know it is unique. Its impact might have influenced some of the self-reforming measures taken by at least one of the 'scuole grandi' in the years immediately after the book's publication to control abuses and expenditure. The issue was the diversion of funds from charity to luxurious 'unneeded' architecture, which did nothing to inhibit the passion of the patriciate for palace-building. If Caravia

13 Venice. Scuola Grande di San Rocco. Begun 1515, completed 1549. Architects
Bartolomeo Bon, then Antonio Scarpagnino.

14 Venice. Scuola Grande di San Marco. Begun 1485, completed c.1495. Architects Pietro
Lombardo, then Mauro Codussi.

caused any serious upset, it would have been amongst those Venetians of many classes who were devout benefactors of the 'scuole grandi' in preference to the church. They expected and relished splendour in these buildings. The magnificence of the *scuole grandi*, however imperfectly attained, was an outstanding reflection and endorsement of the patriotism of a spectrum of Venetian society.

As Francesco Sansovino makes abundantly clear in his ever-useful guide *Venezia Città Nobilissimà* of 1561 and 1581, the substance of modern achievement in Venice is seen in the glories of painting and architecture that made the genius of Venice supreme. In Aristotelian terms, it is not just the state, but every citizen who gains praise and prestige by association with such glories. Without Caravia we would have no inkling of a moral or ethical aversion to lavish building in Renaissance Venice. The title of Sansovino's book calls the city itself noble. More than anywhere in sixteenth-century western Europe Venetian society as a whole seems to have been most receptive to and enthusiastic about lavish building as a reassurance of collective status. In large measure this can be accounted for by the special, insular concentration of the city that was unique. This outlook might only be paralleled in much later times by Manhattan, and the pride of New Yorkers in the buildings of mammoth corporations.

Magnificence versus luxury in northern Europe

Traditions of social criticism in Northern Europe were much more open and vigorous than was ever the case in any Italian city-state. Anti-clerical satire was a well established literary genre, before it was given an enormous boost by the Reformation. Two schools of writing are highly informative about theories and attitudes involving architecture and building. The first might be called the 'magnificence school', which comprised writers concerned with the elucidation and defence of a monarch's right to exceptional material splendour. The second is the 'anti-courtier school', which aimed to alert the public to vain, socially and economically destructive expenditure amongst the old aristocracy and the newly wealthy. The newly wealthy were usually categorised as exploiters of government offices, or 'men of the King's money', as they are described by Robert Dallington, writing of France and England in the late 1590s. This school of social criticism gathered real momentum only in the second half of the sixteenth century.[33]

There are compelling reasons for casting Renaissance theories of magnificence as an antithesis to luxury. Magnificence was the expression in material splendour of a State, which was bestowed by right and political need on the ruler. Subjects might accumulate some degree of magnificence in the service of or by association with the embodiment of the Nation. Fifteenth-and sixteenth-century literature frequently portrays magnificence as the fruit of successful rule in peace and war.

In kingdoms magnificence was an essential property of majesty. In Italian city-states the concept was more pervasive. 'Il Magnifico' was a common title of respect accorded to anyone in a position of political authority without being of princely blood. Lorenzo de' Medici was so-called by his admirers, whilst Savonarola might have titled him unjustifiably 'the Luxurious' in his attacks on materialism and the misuse of power, which cost him his life.

The tarnished image of Rome and its discredited Court was certainly a key factor in the image and style of monarchy cultivated in the first half of the century by the Emperor Charles V, King Francis I of France and King Henry VIII. Charles was no great builder of palaces, but Francis and Henry were passionate builders; unfortunately all we have are panegyrics and nothing in the way of polemics against their architectural enterprises. No important writer of the first half of the sixteenth century ventured a full political and social biography of a living monarch or leading statesman. The more interesting texts deal with big moral and economic issues in ways which avoid direct or singular criticism of heads of state. The defence of a king's magnificence did not preclude warnings and advice on the administration and control of the Court. But there is no substantial text which describes in any detail the social or political objectives in building 'pleasure domes' such as Chambord by Francis I or Nonsuch by Henry VIII (figures 15–17).

The view from France

An influential book like Claude de Seyssel's *Monarchie de France,* written in 1515, the year of Francis' accession, is solidly Aristotelian with a large measure of Cicero added.[34] He does not consider the morality or cost of a king's 'magnificence' which, he argues, should include building. Competitive expenditure and luxury amongst the aristocracy are very serious economic and social problems of concern to a monarch. Seyssel (1450–1520) singles out costly food and plate, furniture, luxurious clothes and ruinously expensive building as actual causes of damage to the social order and a threat to the economy. In the section of the book where he boldly announces 'how display should be humbled', Seyssel writes with passion, assurance and a keen sense of realism rare in writers before him. He insists:

. . . care also must be taken that trade, the third calling of the people of the middle estate, does not destroy and impoverish the nobility. The sole cause of such impoverishment is the great displays that the nobility want to engage in and maintain, and the excessive outlays that they make on their food and everything else. But their outlay on clothes and other luxuries is the most pernicious of all, both to themselves and to the commonwealth of the realm, for thereby money goes out of the kingdom in great quantity. This is the worst evil that can be done to the kingdom, because money

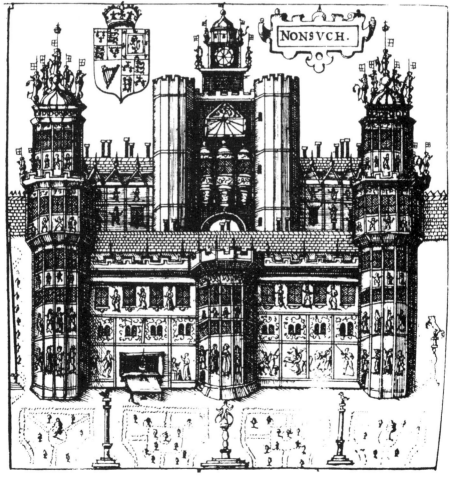

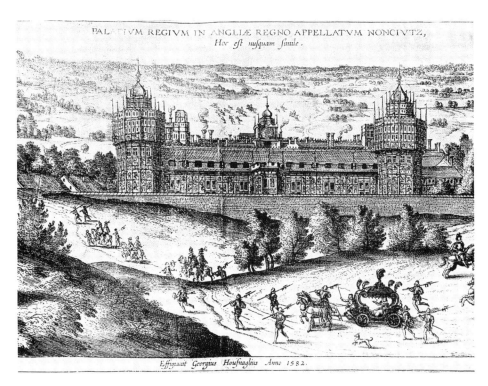

17 Nonsuch, Surrey, from the south-east.

15 *Opposite top*   Chambord. Begun 1519, main building campaign 1526–38.

16 *Opposite bottom*   Nonsuch, Surrey. Begun 1538, completed 1541. Demolished 1683–3.

is its blood and nerves. Therefore the king can do nothing more useful for the realm in a political way than to restrain these excesses of display, which besides their harmfulness are displeasing to God. Moreover, a whole group of other evils rise from them, for the king must give his very numerous servitors greater stipends or make them particular gifts in order to maintain this lavish display, or they would be ruined in his service. For this reason he has to tax people more heavily. On the other hand, those gentlemen who have no stipend or benefice from the king, or only a little one, want to imitate completely or in part the style of the court. It could not happen otherwise, for never have the remainder of the subjects yearned to do anything other than live according to the example of princes and their courts. By this means the nobility is destroyed from lack of proper ordering, and thereafter cannot serve as needed, but is forced to live ill. This is especially true of those in the regular cavalry . . .

It is finely ironic that the new king to whom Seyssel addressed his book was to spend more money on clothes and armour than on his buildings. Francis was in every way the personification of a 'magnificent' monarch in his personal style as head of state and in his pleasures. He was not one to set an example of austerity or moderation. If we are to believe Seyssel, the proliferation of splendid châteaux was already well under way even before the beginning of Francis' long reign from 1515 to 1547. It saw building booms in the Loire Valley and after 1528 in the Ile-de-France, when the focus of the king's building ambitions changed to the area around the capital. It is a pity Seyssel does not identify his examples, when he laments:

One sees all over the kingdom many buildings on the grand scale, public and private buildings replete with gilding not just on the walls and ceilings of the interiors, but also on claddings, roof turrets and reliefs on the outsides; and these houses are stuffed with furniture more sumptuous than has been seen before. Every establishment uses silver plate of such excessive cost, that there has been the need to legislate against such wastage. None from any of the classes do not yearn for cups, goblets, ewers and spoons made of solid silver at the very least. In the minds of prelates, nobles, and other uncouth types, they can never be happy unless they have got all of their table as well as their kitchen ware of silver if it cannot be gold plated; and there are still plenty who own large objects of solid gold; the same can be said of clothes and of the style of living, which is more lavish than ever has been seen.

Savaging the great and grand as being 'uncouth' is astonishingly provocative given that Seyssel's audience was the upper order. All that dazzled dismayed him, and many at the time must have shared his distaste for the frivolity of gilding 'claddings, roof turrets and reliefs on outsides', wherever they may have existed. An important feature of Seyssel's thesis on the responsibilities of the French monarch was that he should be the scourge of luxury, but such an idea certainly fell on deaf ears.

Two forms of absolutist thought were current in France when Francis became king. Seyssel epitomises the moderate form, whilst Guillaume Budé's *L'Institution du Prince* of 1518 mirrored Francis' outlook. To the nobility and institutions such as the senior judiciary are due social and material privileges, but they are not entitled as of right to any share of authority. 'Largesse' from the crown was an important instrument of policy, which Seyssel viewed as an incitement for much of the nobility to take a road to ruin. Guillaume Budé (1467–1540) considered a knowledge of history to be essential for the political success of the king; he strung together a series of stories selected from the scriptures and ancient history, which he hoped would be useful object lessons for the new king. None of the examplary tales chosen by Budé contain episodes in which a ruler curtails extravagance amongst favoured followers or the upper classes. Indeed Francis never showed any inclination to inhibit any at Court from vying to outdo each other. He enjoyed, and probably encouraged, competition in entertaining, art collecting , horse breeding and building amongst those in his service. No humanist preaching economy or utility in his own building programme would have been tolerated. His example ensured the continuation of the arguments formulated by Seyssel amongst later writers and anti-courtier polemicists, when France's religious turmoils of the second half of the sixteenth century began to wreck the economy and, just as Seyssel had warned, fractured the loyalty of the greater part of the old nobility to the Crown.

During the French civil wars of religion of the second half of the sixteenth century internationally influential work on constitutional theory and economics appeared. In these luxury and architecture occur as occasional themes in analyses of the malaise of the times. It is remarkable that writers on both sides of the religious divide assessed the causes for monetary inflation in much the same way. Mercantilism was well established in France before Colbert. The illustrious Jean Bodin in all his output of the 1560s and 1570s warns of the social and economic damage done by the import of luxury goods, and the admission of foreigners to positions of power and influence.[35] The events of the 1570s and 1580s stimulated several at Court and in the country to revise the propositions of Seyssel and Bodin in the light of the deepening crisis. The tone of much of this literature is aggressive but reasoned, and two examples are especially useful in this context. Bernard de Girard, seigneur du Haillan was a secretary to Henri, duc d'Anjou, the future Henri III, and historiographer to Charles IX, when he wrote a brochure called *Causes de l'extrême cherté qui est en France*. This was printed some twelve years later in 1586. With brio he challenged his readers:

. . . Let us now turn to the buildings of present times, then to their furnishings. It was but thirty or forty years ago (that is during the reigns of Francis I or Henri II) that this excessive and magnificent manner of building came to France. Formerly our fathers were content to build a good house, a pavilion or a round tower, a menagerie and other accommodation needed to house themselves and their family, without erecting the superb structures as today with large main blocks, pavilions, courts, rear courtyards, service courtyards, galleries, halls, porticos, flights of steps, balusters and other such things. Not the slightest care is taken with the geometrical proportion in the architecture of the outside, which in many buildings has upset the commodiousness of the interior; once one knew nothing of confecting so many friezes, cornices, frontispieces, podia, pedestals, capitals, architraves, stylobates, flutings, mouldings and columns, and, in brief, one was not aware of all these antique manners of architecture, which mean spending great sums, and which more often than not, make the interior ugly in order to embellish the exterior; once one knew nothing of putting marble or porphyry on fireplaces or around the doors of houses, nor of gilding beams and joists.[36]

De Girard rattles through some classical architectural terms as if they were wholly alien to French language and culture. Scorn is reserved especially for those whose recondite tastes have lured them into dressing up their residences to look as if they were neither French nor even in France. In using the vocabulary of the architectural treatise he mocks, but he has serious complaints. For example, where he complains of no care being taken with the 'geometrical proportion of the outside, which in many buildings has upset the commodiousness of the interior . . . which more often than not, makes the interior ugly in order to embellish the exterior . . .', it is clear he sees a house as a structure to be planned from the inside out. The needs of the users must be the foremost consideration. Sacrifices of convenience and practicability had to be involved, when symmetrical, richly ornamented facades were imposed on the essentially varied spaces required in a well-organised family house. Show with undesirable foreign connotations was, in de Girard's view, taking precedence over a tradition of good household organisation. To him it was all a fad and a wasteful nonsense.

Seyssel and de Girard were of very different social status and backgrounds. Neither was associated with building or architecture in any professional capacity, which makes their opinions appear to be of great objective value. Nevertheless, there is a real and obvious frustration in using them as spokesmen. They write at length, but meticulously confine themselves to descriptive generalities. Their contemporary readership in any part of France would have had no difficulty in seeing the evidence of the change in building and architecture. To make a fuller use of their texts we should do something of the same, and we might as well elect to make ourselves Parisians.

De Girard's utterances bring to mind two Parisian town houses of the late 1540s and 1580s. The Hôtel des Ligneris (now the Musée Carnavalet) and the Hôtel d'Angoulême (now the Bibliothèque Historique de la Ville de Paris) make an excellent comparison and contrast. They are buildings of very similar size, but whose architectural trappings are very different (figures 18–19). The Hôtel des Ligneris was built for a senior magistrate, président of the Parlement de Paris, and its neighbour across the Rue des Francs-Bourgeois was built or remodelled for the illegitimate daughter of Henri II, Diane de France. Blood and rank of the honoured 'Madame la Bâtarde' as distinct from the wealth of the jurist are defined in the degree of pretension on the facades of these buildings of like scale. Des Ligneris' social quality is well expressed to the passer-by in the rustication of the gateway facing the street, which denotes strength and possibly fortitude. For those who passed into his courtyard the fine quality of the plain dressed stone and the reliefs of the seasons on the main block ahead are impressive but not pompous. The careful stages in which the house was built, revealed in the documents, and the absence of the 'friezes, cornices, frontispieces' and so on, which dismayed de Girard, ought to have commended the house to him and others who shared his views.[37] The Hôtel d'Angoulême is altogether different with a maximum of classical ornament. As a badge of rank such a display must have passed as appropriate to the builder. It is justifiable magnificence. De Girard would have deplored the proliferation and imitation of such style by the bourgoisie and gentry. Those who felt compelled to follow the fashions and luxury of the great were falling into a well-known trap.

The Catholic de Girard was the most virulent of the critics to single out classical style in architecture as socially and economically undesirable for the 'middling sort'. Others were less assertive, but, prompted by nationalist sentiment shared his dislike of what was seen as a foreign, alien fashion. De Girard was exaggerating when he claimed that conspicuous, ostentatious extravagance on luxuries including building had caused the ruin of eight out of ten noble families. Inflation, depreciation of the value of land and continual warfare were the real causes of trauma and distress amongst the old nobility. Abroad the most widely read book on the plight of France was the Protestant François de la Noue's *Discours politiques et militaires*, which was written in 1580 and published in French and English editions in 1587. His list of 'vain expenses' is by now familiar: they are clothes, architecture, furniture and food in that order. De la Noue (1531–91) is pithy throughout. The passage he devotes to architecture is a curious blend of the principles of Seyssel written with the narrative gusto of Rabelais, to whom de la Noue pays homage. Serious matters are pondered in jaunty prose, and he is worth quoting at length.

Let us now come to the second article of our vain expenses, consisting of the immoderate affectations that sundry have for stately buildings. For although it has been so from the beginning, yet it was little compared to our own times, when we see the qualities and the number of buildings surpassing olden times. And especially our Nobility have exceeded in this, rather for vain glory than any necessity. I suppose that it was not more than sixty years ago that architecture was restored in France, where before men had lodged grossly. But since then the fair traits of this art have been revealed, many have endeavoured to put them into practice. If none but some of the great and rich had employed the abundance of their crowns upon such works, that would not have been reprehensible, considering they were ornaments both for the town and the countryside. But following their example the lesser rich, even the poor, have wanted to set their hands to such work, and without thinking were obliged to take on much more than they foresaw, and that not without repentance. The lawyers and above all the treasurers have increased the ardour

18 Hôtel des Ligneris, now known as Carnavalet. Begun after 1546, in-building during the 1550s. Architect unknown.

of the lords for building. For they say 'How is this? These men that are not so well established as us build like Princes, and shall we sit still?' And so envious of one another, a multitude of fine houses have been built, and often by the ruin of revenue, which has gone into other hands, because of this vehement passion which they have for putting one stone on top of another. How many are they that have started sumptuous edifices, which they have left unfinished?, having come to their senses half way through their folly. In every province we see but too many examples. It may be that some when they see themselves so well clothed and spangled in gold have said 'This cage is too small for so beautiful a bird, it must have a more stately one.' To this reasoning some flatterer may have replied 'Sir, it is a shame that your neighbour, who is no better than yourself, should be better housed. But take heart, for he that begins boldly has already done half of the work, and the means will not elude the wise man.' He, feeling himself scratched where it itched, forthwith conceived in his imagination a design, which he began with pleasure, continued with pain, and completed in sorrow. Often it comes about that he who has built himself a house fit for a lord with an income of twenty-five thousand livres, which his heir, finding himself with one of only seven or eight hundred, and being ashamed to lodge his poverty in such stateliness, has sold it to buy another more suited to his income. And he that would not sell has been driven 'to feed upon small loaves' (as one says) and he feasts his friends when

19 Paris. Hôtel d'Angoulême, now known as Lamoignon. Built *c*.1550–*c*.1560. Remodelled between 1580 and 1600 for Diane de France. Architecture attributed to Louis Metezeau.

they visit with discourses on architecture. When Father Jean des Antomeures [the head of Rabelais' fantastical, pleasure-loving order of Thélèmites], who was one of the most worthy men of our times, entered these magnificent houses and châteaux, where he saw lean kitchens, he used to say 'Oh, to what purpose are all these fine towers, galleries, chambers, halls and closets, with the cauldrons cold and the cellars empty? By the Pope's worthy pantofle (for that was his customary oath) I would rather dwell under a small roof, and hear from my room the harmony of the spits, smell the savour of the roast, and see my cupboard glorying in flagons, pots and goblets, than to dwell in these great palaces, to take long walks, and to pick my teeth fasting in the Neapolitan fashion.' I accept the opinion of those who advise that if they build, it is on the condition that they sell little or nothing of their goods, and he who does otherwise I refer him to the censure of Father Jean des Antomeures. I am well aware that one of the most remarkable things which one notices in France are the fine buildings strewn across the country, which are not to be seen elsewhere. But if one counts how many such splendours have reduced men to beggary, one will say that the product is indeed costly.

The history of French Renaissance architecture indeed is littered with projects begun, but never finished. The notarial archives in Paris are rich in litigation over inheritances, in which buildings under way, incomplete or abandoned are involved. Specialist architectural writers like Philibert de l'Orme in his *Architecture* of 1567 or the populariser Jacques Androuet du Cerceau (*c*.1515–85) in the forewords for his *Livres d'Architecture*, folio pattern books of 1559, 1561 and 1582, both warn of the dangers of overspending. De l'Orme urged potential patrons to seek competent advice from a member of the fledgling profession of architect. In many parts of France those who wanted to build well traditionally turned to their notary to vet many or all questions of costs, preparation and procurement of materials. De la Noue tells us what we suspect, when we look at some of the stranger artisan products of the architectural Renaissance in the provinces. Many an affluent or even impecunious gentleman thought up the forms and details of his house for himself. Of all the writers who chastise the folly of vain building, De la Noue is the most constructive and dispassionate. His wish was to persuade by gentle scolding and piquant mockery.

The view from England

De la Noue's Puritan readers across the channel would have taken succour from a vision of the Catholic French nobility squandering their wealth on clothes, furniture, food and building. Amongst the earliest and most striking Puritan denunciations of 'sumptuous edifices' can be found in the printed version of *A Sermon preached in the Fourth Sundaye in Lente before the Kynges Majestie, and his Honourable Counsell* by Thomas Lever, which appeared in London in 1550.[38] Lever must have had some courage to stare the Court in the face, and pronounce that '... the chief cause why the commens doe not love, trust, nor obey the gentlemen and the officers, is because the gentlemen and officers buylde many fayre houses and keepe fewe good houses.' By 'fayre' Lever means imposing or richly ornamented, and by 'good' he means well-ordered and welcoming. The brief reign of Edward VI, from February 1547 to July 1553, is of considerable interest for the precocious and highly individual buildings constructed for men close to the throne. The Protector Somerset made his mark on London with his palace on the Strand, and two of his protégés who might have been listening to Lever, Sir John Thynne and Sir Thomas Smith, were to build the famed Longleat and the much less-known Hill Hall (figures 20–1).[39] Search as we may, there is not a single focused lament or polemic, French or English, about the great house of a particular individual. If such a text were found, it would be invaluable. All the despondency and vitriol is generalised, whilst flowery panegyrics are usually personal tributes, which provide little or nothing about the style and function of outstanding town or country houses.[40] The widespread disaffection of the common people towards the rich and powerful of Tudor England took many forms from rebellion to pamphleteering, but when 'fayre houses' are a matter of

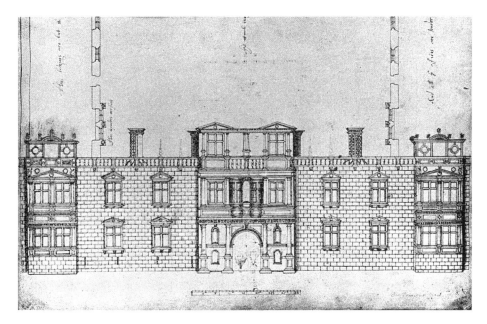

20 London. Somerset House. Street facade to the Strand, built 1547–52. Demolished *c*.1777.

contention, it is because of their shamness or falsity and the neglect of traditional hospitality by the rich towards the poor. From the end of our period a typical example is *The Poore Mans Passions* by Arthur Warren (1605):

Its sumptuous lodge, rich vesture, daintie fare, That robbe the purse, and make Revenues bare. Double and treble Chimneis mounting faire Observe the single Hospitality, All spent to build, and buildings repayre, Which should support oppressed misery, Great halls, large tables, gold, plate, little meate, Feed but the eye, while mouth hath nought to eate.[41]

It is presumably an accident that an English Puritan seems to be echoing the sentiments of Rabelais' ever-hungry Father Jean des Antomeures in looking on a 'good house' as a place where there should be open and abundant hospitality. The finery they associate with 'sumptuous lodge' was superfluous. A good host and a popular lord had no need to impress with imposing buildings. They are simply unneeded. Ancient customs of hospitality were for both friends and strangers, and they were the duty of a lord to uphold. The manor-house or castle had fulfilled many purposes, and was only lastly a private home. The phasing-out of this role is commented upon by so many later sixteenth-century writers in both France and England that there can be no doubt it was a widely held grievance. If hospitality had come to mean merely reciprocal entertaining between peer

21 Longleat, Wiltshire. Built mainly from 1572 onwards, but incorporating work from the later 1550s. Architecture of the facades attributed to Robert Smythson.

groups, the critics of display and vain expense had a strong historical case for attacking these new social customs as un-Christian. The Gospels and the Epistles offer an abundance of stories in which an individual or family seek atonement in this life with care for the less well off and salvation in the next by works of charity and benefactions. The indissoluble link between gentility and household generosity was reinforced by the idea that liberality was the particular prerogative of the gentleman, and was the most visible manifestation of true, inner nobility. From troubadour literature of twelfth-century Provence to the grumbles of Samuel Johnson, good housekeeping is at every stage seen to be in decline. The mythical Golden Age of the good host has always just disappeared, and we have to beware of being led astray by a literary stereotype.

England's first civil historian, William Camden (1551–1623), was especially offended by appetites for luxuries. Profligacy amongst the aristocracy he saw as a serious threat to the popularity of Queen Elizabeth I. Her 'progresses' around the country houses of notables in southern England with the Court in tow were creating the need to extend or build new houses on a massive scale, which caused the ruin of several owners. Camden's *Annals of the Reign of Elizabeth* makes great play of the sumptuary proclamation of 1574.

But through the Untowardness of the Times, both this Proclamation and the Laws also gave way, by little and little, to the Excess of Pride, which grew daily more and more unreasonable: and with it crept in riotous Banquetting and prodigal Bravery in building. For now there began more Noblemens and private Mens houses to be builded here and there through England; and those neat, large and sumptuous edifices, than in any other Age before; and verily to the great Ornament of the Kingdome, but to as great Decay of the glorious Hospitality of the Nation.

Household accounts from the Elizabethan period reveal the contraction of many noble households.[42] The great lords of former times who retained 'troopes of idle servants' reformed their establishments, which might have signalled the decline in the style of hospitality, open or closed. The 'prodigy houses' of Elizabethan England, the likes of Longleat, Montacute, Hardwick and Wollaton (figures 22–4) were haughty and phenomenal. Their impact is the more forceful, when we read of the alienation felt amongst the 'commens [who] doe not love, trust nor obey the gentlemen and the officers.' Writing in the 1570s William Harrison (1534–93) neatly sums up feeling amongst the lower orders. 'Each one desireth to set his house aloft on a hill, to be seen afar off, and caste forth his beames of stately and curious workmanship into every quarter of the country.'

Harrison's is a key text. His *A Description of England, or a briefe rehersall of the nature and qualities of the people of England and such commodities as are to be found in the same* appeared in 1577 and again in 1587, serving as an introduction to Ralph Holinshed's *Chronicles*.[43] Holinshed's book is now remembered mostly as the source well-thumbed by Shakespeare for his history plays. Harrison's

24   Wollaton, Nottinghamshire. Built 1580–8. Architect Robert Smythson.

22 *Opposite top*   Montacute, Somerset. Begun *c.*1590, completed 1599. Architecture attributed to W. Arnold.

23 *Opposite bottom*   Hardwick, Derbyshire. Built 1590–7. Architecture attributed to Robert Smythson.

extended essay is the most prominent and the fullest text in which consideration is given to building and to the changes seen by contemporaries. Harrison is not dismissive of people or trends of which he disapproves. He was then a country parson, and tried to be both sympathetic and critically analytical. Nevertheless, his account of how and why circumstances had changed did not disguise his concern about the wider consequences of luxury epitomised by grandiose building.

The ancient manours and houses of our gentlemen are yet, and are for the most part, of strong timber, in framing whereof our carpenters have beene and are worthilie preferred before those of like science among other nations. Howbeit such as be latlie builded are commonlie either of brick or of hard stone, as provision may best be made: but so magnificent and statlie, as the basest house of a baron doth often match in our days with some honours of princes in old time. So that if ever curious building did flourish in England, it is these our yeares, wherein our workmen excell, and are in manner comparable in skill with old Vitruvius, Leo Baptista [Alberti] and Serlio. Neverthelesse, their estimation more than their greedie and servile covetousnesse, joined with a lingering humour, caused them often to be rejected, and strangers preferred to greater bargaines, who are more reasonable in their takings, and lesse wasters of time by a great deale than our own.

Foreign style and foreign workmen, as had been employed at Longleat and Somerset House, were deplored by Harrison. The change from traditional carpentry for building typifies, for him, the weakening of the stability and authority of the upper classes. In a passage where he denounces the use of oak, he expresses his feelings most concisely. In earlier times such quality timber was used only for shipbuilding, the frames of churches and in the palaces of princes. Now it had come into general use, with common woods such as willow and elm being shunned. 'When our houses were builded of willow then we had oaken men, but now that our houses are come to be made of oak, our men are not only become willow, but a great many altogether of straw, which is a sore alteration.'

The memories and opinions of the elderly amongst his poorer parishioners at Radwinter in Essex were canvassed by Harrison, as to how the material conditions of life had changed for the good and for the bad. Following a long paragraph in which he writes of the profusion of furniture, tapestry, fine linen and expensive plate in the houses of knights, gentlemen and merchants, he concludes

There are still old men yet dwellinge in the village where I remaine, which have noted three things to be marvellously altered in England within their sound remembrance; and other three things are too much increased. One is the multitude of chimneys latlie erected, whereas in their young days there were not above two or three, if so many, in most uplandish townes of the realme (the religious houses and the manor places always excepted, and peradventure some great personages), but each one made his fire against a reredosse in the hall, where he dined and dressed his meat. The second is the great (although not general) amendment in lodging, for (said they) our fathers (yea and we ourselves also) have lain oft on straw pallets, on rough mats covered onlie with a sheet, under coverlets made of dagswain or hopharlots (I use their owne termes), and a good round log onder their heads instead of a bolster or pillow. If it were so that our fathers or the good man of the house, had within seven years after his marriage purchased a matress or flockebed, and thereto a sack of chaff to rest his head upon, he thought himself to be as well lodged as the lord of the town . . .

This parish pump or tavern talk goes on with

The third thing they tell of is the exchange of vessell, as of wooden platters into pewter, and wooden spoons into silver or tin. For so common were all sorts of wooden stuffe in old time, that a man should hardly find four pieces of pewter (of which one was peradventure a salt) in a good farmer's house, and yet for all this frugality, (if it so be justly called) they were scarce able to live and pay their rents . . . without selling of a cow, a horse, or more . . .

Harrison's comments give atmosphere and life to the opinions of the lower and middle orders of Elizabethan rural society, especially in the contained, jaundiced view of the rich. All of his remarks encourage closer scrutiny. With his mention of 'curious building', and the jingoistic tone of that passage, we might like to read the word 'curious' as in contemporary Italian, as meaning 'eccentric'. Distaste if not hostility was behind the use of the word in the memorandum of 1440 concerning the Divinity Schools at Oxford, but the term seems to have lost its pejorative sense by the end of the sixteenth century, when Francis Bacon (1561–1626) used the word in his essay *On Gardens* of 1597 merely to denote 'elaborate'.

Classicised, lavishly decorated buildings are attacked by Harrison in another place, where he characterises them as being 'like cut paper'. The new comforts of life, such as bedding, noted by the old rustics of Radwinter, are less significant in a discussion of architecture than is the singling out of the proliferation of brick chimneys in buildings even of yeomen and those of lower status. Indeed the house in which Harrison probably wrote his *Description of England*, the 'Old Rectory' adjacent to the churchyard at Radwinter, is a very compact timber structure with a massive brick chimney-stack in the middle of its north side (figure 25). Historians of housing and social conditions write of 'a fireside revolution' in England in the course of the half-century before Harrison was writing.[44] The greater availability of brick at much lower cost in a region of great agricultural wealth but no stone, is a good barometer of the greater prosperity seen by the old men. Some way to the east of Radwinter is Stoke-by-Nayland, which is an excellent example of a highly prosperous village in Harrison's time. It boasts merchants' houses built of oak, expensively lit with glass and imposing single, double and quadruple chimney-stacks (figure 26). To a Thomas Lever or an Arthur Warren such signs of affluence and comfort were symbols of privacy and selfishness, not to be rejoiced over as beckoning hospitality.

Contemporaries saw the Royal model as irresistible for imitation by the nobility. As the sixteenth century drew to a close, the change represented by chimneys as a

25 *above* Radwinter, Essex. The 'Old Rectory' (probably the house in which Harrison wrote *The Description of England*). The back, facing the courtyard. The grand scale of the chimney is a dominant feature of such a small house, whose front faces south.

26 *left* Stoke-by-Nayland, Suffolk. Timber-framed houses. Late medieval or sixteenth-century, with substantial late sixteenth-century brick chimney-stacks.

standard feature affordable by the 'middling sort' is of of profound historical and architectural consequence. Such convenience and comfort was unimaginable a generation before. The enclosure of fires in brick or stone chimney-stacks made the open hall redundant, releasing the upper space for another floor. This made the subdivision of ground and first floors into rooms with specialised uses practical and desirable. Amongst the consequences of the 'fireside revolution' were cleaner, more comfortable houses with, eventually, much more private space. Harrison and others of like mind believed sincerely that the benefits of better housing did not improve people. On the contrary it gave them ideas above their station. Almost everything which beguiles us about 'fayre' sixteenth-century houses ought not to. For England, France, Italy or Spain the study of the plans of 'fayre houses' newly built or substantially renovated is richly rewarding. Plans and whenever possible inventories offer insights into the management, organisation and conditions of property owners, their families, followers and servants.[45]

The few foreign travellers who saw and wrote about late sixteenth-century England tell us how well-appointed the houses of the upper classes appeared. The 'great amendment in lodging' for the better-off described by Harrison in the second and third quarters of the sixteenth century is confirmed by no less a figure than Erasmus. In the course of his several visits to England between 1499 and 1517 he saw English houses as uniformly insanitary and badly planned with little or no ventilation, to which he attributed the prevalence of the plague and the 'deadly sweat'. Floors were covered with rushes, which were changed only from time to time, Erasmus noted:

. . . but so imperfectly that the bottom layer is left undisturbed, sometimes for twenty years, harbouring expectorations, vomitings, the leakage of dogs and men, ale droppings, scraps of fish and other abominations not fit to be mentioned.[46]

At first reading Erasmus might seem to be talking of the inns of London or the halls and college lodgings of the two universities, which he knew well. However, at one point he refers to exceptionally large glazed windows, which at the beginning of the sixteenth century were a costly luxury exclusive to the most wealthy London merchants and lawyers or the aristocracy in the shires.[47] He complains that they let in light but seal out fresh air. Erasmus may not be the most objective of sources concerning social conditions, for he was well known for extreme fastidiousness in his personal habits. He ate little and amongst other things was nauseated by fish. Cleanliness mattered much more to him than comfort. The clear impression conveyed by Erasmus, leaving aside the many things which offended him, is of houses far more simply equipped if not primitive in contrast to the panoply of chattels in the 'curious' houses of Harrison's times.

Harrison is one of a very small number of commentators to see the compulsion to overbuild as a general human weakness, something which has to be watched. It is a trait which becomes destructive, when the newly rich compete with the nobility, who in turn respond with projects designed to better those of their inferiors or neighbours. Where de la Noue ironically says that 'the lesser rich, even the poor, have wanted to set their hands to such work', Harrison makes the same observation more credibly with:

> . . . every man almost is a builder, and he that hath bought any small parcell of ground, be it ever so little, will not be quiet till he has pulled down the old house (if any were standing) and set up a new after his own devise, . . . their heads . . . never idle, their purses never shut nor their books of account ever made perfect.

This is almost a complete reversal of the Aristotelian tradition; for now splendid, prestigous buildings are not perceived as justifying a man's magnificence and status. Harrison presumably knew of many case histories, and the sum of what he writes shows a reaction of despondency, not delight in the new architecture. We might divide the more informative Italian, French or English writers who were for and against architectural innovation by the upper classes into optimists and pessimists. The optimists believed in the moral and political value of the 'Renaissance' which their dynamic age had produced. The achievements of ancient civilisation were stimuli to reincarnate literature, art and of course architecture in modern forms. At best this should demonstrate the resilience of civilisation and order. In such matters the leaders of society should lead, and there is no question of any social dimension to such activity and expenditure, as might have been discussed from the eighteenth century onwards. Whether writers of guide books or Aristotelian thinkers, the optimists admired and rejoiced in spectacular change in the appearance of grand and ever-grander town and country houses. The optimists talk of magnificence. The pessimists eschewed all the very various forms of inducement concocted by the optimists to commend or legitimise the scale, cost or seeming strangeness of these changes. The pessimists were convinced that they were watching what was at the very least a developing ailment, but probably a real disease, which if left unchecked would contribute to major instability in the economy, and call into question traditional, stable relations amongst the 'haves', the 'have-less' and the unmentioned droves of the 'have-nothings'. The pessimists brood over luxury.

'Quo vadis?'

We have taken a long road from Ancient Greece to far-off England in the wake of the Reformation. Almost always it is Luxury as a contemporary social or economic issue of the times rather than as an artistic matter, innocent of any harmful side-effects, which brings building and architecture into the wider arena of debate. To continue a discussion of the relationship between ideas of defensible luxury or status and architecture in the Renaissance period, it is useful to move from the 'real' world to the world of dreams and ideals. Myths and fables were often said to fuel the passion for building. If history has the authority to warn and instruct, fiction and philosophy have the power to stimulate the imagination and to untangle superstition.

2

LUXURY ARCHITECTURE IN FICTION AND PHILOSOPHY

The classical heritage

The exasperation of the estimable Francis Bacon with fancy architectural descriptions in literature is concisely expressed in the first two sentences of his essay *Of Building,* first published in 1597. He complains:

Houses are built to Live in, not to Looke on: therefore let Use be preferred before Uniformitie: except where both may be had. Leave the Goodly Fabrickes of Houses, for Beautie only, to the Enchanted Pallaces of the Poets: Who build them at small cost.

Such distractions were an inducement to dream of spending. Bacon was not the first, and he is very far from being the last, for whom dreams of fabulous castles and palaces were idle at best and at worst potentially an insidious influence upon the minds of the impressionable and the young. His scorn did nothing to stem a stream of fashionable literary taste in which descriptions of lavish buildings were used either as metaphors for eeriness and evil or as symbols of wealth or of love. Bacon's comment makes explicit the relationship between fiction and taste in architecture, which he believed was highly undesirable. Building was too important a matter in the lives and economies of people to be subjected to perverse, irresponsible, luxurious influences.

To attempt a comprehensive survey of the references to luxury architecture in fiction and in philosophical writing from their origins in antiquity to the Renaissance would take up too much space. It would involve much tedious repetition. The list of ancient, medieval and later texts of interest in this context is very long. These texts are usually fleeting descriptions of imaginary buildings and serve as minor detours or narrative decorations. The purpose here must be to take some account of the role luxury architecture could play, when being used as more than mere background to narrative, where writers expected that it would act forcefully on the imaginations and the ethical thinking of their readers. In creating the city of Atlantis or the Abbey of Thélème, Plato and Rabelais shared a common purpose, to activate the reader's mind's eye. This is serious entertainment, which is immeasurably more impressive than any panegyric or polemic about architecture.

The buildings of fabled or imaginary places need not be thought of as mere adjuncts to the main theme of stories, tales and epics. Often they are assertive symbols, which bring clearly into view issues of power, wealth, community, or of good and of evil, which matter to the main thrust of the story. Bacon might be gently reproached for being unresponsive to a device in classical and modern literature, which at its best could be employed with considerable and memorable effect. It does not and should not matter whether fictional or philosophical musings about buildings were paradigms of excellence or of corruption; their purpose lies elsewhere.

Candescent names such as Atlantis, Athens, Jerusalem, Babylon or Rome do not merely refer to places. In Western literature and philosophy they are symbols of virtue, glory, good or bad government, corruption or of routine vices such as vanity. The association of the names of these real or fictitious cities with issues provided plenty of potential for symbolic reference from the ethereal to the ridiculous. The attributes and trappings of these places were known in general terms to a broad spectrum of men and women who could read or who received their learning and entertainment from an oral tradition. There is an abundance of examples of late Roman, medieval or Renaissance texts with glosses inserted, which hark back to earlier, well-known accounts of this fabled city or that enchanted castle. Indeed, by the end of the sixteenth century, when Bacon was trying to call a halt, the elaborate imagery of many Italian, French or English poets was steeped in sacred and secular visionary writing of all kinds, which of course included architecture. These buildings built 'at small cost', whether of marble or mud, are almost always of central importance for the way in which characters and peoples are to be esteemed by the reader. Orators and poets knew that *ekphrasis* or bold, vigorous description of material things is a means to hypnotise or seduce an audience more effectively than dogma. Few Latin writers could be thought of as personally approving of the motives and consequences of mythical or real luxury architecture. At first sight it might seem paradoxical that writers of romances and philosophers shared a common approach in this regard with satirists, political thinkers and moralists adhering firmly to reality. Fiction and philosophy in this context use very similar means for very different ends.

Paradise and paper myths

Classical and medieval accounts of Paradise usually contain descriptions of enchanted palaces radiating light from jewelled and gilded walls. Indeed the dazzling walls of these structures, made of beautiful and indestructible materials, is one of the few characteristics of Paradise upon which we may rely, because the testimony of those who say they have been there is so consistent on this point.[1] Every culture has invented a vision of Paradise, and as this was invariably enclosed within impenetrable walls, it was natural for writers to incline towards architectural fantasy. However in contemplating such buildings the reader is usually impressed with a sense of foreboding. Paradise was lost, Troy and Rome had fallen. However, court writers and entertainers during the Renaissance attempted to narrow the image of magnificently adorned buildings. They created them as eloquent representations of righteousness and of princely virtue. Here we must always try to distinguish between the aims and purposes behind the writing of dreams and of propaganda.

Troy

The Trojan legend has been such a constant theme in western literature and art, even up to and including our own times, that it makes a natural starting point. Troy to the Greeks was both the gateway to eastern trade and the symbol *par excellence* of wealth and luxury. As such Troy loomed large in European minds well into the sixteenth century as a commonplace for opulence. The fashion for fictitious historiographies for the ruling houses of Burgundy, France or England was based on a free rereading and competitive rewriting of the legend. Trojan ancestry had been a mainstay of Roman political theory. Thus in an anti-Homeric and pro-Trojan spirit Virgil made Aeneas the hero of his version of the epic. The myth of the Trojan origin of the Franks was first formulated by Fredegar in the seventh century, and this set in motion a process of emulation spanning the centuries, which inspired the iconographers of the Imperial House, the Dukes of Burgundy. Kings of France encouraged the promulgation of the story in plays, manuscripts and painting. The invention of epilogues to the story, to exalt the pedigrees of the rival royal houses, helped to make the Trojan legend a literary playground for the imagination of 'Court Society'.[2] Writers whose adaptations of the epic survive rarely shortened episodes from the *Iliad* or the *Odyssey*. The sparkling descriptions of the building of Troy by Priam or the account of the lavish palace of the ever-generous Alcinous, King of the Phaeacians are outstanding.

The story of the building and of the sack of Troy sets momentous events in a setting which traditionally required especial attention to detail for both writer and painter. The fabulous buildings are a challenge to the inventive skill of the artist to satisfy the expectations of readers, who would expect to see something extraordinary (figures 27–9). The forms of the temples and palaces could not be reconstructed or visually rendered by an artist other than in a free-form of the shapes of the ecclesiastical and secular architecture of his time. The magnificent sheets attributed to Jean Colombe are just one marvellous example, where the gate in the middle ground or the palace in the background has tracery as rich,

27 The Building of Troy.

if not richer, and more complex than any which could be found in contemporary architecture or even metalwork. There is relief sculpture everywhere, and even the recognisably north European row of town houses on the right has sculptural and armorial embellishments. Here is an ideal world to appeal to prince and bourgeois alike. Eternal social distinctions are clearly marked and understood, as exemplified in the deferential gesture of the sculptor in the foreground to his lord. All the classes coexist in harmony.

Every description of Troy eulogises the gold, silver and other materials, whose dazzling effects make more interesting and evocative reading than could any account of the particularities of the architecture, such as the form of a cornice or the proportions of a column. The appetites of the reader are to be stimulated by sample tastes of unsurpassable splendour. In ancient epics and medieval chivalric romances the image of the palace represents the hyperbole of man's materialistic dreams. Every child educated in the classics would have read, if not have had to translate, the well-known passage from the *Odyssey* where the palace of Alcinous is described. It was a gift from the gods as a tribute to his virtues.

28 *left*   The Sack of Troy.

29 *below*   The Palace of Priam (detail from figure 27). The form of the building and its crowded skyline looks forward to Chambord, and the wealth of relief sculpture on the exterior prefigures Nonsuch (figures 15–17).

Now is Odysseus come to the palace of the King. / Beside the brazen threshold wondering / Long while he stands. Gleam as of moon or sun / Shines ever through its halls: the bright walls run / All bronze about the palace, from the door / Even to the inmost chamber banded o'er / With steel-blue frieze. Fashioned of fine-wrought gold / The portals are, and silver columns hold / Aloft a silver lintel, but the latch / Is gold. And either side of the door keep watch / Twin hounds, one golden, one of silver – wrought / To guard it by Hephaestus' cunning thought – / Immortal never ageing. Through the hall / This way and that stand ranged along the wall / High thrones, with coverings woven close and fine, / The work of women; there they sit and dine – / The chieftains of the people – from the store / That never fails. And all about the floor, / Poised on firm pedestals, in either hand / Holding a flaming torch, young Cupids stand / Carved all in gold, shedding their lambent rays / To light the feast through the dark wintry days. – / And fifty handmaidens about the halls / Perform their tasks as each her duty calls . . . [Pope's translation]

Readers of all nationalities during and after the Renaissance period would instinc-tively give fuller, more precise form to the palace of Alcinous in their imagination from the scattering of details and objects pointed to by Homer. The sketchiness of the description is deliberate. As it would originally have been told out loud from memory or read out in later times, the other-worldliness of it all would have been forcefully felt. If done by a good performer, embellishments and asides would be added to astonish the audience. In the oral tradition of performance of epic tales, it is impossible to calculate how much of architectural fantasy has been lost and forgotten since antiquity. Plato got the story of Atlantis fourth hand from his cousin Critias, so there must have been an abundance of lesser tales.

Atlantis

The impact of Homer's evocation of the architecture of Troy and of the palaces of those favoured by the gods for their virtue was not intended to impress by vulgarity. Make believe mixed with tales of heroism is innocent fun in comparison to Plato's light-hearted yet serious-minded telling of the legend of Atlantis.[3] The myth of Atlantis, which is compared unfavourably with a semi-mythical Athenian state, is told in order to set out an explicit set of values. A people can be evaluated through their works of art and their buildings, just as by the deeds in which their qualities are expressed. Saint Augustine early in the fifth century reiterated for christians a central tenet of Stoic philosophy, when he argued in *The City of God* that men can be judged by what they love.

Plato refrained from any denunciation of the lavish buildings of the Atlanteans, which the Stoics would not have hesitated to make. He expected future readers or hearers of his version of the tale to think of Atlantis and her buildings in very various terms, from contempt or disbelief to wonder. His aim is to provide a *topos*, which he could disclaim as being of his own making. Yet in drawing the contrasts between Atlantis and Athens the guise of impartiality breaks down, and justice is done with the Athenians of ancient memory repelling the predatory Atlanteans, which led to their subsequent obliteration in mysterious circumstances. Like Homer, Plato activated the mind's eye with architecture beyond the means of any man, but we are left to wonder whether he was not teasing the credulity and the venality of ordinary mortals.

The grandiose palaces of Atlantis were built of three colours of stone: black, white and red, and yet:

Some of their buildings were simple, but in others they put together different stones, varying the colour to please the eye, and to be a natural source of delight. The entire circuit of the wall which went around the outermost zone, they covered with a coating of brass, and the circuit of the next wall they coated in tin, and the third, which encompassed the citadel, flashed with the red light of orichalchum. The palaces in the interior of the citadel were laid out in the following way: In the centre was a holy temple dedicated to Cleito and Poseidon, which was shut off, and was surrounded by an enclosure of gold, a stadium [180 metres] long, and half a stadium in width, and of proportionate height, the whole edifice having a strange, barbaric appearance. All of the outside of the temple, with the exception of the pinnacles, they covered with silver, and the pinnacles they covered in gold. The roof inside the temple was made up in ivory, curiously trimmed here and there with gold and silver orichalchum; and all the other parts, the walls, pillars and indeed the floor were coated with orichalcum. Inside the temple statues of gold abounded; . . . There was an altar too, which in scale and in workmanship perfectly reflected this magnificence, and the palaces in like manner echoed the status of the kingdom and the glorious allure of the temple.

If it were not for the the words 'strange barbaric appearance' in Plato's judgement on the proportions of Poseidon's temple, his summary account of the monuments and the precincts of Atlantis might pass for uninspired or casual materialistic eulogy. The passage is full of paradox and irony. The coverings of the wall might well have looked dazzling when new, but the likes of tin and brass should be read instantly as ridiculous materials for durable and weatherproof walls. In mixing quarried stone of different colours it is not likely that such artificial effects were meant as 'a natural source of delight'. The equation of mining with the rape of a benevolent female, that is to say Mother Earth, was an idea which was ancient when quoted by Pliny in the second century AD, and must have stemmed from Greece. The condemnation of the Atlanteans' materialistic values and garish taste is merely implied, but the remarks that follow tell us that every generation of Atlanteans sought to outshine their forefathers by adding to and aggrandising their private houses. The Athenians admired and were content to inhabit the houses which sufficed for their fathers. The contrast is one of artificiality and flux as the norm at Atlantis, as against the natural life and continuity at an Athens which bore little relation to the truth of the place, with its brash confidence, in the age of Pericles or in Plato's own time, the fourth century BC. Indeed the enormous expenditure on gold and ivory for the giant statue of Athena, commissioned by Pericles for the Parthenon in the century before Plato was writing, was an Atlantean indulgence for people who were supposed to be especially sensitive to the dangers of ostentation, and who were studious practitioners of moderation, order and appropriateness.

Athenian controversies

Plutarch's famous biography of Pericles, written at the turn of the first century AD, paints a picture of Athens and her successful warlords far removed from that painted by Plato in the *Critias*.

But there was one measure above all which at once gave the greatest pleasure to the Athenians, adorned their city and created amazement amongst the rest of mankind, and which is today the sole testimony that the tales of the ancient power and glory of Greece are no mere fables. By this I mean the construction of temples and public buildings; and yet it was this, more than any other action of his [Pericles] which his enemies slandered and misrepresented. They cried out in the Assembly that Athens had lost her good name and disgraced herself by transferring from Delos into her own keeping the funds that had been contributed from the rest of Greece, and that now the most plausible excuse for this action, namely, that the money had been removed for fear of barbarians and was being guarded in a safe place, had been demolished by Pericles himself. 'The Greeks must be outraged,' they cried, 'they must consider this an act of blatant tyranny, when they see that with their own contributions, extorted from them by force for the war against the Persians, we are gilding and beautifying Athens, as if it were some vain woman decking herself out with costly stones, with statues and temples worth millions.' Pericles' answer to these people was that the Athenians were not obliged to give the allies any account of how their money was spent, provided that they carried on the war for them and kept the Persians away. 'They do not give us a single horse, nor a soldier, nor a ship. All they supply is money,' he told the Athenians, 'and this belongs not to the people who give it, but to those who receive it, so long as they provide the services they are paid for. It is no more than fair that after Athens has been equipped with all she needs to carry on the war, she should apply the surplus to public works, which once completed, will bring her glory for all time, and while they are being built will convert that surplus to immediate use. In this way all kinds of enterprises and demands will be created, which will provide inspiration for every art, find employment for every hand, and transform the whole people into wage earners, so that the city will decorate and maintain herself at the same time from her own resources.'

The social and economic philosophy which informs the politics of Pericles was the near-contemporary foil for Plato's text.

Plato's Athenians live on the north side of the Acropolis in winter, and move to the south side in summer, thus fitting harmoniously into the pattern of the seasons. They are almost as fictitious as the Atlanteans, but they are invented to contrast in an extreme fashion the natural with the unnatural. In this exercise the use of architecture is direct and effective. In Atlantis the people enjoyed spectator sports in a hippodrome, whilst the Athenians preferred healthy exercise in a gymnasium.

The kings of Atlantis always tried to surpass their predecessors by adding to their palace, whilst Athenian houses remained unchanged from generation to generation. The luxury of Atlantis is barbarous, the continuity and contentment with bare sufficiency of Plato's Athens is natural and civilised. Plato offers a general account of the layout of Atlantis, with no effort being made to describe a palace or temple in precise detail. The grand absurdity is in the materials of which the city is built. City walls covered in sheets of brass, of tin or of gold can only be thought of as preposterous splendour, and proof that the Atlanteans had no taste. However, gaudiness is only a folly, whilst the sin is the waste of resources involved in the mining, manufacture and assembly of so much metal for such a silly use. Their wealth derives from exactly the sort of tyranny of which Pericles had been accused, but the Atlanteans have no philosophy of power to justify their ostentation. Walls covered with tin, brass or gold could never be imposing in the sense of being effective or forbidding barriers, and might be more of an incentive to pilfering or plunder, than sights which would draw admiring sighs from the imaginary tourist. Dramatic appearance is all that is suggested in Plato's skilful account. He deliberately leaves out anything which might inspire admiration for any special qualities of form or detail amongst the great piles of Atlantis. Mixing a little history with myth Plato leaves his audience with a resolute sense of the virtues of conservatism in matters of building and architecture. Plato's Atlantis has been viewed by many as a key to an understanding of deep-rooted Athenian social and political values which were being brushed aside in a time of victory and international prestige. By representing in terms of its religion, monarchy and use of wealth the antithesis of the just and worthy state, Atlantis became the proverbial symbol for waste and vanity. Later Aristotle confected a conception of ideal states and households in his *Politics*. He found no use for warnings about waste or corruption, using architectural metaphors. Plato's story did not need reworking, even amongst political and economic thinkers who wished to justify great differences in wealth between the classes. Above all Aristotle argued the case for private property. It is remarkable, when we explore change and continuity in ancient literature, to find that the Greeks, who were so richly endowed with utopian fantasy so long before Utopia was invented, created a literary genre ignored by all leading Roman philosophers and political thinkers.

From Athens to Rome

The practical Romans were almost devoid of interest in such unrealistic manifestations of the human spirit. The only traces of such Greek fantasy are occasional glosses. The stagey palace of the Sun King at the beginning of book II of the *Metamorphoses* of Ovid, or more significantly the amazing, magical golden palace of Cupid conjured up by Apuleius in book V of the *Golden Ass* are the archetypes which stand behind all late Latin and medieval literary paradise-castles.[4] The palace of Cupid in the *Golden Ass* is the perfect example of how a writer with flair was disinclined to slow the pace of a flight of pure fantasy with dull architectural detail. Tedious 'discourses on architecture', so derided by the inestimable Father Jean des Antomeures of Rabelais' imagination, would have soured the flavour and dulled the fun of imagining the impact of a supernatural palace. Cupid's intended lover Psyche follows a stream which led her to the heart of a wood:

... where she came upon a royal palace, too wonderfully built to be the work of any other than a god; in fact as soon as she passed the gate she knew that some god must be in residence. The ceiling was exquisitely carved in citrus wood and ivory and supported on columns of gold; the walls were sheeted in silver on which figures of all the beasts of the world were embossed, and seemed to be running towards Psyche as she came in. They were clearly the work of some demi-god, if not of a full god, and the pavement was a mosaic of all kinds of precious stones arranged to form pictures. How fortunate, how very fortunate anyone would be to have the chance of walking on a jewelled floor like that. And the other parts of this immense palace were replete with things just as beautiful and delectable and fabulously costly. The facing of the walls was made up of massive gold blocks which glittered so brightly with their own radiance that the house had a daylight all of its own, even when the sun refused to shine: every room and portico and doorway streamed with light, and the furniture blended with the rooms. Indeed, it seemed the sort of palace that Jupiter himself might have built as his earthly residence. Psyche was entranced. She went timorously up the steps, and after a time dared to cross the threshold. The beauty of the hall lured her on; and every new sight added to her wonder and admiration. When well inside the palace she came on splendid treasure chambers stuffed with unbelievable riches; every wonderful thing that one might imagine was there. But what amazed her more than the stupendous wealth of the world treasury, was that no single bar, lock, or armed guard protected it. As she stood gazing in rapt delight, a voice suddenly spoke from nowhere. Do these treasures astonish your Royal Highness? They are all yours. Why not go to your bedroom now and rest your tired body. When you feel inclined for your bath we will be there to help you, for I am one of your handmaidens.

Seduced by the staggering wealth of the building, and cosseted by invisible staff, it is little wonder Psyche was moved to enjoy the physical love of her invisible husband. Goddesses can be venal, and she was reassured by the tribute paid to her in treasure. Romans who rejoiced in the real luxury architecture of Rome knew full well how real treasure and booty had built the city. Such unfocused, delirious and sensual writing is characteristic Imperial Roman architectural fiction. Roman patriotism was conditioned by grand, seductive building; Roman fictional architecture has none of the subtlety or purpose of Plato's abstractions.

Actual luxury architecture was the issue for writers as different as Cicero and Horace; they felt no need to dabble with fictions. Political orators and poets shared a keen sense of the potential for discord which highly ornate secular buildings could inject into society, especially if they were claimed to be *res publica*.

Now regal villas had few acres left for ploughing; on all sides were ornamental ponds, quoted and adapted innumerable times in the visual arts during the course of the Renaissance.[5] Notorious examples of the 'regal villas' or city palaces, such as the Golden House of Nero, were funded by ruinous taxes and built with forced labour. Roman authors of the first and second centuries AD echo the accusers of Pericles in equating luxury architecture with tyranny. They may have been right.

From the profane to the sacred

The example of Plato and the style of the oral mythology of Greece was enduring in conjuring images of fabulous buildings. It was given new vigour in the Bible, most dramatically in the Apocalypse, or Book of Revelation of Saint John the Divine. The visions of John on Patmos provide a startling conclusion to the New Testament. Their intensity and horror certainly were apposite, being written against a background of the persecutions of Nero or of Domitian. Close to the end of the account the respite for the anxious mortal reader is a description of the heavenly Jerusalem. A mere pagan might well see it as pandering more to earthly, material values than as a place created by the irreproachable Almighty. The chosen will be sent to a city which

> ...was built as a square, and was as wide as it was long. It was measured by his [one of the seven angels who guides John] rod twelve thousand furlongs, its length, breadth and height being equal. Its wall was one hundred and forty four cubits high, that is by human measurements which the angel was using. The wall was built of jasper, while the city itself was pure gold, bright as clear glass. The foundations of the city wall were adorned with jewels of every kind, the first of the foundation stones being of jasper, the second lapis lazuli, the third chalcedony, the fourth emerald, the fifth sardonyx, the sixth cornelian, the seventh chrysolite, the eighth beryl, the ninth topaz, the tenth chrysoprase, the eleventh turquoise, and the twelfth amethyst. The twelve gates were twelve pearls, each gate being made from a single pearl. The streets of the city were of pure gold, like translucent glass.[6]

It is a very bold step to imagine heaven made of materials coveted by man, and many theologians have maintained that such matters surpass human understanding or imagination. The guise of divine revelation is insufficient justification. In this context the passage from Revelation is of greater significance than the more detailed and famous architectural description of the Temple of Solomon by Ezekiel in the Old Testament.[7] The rainbow effect of the walls of John's heavenly Jerusalem built of precious stones was the design of God, and thus rescued glittering architecture from the realms of sin and barbarism to become the reserve of the virtuous. Later Christian writers, who built 'at small cost', were pleased to have such an authority for their palaces of heroes or castles of love.

Moralising fiction

In contrast, Latin writers from Lucretius (*c*.99–55 BC) to Claudian (fl. AD 400) assert that buildings with features such as elaborate gilded ceilings are evidence of wealth allied to evil and eeriness. As an example we might take Lucan's imaginary account in his *Pharsalia* of the setting of Cleopatra's seduction of Caesar, which has all the material and sensual allure characteristic of epic and myth.[8] Lucan has been described as being like an auctioneer in love with his merchandise as he catalogues the marble, alabaster, ebony and tortoiseshell, jewels and fabrics, which comprise the intoxicating place of assignation. The seduction of Caesar is greatly helped, if it is not effected, by the astonishing richness of the banqueting hall and the private apartments. Lucan's account gains momentum when he visualises and rhapsodises over architectural splendours of incalculable cost, the better to discredit Caesar in his depravity, and to vilify Cleopatra and her household. It is worth reminding ourselves that Cleopatra was a woman who impressed Cicero with her knowledge of philosophy, and who had the business acumen and technical knowledge to run a wool-mill. The school of philosophy which made the most concerted attack on luxury architecture was Stoicism, and Lucan can be judged to have been amongst the most outspoken of Stoics.

To the Stoic eye all craft is suspect as an illegitimate reordering of natural forms and processes.[9] Plutarch records in his life of the Spartan Lycurgus, a Stoic proto-type: 'It was because he was used to . . . simplicity that Leotychides the Elder, as we are told, when he was dining in Corinth, and saw the roof of the house was adorned with costly panellings, asked his host if trees grew square in that country?' This anecdote has a clear purpose, to make an example of a luxury that is not simply a matter of excess but a question of the order and fitness of things. The implication is that a properly panelled ceiling should restate the natural forms of the trees. Coffers would be acceptable, were trees square.[10] Columns are no longer recognisable as tree trunks, and are made of materials other than wood; walls of refined metal or rare stones in heaven or on earth speak of the most ambitious architecture exceeding the means of the richest and defying the comprehension of the wisest.[11] The romantic, mystic and Stoic critiques of luxury architecture were literary legacies from antiquity and the early Christian periods, which were rejuvenated in many forms in the fiction and philosophy of the Renaissance.

The Renaissance

The relationship of humanism to the new style in architecture is littered with contradictions and surprises. North and south of the Alps ancient texts on all manner of subjects were read and discussed, translated and copied to be made more widely known. Centres of learning with universities or court academies combed the literary legacy of the ancient world for a great range of knowledge, from the technological to the philosophical. A humanist nurtured with classical culture was not necessarily a partisan of the new style in architecture, and very many were more concerned with the ethics of privilege and the dangers of excess. The learned were more commonly cautious, if not critical, of the classically styled architectural ambitions of princes and gentlemen. This did not preclude a keen interest in the monumental remains of antiquity.

Petrarch, Boccaccio and their disciples brought about a radically different attitude, dispelling medieval superstitious traditions that they had been built by pagan magic. To Boccaccio the ruins of Rome were 'testimonio della grandezza, dell'anima di collui chi edificio'.[12] These writers were sensitive to the emotional impact of the great structures of a fallen civilisation, but their interest did not extend to measuring them or to any detailed description. In mid-fifteenth-century Italy only Alberti perceived archaeology, architectural practice and ethics to be related subjects. He was no dreamer. The architecture of ideal states and societies invented by his fellow Italians from Filarete to Patrizi, or the Utopias of Thomas More and Rabelais, or the fantasy architecture of 'Roma Antica' found in the *Hypnerotomachia Poliphili* or in numerous artists' sketchbooks, would have seemed to him to be poor fiction and a weak vehicle for philosophic metaphor. Alberti makes no reference in any of his writings to the architectural fantasy, which delighted numerous popular novelists and prominent philosophers of the Renaissance. Paradoxically Alberti's ideal in architecture of a harmony of *commoditas* with *voluptas* – of function and of beauty – was a maxim in a work where some use of his writings was made of which he would have wholeheartedly disapproved; Filarete's manuscript *Trattato d'Architettura* was written at Milan between 1460 and 1464. It was well enough known a century later to be described by Giorgio Vasari as the most ridiculous book ever produced.[13]

Utopia in Milan

Antonio Averlino (1400?–69), whose adopted name 'Filarete' means 'lover of virtue' in Greek, will be forever loved for his creation for Francesco Sforza, Duke of Milan, of the ideal city of Sforzinda. His treatise is an elaborate tissue of fictions with an opening scene, set at table, in which the architect fights off his detractors. Amongst the issues is an elaborate defence of the Florentine style against the Lombard. This is interrupted by long digressions on the discovery of an ancient city plan by Onitoan Nolivera (an obvious anagram for his name), and on hunting parties as well as on problems of construction. This agreeable compilation was probably concocted with a view to its being read aloud to the Duke while he dined, with the *divertissements* making any technical matters of architecture or building the more digestible. Sforzinda, we are told, is to be built by the mythical King Zogalia and designed by his architect entirely in the antique style. The building programme involves a work-force of 102,000 masters and workmen, a total which does not include overseers and additional labourers to assist in laying the foundations. This army of workmen would lay 30,000,000 bricks, and thus raise the city walls in a mere ten days. Private palaces in Sforzinda were to take a little longer, a full twenty days, but more satisfactorily all the radial streets are made up and the canals dug in eight days. It is every despot's dream.

Filarete based the social structure of Sforzinda on the model described in Plato's *Laws*, which is a discussion of every aspect of life in a city community and its surrounding territory.[14] The property rights of the citizen as well as most of the institutions of the imaginary city described by Plato are adopted for Sforzinda. For example both give detailed accounts of schools for boys and for girls, and both insist on the value of competitions and training in the intellectual and military fields. Plato's city has three prisons for three classes of criminal, one in the city centre, one away from the centre and the other in the country, whilst Filarete opts for a single structure in the country divided vertically into three sections. Plato gives no architectural description of his institutions, whilst Filarete not only describes his versions of them, but provides drawings. In the very centre of Sforzinda is an institution the like of which is found in only one other later description of an ideal city-state.[15] The 'House of Vice' is a place where sexual needs could be satisfied, and was to be balanced with a 'House of Virtue' next door (figure 30). There are baths and taprooms and other creature comforts and provision for 'games and other swindles, as is the custom, although an unfortunate one'. Courtesans brought to the House of Vice by their neighbours for violating decent behaviour are accorded a degree of respect in Sforzinda. *Luxuria* is appropriately if tamely condemned in symbolic decorations. Necessary vices are tolerated, and yet this is no wildly licentious society, and there are punishments even in the House of Vice for unspecified 'things which cannot be permitted'. Portraits of Nero, Elagabalus, Sardanapalus and unidentified contemporaries accused of monstrous crimes are displayed to discourage unnatural proclivities amongst the customers of these establishments. The House of Vice rejoiced in a brothel on the ground floor and an astronomical observatory on the top. There is order and pleasure in abundance in Sforzinda, and the architecture of the buildings, Filarete tells us, is intended to reflect that harmony.

The tower of the lord's palace of Sforzinda would have been instantly recognisable to fifteenth-century Italian eyes as a symbol of wealth and prestige (figure 31). Noble towers bristled on the skyline of medieval Siena or Bologna, and the most famous surviving example of competitive tower-building amongst members of a small-town oligarchy is San Gimignano. Modern historians are happy to refer to the 'San Gimignano model' as an easily understood metaphor for rivalry

30   Filarete. The Houses of Vice and Virtue for Sforzinda.

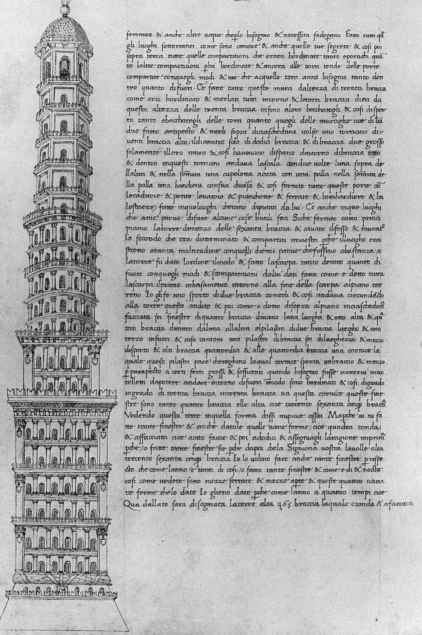

sommita & anche altre acque cheplo bisogno & necessita sadopano tam tum qua
gli luoghi sotterranei come sono comune & anche quelle sue segrete & cosi poi
sopra terra tutte quelle compartitioni che erano hordinate tanto eportichi qua
to laltre compartitioni piu hordinate & ancora alle torri vonde delle porte
compartite conquegli modi & vie che acquelle torri anno bisogno tanto den
tro quanto difuori Et fatte tutte queste mura daltezza di trenta braccia
come era hordinato & merlati tutti intorno & letorri braccia diece da
questa altezza dello trenta braccia infino aloro becchategli & cosi dispor
to tanto ebecchategli delle torri quanto quegli delle muraglie cioe di tai
due fruto antiposto & merti sopra diciaschieduna volse uno torrono di
uenti braccia alto / ildiametro solo di dodici braccia & di braccia due grosso
solamente illoro muro & cosi haueuano dispatio dintorno dibraccia otto
& dentro inquesti torrioni omdaua lascala comdue volte luna sopra de
llaltra & nella sommita una cupoletta acuta con una palla nella sommita de
lla palla una bandiera consua divisa & cosi fornite tutte queste porte co
lecaditoie & ponte leuatoio & pianchette & ferrate & bombardiere & la
lestriere / fatte inqueluoghi cherano diputati dallui Et anche inque luoghi
che anne parue disare alcune cose butili sea Siche fornito tutto prima
piamo latorre dimezzo delle sexanta braccia & cauato ilfosso & murai
lo secondo che era determinato & comparti maestro poche illuogho era
stretto atanta moltitudine conquesti chormi parue chefussino abastanza a
latorre fu dato lordine ilmodo & fatto lascarpa tanto dentro quanto di
fuori conquegli modi & scompartitioni dallui dati fara come e detto tutta
lascarpa ilprimo imbasamento intorno alla fine della scarpa alpiano ter
reno Io glife uno sporto didue braccia comerti & cosi andaua circundado
alla torre questo andito & poi come o detto disopra alpiano inciaschedun
facciata sei finestre diquanto braccia divano luna larcha & otto alta & qua
tro braccia dimuro daluna allaltra elpilastro didue braccia larcho & uno
terzo infuori & insu cantoni uno pilastro dibraccia sei dilarghezza & mezzo
disporto & alti braccia quattordici & alle quattordici braccia una cornice la
quale questi pilastri pare dereghino laqual cornice sporta umbraccio & mezzo
pparapedto a certi ferri grossi & sofficienti quando bisogno fusse meterui man
telletti dapotere andare intorno difuori modo sono hordinati & cosi digrado
ingrado di trenta braccia intrenta braccia ua questa cornice infino alle fine
stre sono tante quante braccia elle alta cioe trecento sexanta cinqu braccia
Vedendo questa torre inquella forma disse mipiace assai Maparche ai tu fa
tte tante finestre & anche datole quelle uarie forme cioe quadra tonda
& affacciata cioe actto facce & poi a dodici & assegnagli lamgione imprimi
poche io fatte tante finestre sie poche dapoi chela Signioria nostra lauolle alta
trecento sexanta cinqu braccia Io lo uoluto fare anche tante finestre prspe
cto che come lanno e tanti di cosi o fatto tante finestre & come e di & nocte
cosi come vedete sono mezze serrate & mezze apte & queste quattro uaria
ti forme chelo date Io glieno date poche come lanno a quattro tempi cioe
Qua dallato sara disegnata latorre alta 365 braccia laquale etonda & afacciata

31 Filarete. The tower for the lord of Sforzinda.

and the quest for status by building in a very small community.[16] Some one hundred and forty such towers in Rome, during a famous campaign in 1257, were *capitozzata*,[17] with similar measures being instituted by the commune in Florence during the late thirteenth and early fourteenth centuries in pursuit of its policy of asserting public authority over private interests.[18] The twenty stories of the Lord of Sforzinda's tower is an emblem of unchallenged superiority, and one which might allude to the many references to towers in the Bible, where towers denote the strength of God vested in a mortal. Towers will reappear in our discussion of luxury architecture.

Utopia in the Veneto

The image of social order and architectural wonder which Filarete created for the Duke of Milan was not accessible to a wide readership. That aim was fully achieved in the *Hypnerotomachia Polifili* (Polifilo's Strife of Love in a Dream), a fantasy written by a Dominican monk, who might have known or been known to Filarete. The text is signed Treviso, May Day 1467, but most scholars agree that it dates from the 1480s or 1490s. It was published in Venice by Aldus in 1499, and its author was surely Fra Francesco Colonna of Venice (1433/4–1527).[19] It was translated into most of the major European languages by the end of the sixteenth century, and there is plenty of evidence of its enduring appeal to writers of escapist fiction.[20] The wanderings of the enamoured Polifilo and his final union with his beloved Polia in the gardens of Adonis, surrounded by nymphs making music, might come from a medieval love allegory. However the *Hypnerotomachia Polifili* is a story which transcends convention and traditional formulae of narrative and of content. The echoes of the *Roman de la Rose*, reminiscences of the pilgrimage of Dante's *Divine Comedy*, and borrowings from Boccaccio's *Amorosa Visione* are woven into the text to make the lover of light reading feel at home. He or she might easily skim through those portions of the book which are its true novelty. Instead of golden pastures and gardens of love the reader is conducted through a landscape of awesome ruins and monuments. The author went to great pains to create a convincingly classical atmosphere. The hero acts as an intermediary between ourselves and a distant mysterious past, some of whose secrets he reveals by brilliantly decoding enigmatic hieroglyphs. In case the reader should find difficulty in visualising the fallen columns, broken friezes or huge gleaming temples which Polifilo measures, Colonna had the book beautified with fine woodcut illustrations to help us through nearly five hundred pages of densely printed text (figures 32–5). The quest for requited love accords with the search for an equally important form of fulfilment, which is to remedy the grievous loss of ancient wisdom. By these means modern men and women should discover a large part of their true selves. A hero is both ardent lover and learned antiquarian. He has

A SPAVENTEVOLE SILVA, ET CONSTI,
pato Nemore euafo,&gli primi altri lochi per el dolce
fomno che fe hauea per le feffe & proftrante mébre dif,
fufo relicti,me ritrouai di riouo in uno piu delectabile
fito affai piu che el præcedente. Elquale non era de mon
ti horridi, & crepidinofe rupe intorniato, ne falcato di
ftrumofi iugi. Ma compofitamente de grate montagniole di non tro
po altreia. Siluofe di giouani quercioli, di roburi, fraxini & Carpi,
ni, & di frondofi Efculi, & Ilice, & di teneri Coryli,& di Alni,& di Ti,
lie,& di Opio, & di infructuofi Oleaftri, difpofti fecondo lafpecto de
gli arboriferi Colli. Et giu al piano erano grate filule di altri filuatici

32   Polifilo's dream begins.

arbofcelli, & di floride Genifte, & di multiplice herbe uerdiffime, quiui
uidi il Cythifo, La Carice,la commune Cerinthe. La mufcariata Pana,
chia el fiorito ranunculo,&cceruicello,o uero Elaphio, & la feratula, & di
uarie affai nobile,&de molti altri proficui fimplici,&ignote herbe & fio
ri per gli prati difpenfate. Tutta quefta læta regione de uiridura copiofa,
mente adornata fe offeriua.Pofcia poco piu ultra del mediano fuo,io ri,
trouai uno fabuleto,o uero glareofa plagia, ma in alcuno loco difperfa,
mente,cum alcuni cefpugli di herbatura. Quiui gliochii mei uno io,
cundiffimo Palmeto fe apræfento,cum le foglie di cultrato mucrone
ad tanta utilitate ad gli ægyptii,del fuo dolciffimo fructo fercúde&abun
dante. Tra lequale racemofe palme, & picole alcune, & molte mediocre,
&laltre driterano &excelfe.Electo Signo de uictoria per el refiftere fuo
ad lurgente pondo. Ancora &in quefto loco non trouai incola, ne altro
animale alcuno. Ma peregrinando folitario tra le non denfate, ma inter,
uallate palme fpectatiffime,cogitando delle Rachelaide, Phafelide, & Li
byade,non effere forfa a quefte comparabile. Ecco che uno affermato &
carniuoro lupo alla parte dextra,cum la bucca piena mi apparue.

33   Polifilo begins his encounters
with architectural ruins and
debris.

34   A rare and melancholic
survival – a temple of Jupiter.

iuerfi loci appédeua. Gliqli rami & in qua & i la affixi,cú fupflitóe feruata
fina al futuro anniuerfario ftauano. Et ritornato lo anno tute qlle arefa,
cte fronde racogliédole gli facrarii fimpulatori,il facrificio icendeuano.
Finalméte dappo tuto qfto feftuiffimaméte pacto & fúma cú obferuan,
tia celebrato gli ferali officii cú piee fupplice cum religione & cerimonie
degli dii.qualúque malo genio fugato.Il fúmo facerdote Curione primo
& pofcia dicédo lee extreme parole, illicet . Ognuno licentemete & fefti,
uo ritornare poteua al pprio icolato & læti remeare ad la domuitione .
Cú quefto tale ordine la mia magniloqua Polia facondaméte haurdo,
&cú blandicelle parole tanta obferuantia digna di laudatiffima commé
datione integramente exponendo narrato, & mecompendiofaméte in,
ftituto al fpatiofo & harenulato litore di piaceuoli plémyruli irruenti re
lixo,oue era il deftructo & deferto tempio peruenti ffimo.

35   The lovers Polifilo and
Polia contemplate the ruins of
Polyandron.

the ideal combination of qualities to persuade the reader that greatness of spirit is not the preserve of the knight-errant, and that fabulous ancient monuments have some meaning.

Without the woodcuts the architectural apparatus of the book would baffle the most conscientious reader. The amphitheatre on Cythera, the island for lovers, is based in general terms on the Colosseum, and the Temple of Venus is an obvious pastiche of Santa Costanza, which at the time of the writing of the Hypnerotomachia Polifili was thought by some to have been built as a Temple of Bacchus. One of the Seven Wonders of the Ancient World, the Mausoleum at Halicarnassus, as described by Pliny, is the basis of the Temple of the Sun in the dark vaults of which Polifilo loses himself. The woodcut which shows Polyandron is remarkable for many reasons, not least because it is the 'first Renaissance picture of ruins'.[21] Polyandron is a necropolis for forlorn lovers, an imaginary and romantic architectural emblem of melancholia, that is nevertheless based on a description and survey of the ruins on Delos compiled in 1445 by a legendary antiquarian, Cyriac of Ancona (c.1390–1455).[22] This man of boundless energy, whose travels all over the eastern Mediterranean in search of the remains of antiquity resulted in a mass of detailed descriptions and drawings, left a priceless legacy to late Quattrocento antiquarians and artists. His aim was to 'wake the dead' and he sought by his 'potent and divine art to revive the glorious things, which were alive to the living in antiquity but had become buried and defunct through the lapse of ages and persistent injury at the hands of the half-dead; to bring them from the dark tomb to light, to live once more amongst living men'.[23] In a similar but more pessimistic vein Polia talks to her lover. As they approach the shattered pile of the Temple of Pluto (that is to say the temple of 'the rich one') in Polyandron, she says, 'Look awhile at this noble relic of things great in the eyes of posterity, and see how it now lies in ruins ... in the first age of man it was a splendid and magnificent temple ...'. Such things might be rebuilt in the mind, but all these hopes and musings are no more than 'False dreams, all false, mad heart ...'.

The magnificence and melancholy of the buildings of the Hypnerotomachia Polifili provide some of the most potent imagery of the tale. The book can be seen as the watershed between the writing of chivalric romances, where buildings were used as background decoration, and the work of those writers and poets who, in the wake of Lutheranism and the Sack of Rome in 1527, used the relics of Rome poudreuse as the most cogent of symbols of impermanence.[24] The cult of ruins in literature and art was inaugurated by Colonna, and the outcome of his story is the reverse of Cyriac of Ancona's thesis. Cyriac would reknit the fabric of antiquity, which time had unravelled, but in the romance time inevitably unravels love. What use is there to build monuments other than in the mind? Such an attitude forms part of the mental worlds of Thomas More and of François Rabelais, who built 'at small cost' the most enduring architectural fictions of the sixteenth century.

More's Utopia

Throughout his life Thomas More suffered prolonged periods of black despair, and at such times his gloomy and contemptuous view of his fellow man made him weary of existence. The father of a whole genre in western European thought was a man often at odds with himself. More's complexes made him ideally suited to write about harmony. His voluminous writings and copious correspondence are the preserves of specialists, whilst the little book *Utopia* has a giant reputation. It was published first, in Latin, at Louvain in 1516, then at Paris in 1517, and again at Basle in 1518, with a German translation appearing in that city in 1524. An Italian translation appeared in 1548 at Venice, with a translation into English 'of melodious charm' finally being printed in 1551.[25] The success of the work in Latin made the paradoxical world of *Utopia* common ground for the imaginations of the educated throughout Europe. Translation into the major vernaculars produced innumerable echoes in political pamphlets, popular plays, novels and satires. Thoughtful folk have been arguing over meanings in *Utopia* ever since.

Utopia means literally 'no place', and the towns of the realm are described at the start in discouraging terms. '. . . when you have seen one of them, you have seen them all, for they are as nearly identical as local conditions will permit'. A few paragraphs further on comes the famous description of the leading town, Aircastle.

The streets were designed both for traffic and protection against wind. The buildings are far from unimpressive, for they take the form of terraces running the whole length of the street. The fronts of the houses face each other across a twenty foot carriageway. Behind them is a garden, also as long as the street itself, and completely enclosed by the backs of other streets. Each house has a front door leading to the street with a back door out to the garden. Both sets of doors are a double swing type, which open at a touch, and close automatically behind you. And so anyone can go in and out, for there is no such thing as private property. The houses are allocated by lot and change hands every ten years. The people are extremely fond of their gardens, in which they grow fruit including grapes, as well as having grass and flowers. They are kept in wonderful condition, and in all truth I have never seen anything to beat them for beauty and prolific growth. The people of Aircastle are keen gardeners not only because they enjoy it, but are given even greater incentive to excel by the competitions which are held between streets for the finest garden. Certainly it would be difficult to find any feature of the town better calculated to give pleasure and profit to the community, which makes me think that gardening must have been one of the founder's special interests.

By the founder I mean Utopos himself who, it is said, designed the layout of the town. However, he left posterity to embellish it and add the finishing touches, which he realised would take more than one lifetime. According to their historical records, which cover a period of 1,760 years from the conquest and which have been most carefully written up, the earliest houses were merely small huts or cottages built hurriedly with the first timber which came to hand. The walls were plastered with mud, the roofs were ridged and thatched. But nowadays every house is an imposing three storey structure. The walls are faced with flint or some other hard stone, or else with bricks and lined with roughcast. The sloping roofs have been lowered to the horizontal, and covered with a special sort of concrete which costs next to nothing, but it is better than lead for resisting bad weather conditions, and it is also fireproof. They keep out draughts by glazing the windows. Oh yes, they use a great deal of glass, or alternatively they fit screens of fine linen treated with clear oil or amber, which has the effect of making it more transparent and also more airtight.

Much if not most of book II of *Utopia*, in which the imaginary society is described, was written during More's diplomatic mission of May to October 1515 to Brabant and Flanders. It was a momentous time in his political career and intellectual life. Amongst many others he met Erasmus in Bruges, Peter Gillis in Antwerp and Jérôme Busleyden in Malines.[26] Erasmus was uninterested in architecture; Peter Gillis's garden is the setting for the telling of the great tale. The polymath Jérôme Busleyden (1470–1517) was a great builder (figure 36), which makes it far from straightforward to relate the social as well as the actual architectural setting in which More wrote *Utopia* to the architecture of Aircastle. More admired the orderliness and character of bourgeois houses in the Flemish towns, which perhaps provides a clue to the form of the houses of the capital of the Kingdom of Utopia. The terraces of the three-storey houses of Aircastle are solid, uniform and with flat roofs. All the major trading centres of the Low Countries have quarters containing attached merchants' houses, which are well built, but have pitched roofs. In the richest quarters facades of neighbouring houses vie with each other for attention. Rapidly changing fashion in applied ornament and ever-revised forms of the scrolled gable to crown the front of the often narrow fronts of houses in the booming towns of the southern Netherlands make their study a bewildering task (figure 37).[26] Such a background of variety and competitive ostentation in domestic architecture stimulated More to invent plain, uniform three-storey terraces.

A further paradox to amuse his more learned friends in matters of architecture may have been the imposed grid pattern of straight streets. Alberti in the *De re aedificatoria*, a book which we cannot be certain More had read but of which he must have heard much, argues that streets with curves and bends are to be preferred. The Florentine favoured variety, multiplicity and complexity in the make-up of towns. On the correct assumption that wealth stimulates growth, which brings change, Alberti comments 'I ask you to consider how much more pleasant the view will be if at every step you see new forms of buildings.'[27] Learned mischief abounds, given the immediate background against which More

36 Mechelen (Malines). Jeronimus van Busleyden's house. Built *c*.1500–*c*.1510. Architecture attributed to Antoon I and his son Rombout II Keldermans.

37 Ghent. Merchants' houses on the Graslei. Fourteenth to seventeenth centuries.

was writing. He would have been bound to amuse more than his friends and correspondents, who were in tune with his private jokes. The uniformity of the houses of Aircastle is a logical consequence of one of the most fundamental principles of Utopian society, equality amongst the citizens. The abolition of private property is in tune with Platonic and contrary to Aristotelian thought. The abolition of classes and of the privileges which go with rank, responsibility and wealth would have confounded More's friends and colleagues in government. In Utopia there are decent honours for elected magistrates, priests and scholars, but their status is not to be expressed to their contemporaries or posterity in distinct or distinguishing private houses. In Utopia evil is a lust for possessions. In a more credible manner than for the people of Sforzinda, More invented a hierarchy of tolerated pleasures to satisfy intellectual aspiration on the higher level and to appease, within agreed limits, the baser desires to eat and drink well, to defecate, copulate or scratch. Pleasures are matters constantly debated by Utopians, who have one overriding principle, that the pleasures of one should not hurt another. 'Hurt' in this context might also or imply 'corrupt', for competition for material things stimulates the vices of pride and jealousy. Thus Utopians co-operate with their neighbours in their gardens, but also allow themselves the pleasure rather than pain of competing to improve them. The enclosed garden is the standard metaphor for Eden or Paradise, both of which are long gone, but

More with consummate subtlety invented gardens which were both open and closed, public of access as well as private.

There is, however, a very good case for excluding the housing of Aircastle from a discussion of luxury architecture in fiction and philosophy. Although it is not specified how spacious was the accomodation, nor is there any account of the equipping and comforts of the houses, it is certain that More intended his readers to understand that they were not luxurious inside or out in any way which might allow ethical reproaches by Platonists. Only Stoics might find cause for complaint, but More gives no information on the chattels used by the Utopians. Life in Utopia is not austere, and so the buildings need not be imagined as austere, and part of the success of More's creation is that it could commend itself to contemporary philosophies and social ideologies which were at odds with each other. Conditions have improved from the time of huts, but good housing does not corrupt with luxury.

The active humanist life ruled by virtue and motivated by the pursuit of learning was an ideal existence. All the conventional classes of luxuries such as fancy food, fine clothes and furniture, or large and ornate building are too mundane to be considered even for condemnation in More's other mental world. The essence of Utopia is to conjure a society provided with everything it needs, not one which is rich in the unneeded. This would have been difficult to imagine without his obsession with the qualities of prudence, integrity and *suavitas* or the evenness of his temper. More acquired a contemporary and posthumous reputation which amounted to a personality cult, unmatched by any other sixteenth-century writer and thinker.[28] His execution in 1535 for his refusal to swear to the Supremacy and his silence over his reasons made of More a martyr of conscience. *Suavitas* was not an aid to survival.

More's behaviour was and is a primary factor in the impact and influence of the colossal paradox of *Utopia*. It was written both to entertain and as a context in which he could say what he liked. Utopia is this world turned inside out, where prisoners wear chains of gold, because it is a material of no value to Utopians. Just like the predatory hares of Vienna, the harmless lamb is transformed into a monster that devours men. More aimed to ridicule human venality on the one hand, and condemn tyranny, manifest in the enclosure movement of his times, which continued to displace farmers, on the other. More did not invent perfect men to populate Utopia. Its laws were drafted with clear principles of communal discipline and the necessity of rigorous work as the basis for social order and harmony. His personal inclination towards the monastic life is manifest in the ambiguous and unbelievable ways in which pleasures are accommodated and minor abuses tolerated. Without More's Utopia the most outlandish and sophisticated architectural fantasy of French Renaissance literature, that of François Rabelais (1493?–1553?) could seem disconnected from ethical thought.

In *Gargantua*, published in 1534, the account of the buildings of the Abbey of
Thélème and of its cosseted denizens surpasses in extravagance anything imagined
before. A lengthy inscription over the main gate warned off 'sots, imposters, snivel-
ling hypocrites and bigots' and welcomed 'all noble sparks, endowed with gallant
parts . . . here you shall not want for anything, for what you ask, we grant'. The
order recruited for the abbey was to be 'contrary' to all others, made up solely of
good-looking men and women, who might marry should they wish. On numerous
occasions Rabelais shows that he has Utopia in mind; Gargantua addresses letters
to his father from Utopia, and all of Rabelais' social structures flagrantly violate
all monastic or Utopian rules. The contrariness of Rabelais in his satiric tribute
to More might be exemplified in a digression in *Pantagruel* in which Panurge tells
of a wonderful city of debtors where, because everyone owes something to everyone
else, harmony and peace prevail with all cherishing, protecting, and speaking well
of one another to safeguard their loans. Likewise Thélème is a grandiose paradox,
a literary conceit played out to the limit of the reader's credulity. With a massive
endowment from the goodly Lord Gargantua, their lives were to be of exquisite
comfort. The great complex, both within and without, is described in some detail
by Rabelais, who intended the mind's eye to see and be seduced by trappings which
would never have been sanctioned in Utopia.

The building was hexagonal, with at each angle a great round tower of threescore feet in
diameter; all these towers were alike in scale and style. The river Loire ran along the
north side, and on its bank was situated one of the towers called Arctic, and facing to the
east was one named Calaer; the next in line was Anatole, after which came one called
Mesembrine, Hesperie and lastly Cyrere.[29] Each tower was distant from the other by
three hundred and twelve paces. The whole edifice consisted of six stories, which
includes the basement cellars. The second storey had arches after the fashion of basket
handles with vaults behind. The rest of the ceilings were of the best wainscot
embellished with pendentives of Flanders fretwork in plaster in the form of the foot of
a lamp. The roof was covered with the finest slates trimmed with lead, where antique
style figures of puppets and animals of all sorts were to be seen, all of which made
up a wonderful combination. They were gilded, and the gutters which projected from
the walls between the casements were painted with gold and azure zig-zag patterns,
reaching to the very ground where they joined the great conduit that carried all from
the house to the river.

The building in question was a hundred times more sumptuous than ever were
Bonnivet, Chambord or Chantilly.[30] For there were within nine thousand, three
hundred and thirty two sets of chambers; each one was provided with a withdrawing
room, a handsome closet, a wardrobe, an oratory and each of these apartments were
neatly connected by a spacious passage leading to a great hall. Between each of the
towers, in the middle of the wings was a pair of winding staircases, some of whose
steps were of porphyry, some of Numidian stone and others of serpentine marble; each
of those steps was twenty two feet in width, three inches thick, with flights of twelve

steps between each landing or resting place. At every resting place were two fair antique arches through which the light came in; and through these one entered a lattice-windowed closet of the same breadth as the stairway, and at the top of these pavilions were conical roofs, which were reached by the spiral stairways. By these same stairs were entrances on each side into a great hall and from the halls was access to the apartments. Between the Arctic tower and the Cryere were the great and fair libraries of Greek, Latin, Hebrew, French, Italian and of Spanish books, with each of these stocks of books in the different languages housed on successive floors. At the heart of the complex was a marvellous spiral staircase, the entrance to which was on the outside of the building through an arch thirty six feet in width; and this was built of such a size and symmetry that six men-at-arms with their lances in their rests could ride abreast up to the very top. The tower called Anatole and that called Mesembrine were connected by spacious galleries, richly painted with scenes of ancient prowesses, histories, as well as views of many parts of the world.

The mind's eye has much work to do, and might well be strained to complete the picture of the building by filling in particulars of both the architecture and the style of the elevations of such a spectacular structure. As long ago as 1840 Charles Lenormant felt that the imaginative veil drawn over the external architecture of Thélème by Rabelais' outline needed lifting. The *restitutions* done for his little book are based on the specifics and the stylistic clues provided by Rabelais, but such an exercise violates the spirit of the narrative, with which he sought to entertain and stimulate his readers (figures 38–9).[31] In the first edition of 1534 mention is made only of Bonnivet being outshone by Thélème. For the revised edition of 1542 Rabelais added Chambord and Chantilly for extra effect and emphasis, in case the reputation of Bonnivet as a paradigm of splendour had not spread throughout France (figure 40). Every loyal subject of Francis I would have heard of his great building enterprise at Chambord, even if they had no idea nor special interest in what it looked like. Grafting the architecture of Bonnivet to serve for the elevations of Thélème, with simplified versions of the famous central spiral of Chambord tacked on as the structures up which six men-at-arms could ride abreast, makes a banality of Rabelais's contraption (figure 46).

Every trick of exaggeration and descriptive hyperbole is employed. The interiors and living quarters for these lucky, beautiful people are packed with luxuries, and no mere mortal could be expected to opt for Utopia, when offered such ease for the body. Outside there were pleasure gardens, tennis-courts, a tilt yard and a riding ring, a theatre and swimming-baths in a three-tier structure, all for the recreation of the inhabitants when they were abstaining from the pleasures of the chase. Inside

All the halls, chambers, and closets were richly hung with tapestry, and hangings of many kinds, which were changed according to the season of the year. All the pavements and floors were covered in green cloth; the beds were all embroidered. In every withdrawing room was a crystal mirror set in a frame of fine gold, garnished all around the frame in pearls, and it was large enough to give a true reflection of the whole figure. At the outer doors of the ladies' lodgings were perfumers and

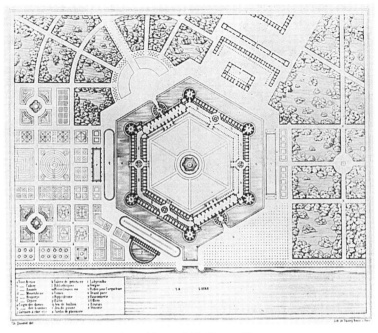

38   The Abbey of Thélème. Plan.

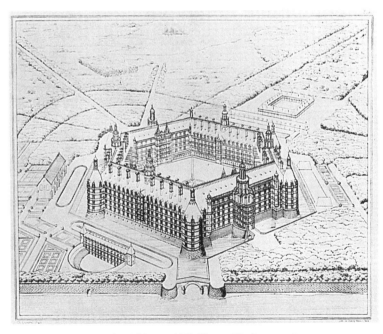

39   The Abbey of Thélème. Bird's-eye view.

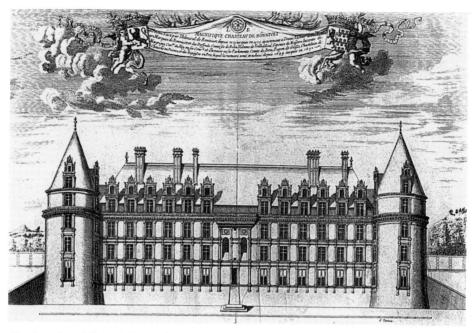

40 Bonnivet (Vienne). Begun between 1513 and 1516, demolished in the course of the early nineteenth century.

hairdressers, through whose hands the gallant men passed on their way to visit the ladies. These sweet artificers provided each morning for the ladies' rooms rose-water, orange-water, and angelica; also they brought in for each a precious little casket, from which exuded the vapours of the choicest aromatic scents.

How the luxury of life at the Abbey of Thélème is supported is left to the readers' imagination. There is a mention only of two types of functionary, amongst what must have been an army of servants. Charmed worlds for men and women wholly at leisure, without powers of magic, need servants if not slaves, but here the idea of luxury in some being inevitably exploitative of others is put aside. Those who would be beguiled by Thélème are naïve. Thélème is a tease.

François de la Noue, in his jaunty broadside of the 1580s, quoted above, deploring those who would impoverish themselves by building, made shrewd use of Rabelais. De la Noue expropriated from *Gargantua* Father Jean des Antomeures, the head of the Order of Thélèmites and 'one of the most worthy men of our times', to act as his advocate. Most memorable of all the quips which de la Noue puts into the worldly monk's mouth is that passage where a lord who 'lodges his poverty in stateliness' can do no more than to 'feast his friends when they visit on discourses on architecture'. Such inventive use of Rabelais shows the immediacy and enduring popularity of his tales. If the estimable *bon viveur* Father Jean

78

des Antomeures found architectural theory boring, then those who might want to know about any stylistic intricacies of the exterior of Thélème fall straight into a trap set expressly for pedants and windbags. Luxury architecture with its pseudo-academic status and materialistic allure is an ideal target for mockery. Only the stupid set no store in honest pleasures such as gluttony, good clothes and sex. The reader who wishes something like Thélème could exist is fooling himself, whilst a reader who yearns to be a Thélèmite is just a fool. Or is he or she?

Vivès, architectural parody and women

The gullibility of those who are overawed by ostentation in building and who covet luxury is acutely satirised by the educationalist Juan Luis Vivès in a book published in 1534, the same year as *Gargantua*. Vivès (1492–1540) was a Spanish Jewish *émigré*, a friend of Erasmus and was a protégé, during an English sojourn, of Thomas More. He is an eminent figure in the humanist world of the 1520s and 1530s.[32] In one of his *Dialogues*, which is a series of parallel texts in French and Latin 'pour l'exercice des deux langues', we find a passage which exemplified the scorn for luxury and Renaissance architecture amongst his circle of polymath friends. A concierge called Vitruvius, a humiliating social demotion for the one surviving ancient authority on architecture, conducts two delightfully credulous boys called Jocundus and Leo through the town house of a great and rich man, whose name is never mentioned. The boys' names are a spoof on Fra Giocondo, who was responsible for the first illustrated edition of Vitruvius, of 1511, and on Pope Leo X. The tour of the 'ample, beautiful house, standing apart from those around' begins at the imposing entrance gateway, where the boys are especially impressed by an entablature of alabaster. The concierge Vitruvius tells them that at one time a figure of Hercules would have been placed above the gate to guard against evil-doers. However, now that Hercules is seen as having been a cruel hero and a wrong-doer, he has been replaced with a statue of Jesus Christ. The boys and the concierge cross the forecourt and enter the ground floor of the main block. Here they see a room with a painting of the sky on the ceiling. Landscapes and sea-scapes line the walls, amongst which are some views of the new lands found by the Spanish navigators. Slightly out of keeping with the theme of land, sea and sky is the inclusion of a picture showing the suicide of Lucretia, to provide a note of Stoic melancholia. Lastly there is a painting showing the full, unrealised project for the house, which is coyly covered by a curtain. The implication of this is that the anonymous master has been guilty of the folly of yearning for a building greater than he could afford, or for one which was inappropriate to his station. As with all the other rooms there is no mention of furniture. From this picture-room cum entrance hall they climb a wide, spiral staircase whose steps are fashioned out of iron-coloured marble. They reach the master's apartment at the top, which makes of the

79

first floor a true *piano nobile*. In one particularly tall chamber, the boys are told, the master greets travellers of whom he would ask no money for lodging. The other function of the room was for entertaining his own friends. Vitruvius emphasises that at all times the room is ready for private gatherings, as well as a refectory when there are miscellaneous visitors. The nameless master of the house is portrayed as keenly conscious of ancient attitudes and modern traditions of lordly hospitality.

At this point Jocundus goes into a transport of delight over the painted glass in the windows of the tall chamber, which portray scenes from Boccaccio's fable of Griselda, to which the master had chosen to add a true story of Godeleine of Flanders and one of Katherine, Queen of England. (Griselda is the superhumanly chaste and patient heroine of the last of the tales of the *Decameron*; Godeleine or Godelive is the eleventh-century saint especially venerated in Flanders as an inno-cent sufferer, and her inclusion makes it certain that this text was written at Bruges, where Vivès died; Queen Katherine of England is Katherine of Aragon, a compatriot *émigrée* who patronised Vivès and to whom he dedicated his key work of 1524, *On the Instruction of a Christian Woman*.) These good women are followed by a series of saints beginning with St Paul the Apostle. After admiring these Jocundus asks the concierge what is the basic theme or argument of these images. He replies, 'I am what I am by the grace of God: the grace of God has not been wasted on me.' The further panels of glass showed Helen and Homer, with Homer saying to Helen 'That which you have done wrong I have described fully.'

Vivès' *On the Instruction of a Christian Woman* shows the importance he attached to the proper education of women. More taught that 'not content to have them [i.e. his daughters] good and very chaste, would also that they should be well learned'. Vivès gives women a domestic role only, insisting on the importance of stocking their minds so they would avoid 'fantasies', while fulfilling their household tasks. The fiction of the castles in chivalric romances is parodied by Vivès. Glamorous materials abound, but there are no scenes of masculine glories. When present the owner is master, but the figurative imagery is for the benefit of weak women in their domestic precinct.[33] The concierge Vitruvius is too obtuse to see much mean-ing in the expensive glass and the array of virtuous women. Domestic order and discipline are essential in the establishment of an important man. Why such a house should be totally deserted is not explained, but its emptiness adds a touch of eeriness.

The chamber of female worthies and saints has gilded panelling decorated with pearls, which is just the sort of trapping singled out by a long line of moralists as the product of a reprobate spirit.[34] Vitruvius here makes a very Utopian observation. He says that the pearls are of no particular value. Pearls cluster the mirror frames of the womens' apartments at Thélème, and once again a reader is made to feel uncertain whether the text is satirising or pandering to venal values. One side of this room looks out over the forecourt with the other offering a view of the garden.

The bisection of the site with the *corps de logis* allows Vivès' town house to be imagined as a proud late fifteenth-century or early sixteenth-century *hôtel* anywhere from Bruges to the Mediterranean.[35] He would have been especially familiar with the grandest town houses in the southern Netherlands, such as that of his friend Busleyden at Mechelen (Malines) (figure 36). Adjacent to the main hall of the first floor is a group of rooms including a dining-room for summer time. This is a remarkable feature, for it is the first mention in post-classical literature of a room in a private house set aside especially for dining. Next to it is a room and ante-room both with matting covering their walls. Here the boys see pictures of Christ and the Virgin Mary, mixed incongruously with paintings of the fated Narcissus, Adonis, Polyxena and Euryalus. An inscription over the door reads 'Retreat from attachments to the heaven of tranquillity'. The need for an explanation of the mass of imagery in the house is helped neither by the inscriptions nor by Vitruvius' often abstruse commentary. In the ante-room to the summer dining-room is a locked larder, where all the *utensiles* of the house are kept. On the other side of a lateral passage from the summer dining-room is a group of rooms for winter time, which face in a direction away from the path of the sun. It is as if the house is a metaphor for Plato's Athens, where people lived facing north during the winter. These winter apartments are heated by one large stove rather than individually with fireplaces, which confirms our hypothesis that this household should be pictured as Netherlandish in character. Montaigne amongst others records a strong dislike amongst Frenchmen of the humid atmosphere generated by large domestic stoves which, it was said, made one shudder and risk a chill on going out into the cold air.[36]

In a vaulted room attached to the winter quarters members of the family and visitors devote themselves to 'sacred things'. Immediately after visiting this chapel the conversation turns to baser matters. Jocundus asks where are the privies, and is given a peculiar answer. For the general public they are in the attic, whilst the master keeps chamber-pots for both types of function in his room. After visiting the kitchen in the basement, where Vitruvius complains of the constant nuisance caused by rats and weasels, the three emerge from the building to admire a grandiose attached portico. It is not stated whether this is on the courtyard or garden side of the house. Jocundus exclaims 'O, look at these giant columns, a portico full of majesty. See how these Atlantides and these Caryatids really look like people being forced to hold up the structure.'

By the time Vivès was writing the great Caryatid portico of Athens, the Erechtheion, described only in passing by the real Vitruvius, had been twice illustrated by woodcuts for the first chapter of Book I. The impassive Caryatids and Persians for Fra Giocondo's edition of 1511 (figures 41–2) do not correspond to the straining figures seen by Jocundus. Vivès must here be satirising a certain sort of bookishness, for the woodcut he must have had in front of him is the bizarre

41 Caryatid Portico.

LIBER

42 Persian Portico.

43 Caryatid Portico.

image from Cesariano's Italian translation of Vitruvius of 1521 (figure 43), where the figures really do express their torment. Such a structure would have looked most peculiar on the walls of the home of any great and so-called generous lord. Leo's response to Jocundus' admiring words comes as a real surprise. 'There are many such, who seem to do great things, despite which they live a life of idleness and sloth: lying they consume the fruits of the labour of others.' With that he turns his attention to a run-down house next door, and the dialogue ends with Vitruvius saying that it will be demolished shortly, for it is out of keeping with the quality of the building of his master's house.

Vivès' text is first and foremost a translation exercise for the young, and does not pretend to be a methodical social and architectural analysis of a very substantial town house. However the one theme which runs all through the dialogue is a moral evaluation of the master through an examination of his building and possessions. It is a picture of luxury and architecture drawn in outline and with just enough detail for a reader of any nationality to imagine the house and its rooms in terms of the aristocratic architecture of his own country. The demotion by Vivès of Vitruvius to play the part of a concierge is a forceful attack on the Renaissance of architecture in its many national and regional guises. The apparatus of glory leaves the boys and the reader with mixed feelings. The concierge Vitruvius is not a guide of learning and vision. He understands but superficially the culture of his absent master. Neither boys nor reader can fathom the meanings of all these splendours. The masculine image of conquest of the Caryatid portico on the exterior is today a startling contrast to the symbols within the body of the house.

Renaissance best sellers

Vivès does not pile up superlatives to fire the imaginations of those impression-able creatures prone to 'fantasies'. Several Spanish poets, humanists and churchmen of the sixteenth century warned of the ill effects of escapist literature, which panders to the romantic whims and materialism of women. The principal target of their criticism is the chivalric romance, in particular *Amadis de Gaule*.[37] Leaving aside religious and devotional books the epic cycle of the deeds of *Amadis de Gaule* was the greatest popular international publishing success of the sixteenth century, and its many volumes are so replete with intoxicating imagery of palaces, castles and gardens as to make a Thomas More or Francis Bacon despair.

It is a pity that the size of print runs or sales figures, which are the means of measuring the impact or reputation of 'best sellers', do not survive from this period. By the middle of the century *Amadis* had grown into twelve folio volumes from the pens of a succession of Spanish writers; by 1581 it had been translated in part or whole into Italian, French, German, Dutch, English and even Hebrew, and some of these translations could run to twenty-one volumes where the native readership showed no sign of wearying of it.[38]

Forty or more protracted and marvellous sagas of knight-errantry were churned out by Spanish and Portuguese literary impresarios, of which by far the most prominent and lengthy are *Amadis da Gaula* and *Palmerin da Oliva*. These first appeared in 1508 and 1511 respectively. An anthology of all the architectural descriptions to be found in sixteenth-century romances would be a substantial volume in itself, but amongst this mass of material one account of an amazing palace deserves special attention. For the French edition of Book IV of *Amadis*, published in 1543 at the instigation of Francis I, the translator Nicolas de Herberay, Baron des Essarts, added a substantial passage describing the fabulous palace of Apolidon (see Appendix 1 for the whole passage). To render this tortuous description more manageable (for readers with above average appetites for stodgy prose), de Herberay commissioned two woodcuts to ease the digestion (figures 44–5). This modern Spanish epic of a mythical Gaul was an ideal foil to cheer a French audience. Francis I's Chambord is cast as the ultimate palace of a world of luxury, romance and heroes. This was calculated by de Herberay to please the readership and to flatter the king. After his defeat by the Emperor Charles V at Pavia, Francis I was held in captivity at Madrid between February 1525 and March 1526 when, it is reported, he enjoyed Spanish romances in the frustration of his confinement. In make-believe a great warrior-king in such a predicament always finds a heroic solution with a happy ending, and Francis in happier times, as a part of his policy for literature, encouraged or commissioned de Herberay to make his translation.[39] The excellence of the translation helped to make *Amadis* a surprisingly controversial book. The poet Joachim du Bellay praises the beauty of the prose, but François de la Noue was so upset by its pernicious influence that he devoted an entire chapter of his *Discours politiques et militaires* to it.[40] The palace of Apolidon is a cornucopia of unnatural architecture designed to outrage Christianised Stoics and Puritans alike.

Apolidon is the son and heir of the Byzantine Emperor, and on the 'Isle Ferme' he found paradisical bliss with his beloved Grimanesa, before the arrival of Amadis. In her memory, he builds a miraculous and dream-like castle on the site. It is confected of precious materials and has a series of magic defences to test the visitor and to ward off unworthy lovers. We are reminded of the Heavenly Jerusalem of the Apocalypse, when the materials of the four great angle towers are described as built variously of 'pierre d'Azur, pierre d'Iris, de Grisolite et de Iaspe', with architraves of gold, bronze, alabaster and even porcelain. As it progresses the image of the palace becomes more and more stupendous as we are guided across floors '... of Chrisolite, carved in love knots, enriched with Coral and Cypress, cut in little scales, and fastened with threads of gold'. De Herberay rhapsodises over doorways of alabaster with pediments of amber, agate and silver-gilt, each and every

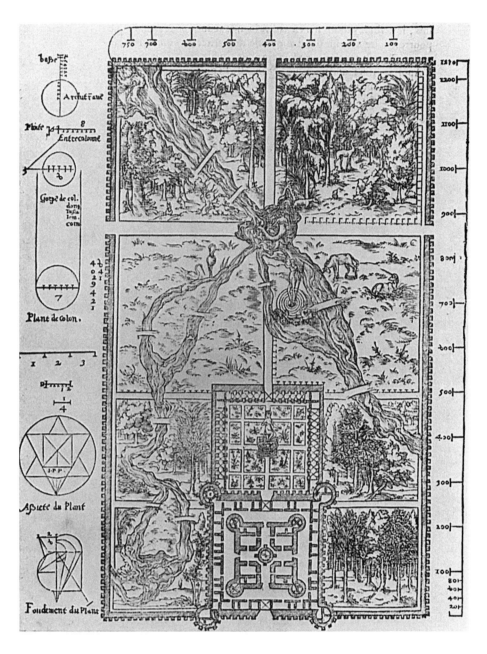

44 The 'Isle Ferme'.

86

Ce baſtiment ne vient à la raiſon
De noſtre plant, pour n'auoit placé entieret
Puis le maçon n'a pas eu la matiere,
Pour eriger vne telle maiſon,

45 Elevation of the palace of Apolidon.

detail of which is carved in the best antique manner. We might be reminded of Utopia, when we read 'Apolidon specified that the mouldings of these doorframes should be made of magnetic stone and the doors themselves of steel, so that when they were opened they would close again on their own by virtue of this stone.' Indeed the planning of Chambord and its fictional offspring, with thirty-two self-contained *apartements*, gives the same accommodation as that provided for the pampered Thélèmites.[41] It was a short step from a real world of luxury to one of dreams.

Descriptions of other wondrous palaces crop up elsewhere in *Amadis* to give the reader respite from the hurly-burly of battles, grand deeds of heroism and countless flamboyant wooings. Such interludes are found in the accounts of the Palace of Axiane in Book VII and the Palace of Mars in Book XI. Both dream-châteaux are lavishly furnished, with stained glass and, in the Palace of Mars, appropriate quantities of parade and battle armour and marvellous engines of war worthy of Leonardo. However, none of these descriptions has the architectural significance of the Palace of Apolidon, nor are any of the other dream palaces and gardens illustrated. Chambord, in the guise of the Palace of Apolidon, is no stranger a metamorphosis than is the person of the King playing a lead role in a Court masque. In the case of Francis I, Chambord and the Palace of Apolidon were simply expressions of actual and imagined eminence.[42]

The sixteenth-century *fortune critique* of *Amadis de Gaule* is in itself a huge subject. There are literary echoes and entanglements in the prose fiction of most western European countries, and the popular assimilation led to letters of cartel and poorer quality love poems being couched in Amadisian language.[43] California acquired its name because the landscape reminded the conquistadores under Cortez of an island of that name in *Las Sergas de Esplandian* in the fifth book of *Amadis*.[44] On a wet evening in February 1555, it is noted in the diary of a Norman gentleman, Gille Picot, *Amadis* was read all evening, so fond were Picot and his family of the intoxicating imagery of the saga, which took their minds away from the gloom outside.[45] This is a very rare record of a family audience for romances, as a distraction from ordinary drudgery.

The earliest known detailed description of Chambord was written in the spring of 1541 by Francisco de Moraes (1510–72), the secretary to the Portuguese ambassador to the French Court.[46] Three years before the publication of de Herberay's metamorphosised Chambord, de Moraes went through the château measuring and noting the functions of rooms and describing decorative features with the eyes of one intent on making future use of his research. Francisco de Moraes was to be the author of the other great chivalric cycle, the *Palmerin romances*.[47] His volume for the series appeared in Portuguese in 1544 or 1545, in Spanish in 1546, in French in 1552 (entitled *la Chronique du fameux et très vaillant chevalier Palmerin d'Angleterre fils di roi D. Edouard*) and in Italian in 1553. De Moraes' keen interest in Chambord might be expected to surface in his telling of the tale, but with de Herberay's fanfare of architectural nonsense being prepared at the same time for the rival *Amadis* he might have been put off. De Moraes does not stop to describe any one castle or palace in great detail, but his experience of Chambord can be read into the imaginary castle of the giant Califournie. It had been built for the hunt like Chambord, or the house of the wise Urgande, with its incomparable staircase, which appears later in the text. The unique double spiral of Chambord had to be in his mind (figure 46). Only of Chambord are there so many echoes in fantastical literature of an ideal life lived in the surroundings of a superb architecture which had actually been built. Only the materials, trappings and magical powers of the castles of the romances differ.

Other imaginary palaces in Renaissance fiction were and are understood as 'no place'. One of the finer ironies of Chambord as a foyer for a society devoted to all the accomplishments of peace and gallantry is that unlike 'the Enchanted Pallaces of the Poets: Who build them at small Cost', this wonder was built at great cost by a poet or king who never managed, by force of circumstance and call of duty to make any significant use of the edifice.[48] It was usually deserted, and to all who saw the great house, it must have seemed as grand a symbol of forlorn hope as any writer of fiction could invent.[49]

In the course of the second half of the sixteenth century there is a proliferation of descriptions of fabulous buildings in chivalric poetry and prose. In Italy the elitist and ambitious poet of Ferrara, Lodovico Ariosto, produced his *Orlando Furioso*, published in three versions in 1516, 1521 and 1532, and the basis of numerous pastiches. The most famous and least servile of Ariosto's tradition was Torquato Tasso. His *Gerusalemme Liberata* of 1581 is no radical rethink of how to write dazzling architectural descriptions. Usually they are brief, concentrate on a conventional accumulation of costly materials, and are never accompanied by illustrations. Palaces in Italian romances throughout the sixteenth century are closer to the unimaginable exaggerations of the ancient epics, ignoring the archaeological and topographical allures of the richly illustrated *Hypnerotomachia*.

It was in France that the most elaborate and dramatic architectural fiction of the second half of the sixteenth century was written. Now it is little known. *L'Ombre et Tombeau de Trèshaute et Très puissante Dame Marguerite de France/ Duchesse de Savoie & de Berri / Description tant de l'ichniographie que de l'orthographie, plan et montée de la sépulture et mausolée &c.* written, according to the title by one R. dER in Latin, translated into French by ENDI, and printed at Turin on 17 October 1574 by Baptiste d'Almeida is an extraordinary literary obscurity.

The author's name is an obvious and intriguing *nom de plume*. This anonymous sixteenth-century architectural erudite wears a strange literary mask for his description of a giant mausoleum. Er is a hero from a mythology already ancient when Plato

46 Chambord, the double spiral staircase.

recorded the 'Myth of Er' at the end of *The Republic*. It was the mortal Er, according to Plato, who was made immortal and appointed by the Gods to guide the souls of the chosen and blessed back to life after death. As a steward for reincarnation his status, for a neo-platonist of the Renaissance, as an authority to describe the ideal mausoleum, would be unmatched. The other names in the title credits are mysterious, for what ENDI signifies has not been clarified, and those who are expert in the history of printing are categorical that no such printer as Baptiste d'Almeida existed at Turin in the 1570s or, indeed, at any other time.[50] One scholar has concluded that it was printed by the widow Berton at La Rochelle.[51] The title of the pamphlet concludes by telling us that it has been translated from Latin into French '... pour gratifier les studieux de l'Architecture'. There are no illustrations, to ensure that the recondite text would stretch the most studious in matters of architecture. To make this fabulous architectural fiction more accessible and better known the full text is printed here as Appendix 2, and a reconstruction drawing by the late A. Don Johnson is shown in figure 47.

Marguerite de France was the youngest legitimate daughter of Francis I. She died at Turin on 17 September 1574.[52] Her praises were often sung by French court poets before and after her departure from France in 1559 to marry the Duke of Savoy, and few can doubt when reading the verses of Ronsard and especially the many lines of prose and verse written in her honour by Jodelle, that she was exceptionally well-read and a wise and generous protectress of writers.[53] Her loss was keenly felt and mourned in literary circles. The mausoleum for her as described by 'Er' might be accused of being gross and macabre. He envisions the great edifice as standing on open ground, and built on a great platform 179 feet square. Five steps of black marble bring us to a walkway on which the visitor can make the tour of a closed peristyle of sixty-four giant coupled Corinthian columns. Then follows a description of the sumptuous materials of the peristyle and the multitude of decorative intricacies woven into the design. 'Er' must have been writing surrounded by piles of decorative engravings and a miscellany of ancient texts. The outside has an array of statues on tall podia, which include many members of Marguerite's family, and about a quarter of the length of the account is taken up in describing their distinguishing features. At last we are taken into the inner precinct, where 'Er's' itinerary is far from easy to follow as he takes us up a short flight of steps, round a corner, along by this much and down by that much to be amazed by this and struck by that. Through a great bronze door and down a ramp and now the climax of the tour: we are confronted with a tank of spring or possibly preserving water, in which float the corpses of the royals stitched and tightly wrapped in boiled leather. Thus they are protected for ever from rotting.[54] Many more marvels and intriguing sights follow. At the end 'Er' reveals his sources of inspiration for his creation on paper of a Wonder of the Modern World. It comes as no surprise, that his point of departure is Pliny's famous description of the Mausoleum, built by the inconsolable

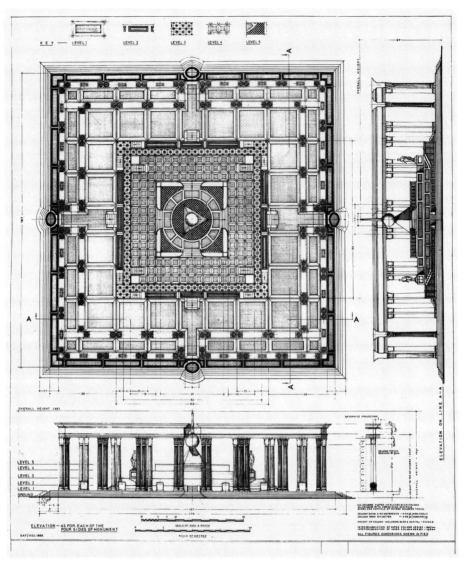

47 The Mausoleum of Marguerite de France. The imagined site must have been Haut-Combe (Savoie), where the Duchess was buried.

widow Queen Artemesia of Caria for her husband, King Mausolus, and one of the Seven Wonders of the Ancient World. No antique coin survived to give a general impression of it, and several draughtsmen, engravers and medallists in the course of the sixteenth century sought to fill the gap with their reconstructions.[55] 'Er' felt that his scholarship had surpassed all previous efforts at reconstruction, and boasts that the colonnade of his creation had come in part from Pliny, but had been completed by a much less well-known text by the fourth-century Libanius on the organisation of columns, of which he tells us he has given an account elsewhere, but without any reference.[56] His last sentence is worth quoting in full, for it reeks of the sour and unsuccessful pedant. After boasting of his learning and his creative use of his sources he grumbles 'These are things which the learned and wise lacking in curiosity have not looked into, for such things are deemed to be of no consequence for the doctrinaire.' Just as the work of Pliny has been glossed over by Ermolao Barbaro (1410–71), all translators and all so-called Pliny specialists and Vitruvius scholars are charlatans. One sees betrayal rather than translation (*trahis que traduis*).

We can leave aside 'Er's' dismissal of translations of Vitruvius into Italian or French as the jealousy of a hack. Contemporary learned opinion is unanimous in praising those who undertook the difficult task. Ermolao Barbaro was the deserved *imperator* of late quattrocento Venetian philology. Barbaro's emendations to Pliny, the *Castigationes Pliniae*, published in 1492, in which nearly six thousand difficult and distorted phrases and passages were elucidated, was a monumental work of scholarship widely applauded at the time and lauded by humanists of following generations across Europe.[57] Pliny's somewhat confused account of the Mausoleum at Halicarnassus is not clarified in all points by Barbaro, but from him emerges a far clearer picture based on his sharp-eyed and thorough reading of Greek texts. Despite his many shortcomings Pliny makes several clear points about the general form of the great edifice, most notably that it was a four-storey structure with the bottom two storeys equal in height to the upper two plus the quadriga. The base of the Mausoleum was about one hundred feet square with a main colonnade of thirty-six Ionic columns, and a stepped pyramid of twenty-four steps above, the whole structure being about a hundred and thirty-six feet high. Given that 'Er's' mausoleum for Marguerite de France does not follow that at Halicarnassus, it is difficult to grasp why 'Er' bothered to complain about poor or inaccurate translation.

The complex described by 'Er' does not emulate any ancient building known from a text, nor does it seem to be an arcane synthesis based on a selection of Latin authors. He might have made a drawing or even a model, which would account for the difficulty the reader has with the itinerary. It is certain that no one ancient or modern building was his primary source. Architectural fiction at its best is made up of paradox with plenty of allures to dazzle and baffle. It is always an intellectual game to challenge the reader's knowledge of history, literature and taste. The mausoleum for Marguerite de France is an outstanding example of a Utopian building, for there is not a scrap of evidence to suggest that such a grand design existed outside the imagination. Maverick literary archaeology can make romance out of architectural fiction. 'Er's' text is a peculiar product of new literary and intellectual tastes. It is not a conventional entertainment, and it is certainly not entertaining to read. Nevertheless, it is a novel erudite game of a kind unimagined before. With a reconstruction drawing we have cheated by lifting the veil which 'Er' drew across the eyes of those who are not in his terms *studieux de l'Architecture*.

The cost of building at small cost

From the later sixteenth century there are plenty of examples in courtly literature where we can feel the return of the cold draught of disapproval of lavish building, even where they masquerade as nothing more than dithyrambic entertainment. In England those who most benefited from Henry VIII's 'Age of Plunder'[58] and consolidated power and wealth under Elizabeth built, as William Harrison has told us, '. . . to be seen afar off, and caste forth his beames of stately and curious workmanship into every quarter of the country'. The image of the lofty, luminous, radiant palace of ancient and modern fiction is evoked. In the context of the later sixteenth century in England, the author's intention can be judged only as a warning of the jealousy which such creations engender. A most interesting example of the conflict between taste for the splendid in fiction and distaste for the emulation of such things in real life is found in the writings of George Whetstone (*c*.1544– *c*.1587).[59] This soldier, traveller and gentleman of letters at the start of the 'First dayes exercise' of his *Heptameron of Civil Discourses &c.* of 1582 gives a description of the imaginary, lavish palace of 'Segnior Phyloxenus'.[60] The list of its allures is concluded with the following douche.

And to be briefe, this Pallace, with all her conveinces, as well necessarie as of pleasure, fully matched the statelyenesse of Cardinall Farneses Pallace, buylded and beautified with the various Monumentes of Rome, in her pride: so that the curiousness thereof, was of power to have enchanted my eyes with an immodest gaze, had I not remembered, that it belongeth unto a Gentleman to see, and not to stare upon, the straungest Novell that is: for base is his mynde whose spirit hourely beholdeth not greater matters than either beautie, buylding, or braverie. And certainely, at this instant, I delighted more to contemplate of Segnior Phyloxenus' virtues than to regarde his sumptuous buyldings.

To have one's eyes enchanted even briefly by 'the immodest gaze of sumptuous buildings', and then to shake off the spell, is to have allowed one's reason to have been suspended. That is always dangerous. To insist that a building is a bad medium

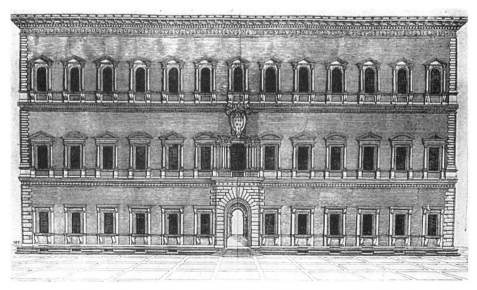

48 Rome. Palazzo Farnese. Begun 1517, major building campaign 1534–5. Architect Antonio da Sangallo the younger. Upper floor, after 1546. Architect Michelangelo. Building of the rear wing and garden facade continued up to 1589. Architects Vignola and Giacomo Della Porta.

through which to evaluate the virtues of a man, cuts luxury architecture out at a stroke as a constructive, didactic context for the activities of the great in fact or in fiction. Whetstone's reference to an actual building, the Farnese palace (figure 48), is especially piquant. He charges that it had been assembled out of the remains of ancient buildings. This was not true, but his point is clear, that such building will in its turn crumble and be forgotten, as surely as will the likes of the Farnese. Likewise the great palaces of fiction have just as much permanence as is allowed by the imperfect memory of mortals. A good night's sleep is quite enough to lessen and make fade away the excitement of any astonishing building seen or imagined. Writers of fiction who build palaces, castles and temples 'at small cost' pose their readers a specific ethical question. Do you admire such magnificence, and if so why? To be impressed at first, and then to shake off the spell cast by real or imagined architectural splendour, as Whetstone says he has done, is an act of repentance.

The consensus of opinion amongst writers of the Renaissance who discuss the popular fiction trade, favours the view that the most fabulous luxury architecture is a tolerable auxiliary in a supernatural world of romance. Those with the privilege of literacy need to be warned: they can demote themselves to fools. Men's and women's material values and sense of social order might be briefly suspended for the enjoyment of extravagant nonsense. Only the Protestant Frenchman de La Noue went so far as to claim that the magic of the castles and palaces of fiction may cause readers to investigate black magic, which must lead to the loss of their souls. This literary opium of the old romances such as *Lancelot* and *Tristan*, which he singles out, 'attest to ancient vanity', and thus if the trappings of the romance, such as the fabulous castles, are not clearly understood as insidious follies, the public should be warned.[61]

Unless we are told, fictional architectural marvels cannot be taken as straightforward symbols of good or of evil. It is unusual in ancient literature, as happens in the case of the description of the palace of Alcinous in the *Odyssey*, for there to be an unequivocal pronouncement that the palace was a gift of the gods as a tribute to his virtues. The gods themselves can behave in ways not always in keeping with the qualities they demand of their servants or followers. Apuleius' account of the palace of Cupid should produce very mixed feelings in the reader, especially as all that glory was a setting for the clandestine pre-marital delights of Cupid and Psyche. More or Rabelais dreamt up their architectural fictions as incredible creations to disturb any reader's norms of how life ideally might be managed. The clearest consequence of More's or of Rabelais' or even 'Er's' bizarre architectural fictions is that societies are conditioned and can be judged by their buildings.

Uniform and austere as are the buildings of Aircastle, or lavish and complex inside and out as is the Abbey of Thélème, the unreality of these architectural inventions is designed to stimulate reaction to what there could and should be in the architecture and building of society reformed. The language of imaginary architecture in fiction and philosophy has a shared goal in attempting to stimulate the mind's eye, but the effect on the heart of mellifluous entertainments and of ideal and impossible worlds is very different. Had there been no controversies attacking and defending architecture and luxury in the fifteenth and sixteenth centuries, there would have been little incentive to challenge the credulity of literate people with fantastical buildings 'at small cost'.

'Quo vadis?'

Dreamers and lovers of harmless luxury on paper probably did not influence the course of architectural history. Architecture has always been a client of history as much as technology. Now it is worthwhile to turn to what happened, or was supposed to happen, with a discussion of 'Renaissance Architectures'.

3

RENAISSANCE ARCHITECTURES
AND PEOPLES

The problem of authority

Antiquity was both a problem and a joy for Renaissance patrons and intellectuals. The problem centred on how to use antique art, architecture or literature in a cultural climate of emancipation. The joy was the invigoration of modern language to prove it. Architecture was always an important vehicle of expression, but it was hoped that it would not be mute to future generations, including us.

Extravagant, other-worldly building in fiction and philosophy are mostly symbols of a genuine, human, uncontrolled ambition dressed as literary flights of fancy. In the real world such temptations were an inducement to disorder. One symptom of the disease caused by the vice of luxury is the compulsion to overbuild, and the cure had to be found both in legislation and in responsible writing by experts in building and architecture. Realistic architectural writing had to account for the different material circumstances of men within any given nation, and care also had to be taken to assimilate cultural traditions and geographical conditions. No single architectural book could provide a universal doctrine, just as different languages made men more impressionable to innovations and achievements from within rather than from outside. Alberti joked that Vitruvius spoke Greek to the Romans and Latin to the Greeks, which encapsulates a serious point. Different peoples comprehend their needs and express their aspirations in contrasting and possibly contradictory ways. In this context the forms, potential and limitations of expression are common factors in discourses about architecture and language. If dialectics were ill-suited for the evolution of language or of architecture, arguments about luxury, licence or the abuse of free will would persist.

The Roman Vitruvius (46–30 BC, active) often reveals himself to have been a reactionary. His heart and thought were bound to the achievements of the Greeks of two hundred years and more before his time. Probably his best known and most often quoted passage is where he expresses his resistance to novelty in an attack on contemporary fashions in mural decoration.[1] He yearns for a return to the depiction of heroic episodes from the legend of Troy, or scenes from the wanderings of Ulysses. He bemoans the passing of 'the grand style' of landscape painting, with its richness of detail, and its replacement by a decadent style. Vitruvius thoroughly disliked 'paintings of monstrosities, rather than truthful representations of definite things'. With this he is denouncing the exotic hybrids of animal and plant forms, a genre of decorative fantasy which is known by the much misused word 'grotesque'. (That is to say 'of a grotto', and not 'horrible' or 'grim.') (Figures 49–51)[2] He moans 'Such things do not exist and cannot exist and never have existed . . . it is this new taste which has caused bad judges of poor art to prevail over true artistic excellence'. This theme of past perfect, present imperfect, and future uncertain helps us to account for the vigorous assertiveness of most of his pronouncements on principle and practice. The second chapter of his first book is a kind of rapid manifesto of 'the fundamental principles of architecture', where he attacks the licence he sees in Augustan Rome. To him 'Propriety is that perfection of style which comes, when a work is authoritatively constructed on traditional, approved principles.' Many have taken this to mean that there is one universal way, rather than different ways depending on means and place.

To exhort patrons and their artists to learn and follow the lessons from tried and tested formulae is far from controversial. Vitruvius goes much further. He frequently asserts that without close adherence to admired and successful models from the past, progress is reversed. Experience and historical knowledge have to be of greater value than experiment without authority. However, 'traditional approved principles' would be interpreted or visualised in utterly different ways by natives of different lands, as they consider Vitruvius' 'fundamental principles' while looking at their own circumstances. This must have led any reasonable reader to conclude that there is no absolutely right way of doing things. The succession of Greek buildings which Vitruvius describes and praises are exemplars for his Roman contemporaries, who have erred. Vitruvius had seen buildings and had read books which were not extant in the Renaissance and are still lost. Chapters twelve to fourteen of book VII are a roll of honour of thirty-three Greek authors, whose writings were his sources. Writing on architecture by Romans, he reports, has been scarce. This Roman steeped in a Hellenic or Hellenistic architectural sensibility was the only witness and guide to serve as an authority during the Renaissance.[3] His pluralism is most succinctly expressed in the ninth and last of his 'fundamental principles'.

49 *above left* Roman 'grotesque' mural decoration.

50 *above* Anonymous Italian 'grotesque' engraving.

51 *left* Agostino Musi. 'Grotesque' composition.

After considering how to choose and cost materials he writes

A second stage in economy is reached, when we have to plan the different kinds of dwellings suitable for ordinary householders, for those of great wealth, or for those holding high office of state. A house in town obviously calls for one form of construction; that into which stream the products of country estates requires another; this will not apply to money lenders and will be much different for the opulent and the luxurious; for the powers under whose deliberations the commonwealth is guided, dwellings are to be provided according to their special needs; and, in a word, the proper form of economy must be observed in the building of houses for each and every class.

Such opinions are far from the stuff of controversy, but it is to be regretted that Vitruvius' text is of far greater value on the subjects of Greek temples, theatres and public monuments than on the 'houses for each and every class'. This meant that there was a precise hierarchical code dealing with the scale, form and style of private houses known to him, but which he does not detail. In his sixth book he deals with domestic architecture, and at the end of his discussion of town houses, and before his account of the arrangement of houses planned in the Greek fashion, he admits that his descriptions are summary. His laziness in this, and his stated but undefined plurality, were the incentives which encouraged the formulation of national theories of domestic architecture during the Renaissance. To complement and supplement the treatises came the invention of the printed pattern book of architecture and decoration. Vitruvius was cast as the originator and the founder of the new architecture in every country of the Christian West, for there was no other known teacher.

The legacy of Vitruvius to the Middle Ages

During the Middle Ages manuscripts of some or all of Vitruvius' text were to be found in many major monastic libraries across Europe.[4] Churchmen and scholars from the twelfth to the fourteenth century who were interested in building were familiar with this unique literary survival. Petrarch owned and annotated a manuscript, but this exercise is nowhere in evidence in the highly emotional way in which he wrote about ancient Rome. For medieval master builders working with their compasses and rules and squares, and who performed arduous and sometimes risky tasks, their 'culture-hero' from antiquity was demonstrably the geometer Euclid.[5] In the stylistic or technical history of architecture from the Fall of Rome to the mid-fifteenth century, Vitruvius' text is of marginal importance. This is not to deny that some of his general pronouncements would have intrigued monks and princes. His thoughts on economy and propriety are not authoritative amongst the classics of ancient literature. There are many ancient authors who could be quoted on such subjects without special reference to architecture. Once dug out of the archives in the early fifteenth century, Vitruvius was progressively raised to a status which makes the generalities in his writings matters of import throughout the Renaissance.[6] As an authority this flawed book had to be assimilated into the architectural thinking of each nation in which classical literature was studied and discussed. To what degree and manner he was to be followed or adapted are issues akin to those confronting writers absorbed in the widespread debate about *imitatio*, in the two hundred or so years which we label the 'Renaissance'. Thinking about tradition, national identity and creativity, and how to make appropriate use of antique sources, are fundamental matters in every one of the western vernacular literatures.

Language, national identity and building

Had not a single Renaissance building survived, the terminology of building contracts would make us believe that all across Europe men were busily and carefully imitating the monuments of ancient Rome. In Portugal the new style is designated with the words *ao bom romano*, in Spanish texts the expression used is *a lo Romano*, in France the customary phrase is *à l'antique*, in Brabant and Flanders *antieksnyders* occurs, and in English texts we read of 'anticke' or of 'Romagne worke'.[7] Such apparent unity of purpose and harmony of taste was viewed by a small number of Spanish writers as a pan-European cultural renewal, rather than as a national revival of antique art and learning with particular relevance to the Imperial present.[8] In contrast not a single advocate or critic of the new style writing in French, German or English takes the view that building in an antique manner will bring nations closer together.

The opposite is true, for in the course of the late fifteenth and sixteenth centuries every major nation had an accumulating literature that was strongly nationalistic. A wide variety of subjects were affected, including law, history and of course epic fiction. The cultural phenomenon which we call patriotism or nationalism may be ancient and recurrent in European history and folklore, but the word 'patriotism' first crops up in the eighteenth century and *nationalisme* in French only once, in 1812. In English the oldest example of the use of the term 'nationalism' occurs as late as 1836. Sixteenth- and early seventeenth-century Europe witnessed powerful movements of messianic religious nationalism, but we have to distinguish these turmoils from much later populist political movements motivated by racial and national emotions.[9] The origin and tenor of most fifteenth- and sixteenth-century writing about national identity might be described as Hippocratic. Peoples are different because of varied climates and diets, and it natuarally follows that differing material conditions will foster different building traditions.

It would be a serious shortcoming in any account of Renaissance mentalities and artistic theories evinced in buildings, if debates and propaganda about contemporary language were left out. Renaissance manifestoes on vernacular language, texts on the aims and techniques of translation as well as architecture books provide a welter of justification for a free, independent and modern use of sources. The classical architectural culture of the Renaissance was not a pan-European acceptance and assimilation of the Roman past nor of the Italian present, just as amongst writers outside Italy every theorist, poet or playwright of note deplored parody of admired ancient or modern authors.

Italian in many vernacular forms had superseded Latin in the peninsula by the thirteenth-century. For vernacular literature it was the fourteenth-century Tuscan of Dante, Boccaccio and Petrarch, the *tre corone*, that set new standards for writing in Italian; sincere belief in the ascendancy of Tuscan in particular over Latin is explicit in many passages in the writings of Alberti in the next century, but for his treatise on architecture his medium had to be Latin, in which he could be more syntactically correct.[10] It has been argued convincingly that Renaissance humanism was basically distinct from vernacular literature in comprising a well-defined cycle of disciplines: grammar, rhetoric, poetry, history and moral philosophy rooted in the study of Greek and Roman authors. Humanism, it has been said, represents a body of scholarship that was secular without being scientific.[11] As written and completed in 1452, and as published posthumously in 1485, Alberti's *De re aedificatoria* tackles many of the problems of the interpretation of Vitruvius, but ignores the question of whether a serious book on architecture should be written in a vernacular. The problems of translating Vitruvius and indeed his own book he deliberately left for future generations. The seeming exclusiveness of his approach to the dissemination of architectural principles and ideas would make his book fit well into a category of humanist literature, that is one which is fully conversant with all useful classical authors and is secular rather than scientific. For the meantime architectural theory was confined to Latin until the *questione della lingua* gathered momentum in the first quarter of the sixteenth century in Italy, and was emulated in other countries.[12]

The thinking of grammarians inclined to the present clarity and future health of vernacular language. As a choice early example in print, Antonio Nebrija's *Gramatica castellana* of 1492 has a grandiose prologue addressed to Queen Isabella. Nebrija makes a crucially important and original point. To him political power and true contemporary language are companions. They begin, flourish and risk decay together.[13] Since the Spanish realm was now secure from the military oppression and cultural contamination of heathens, he concludes, the time has come for the arts. Such a sense of freedom could not inspire any of the contributors to the *questione della lingua* as it unfolded in the disunion that was Italy. Castiglione in the *Book of the Courtier* of 1528 produced a very conciliatory series of proposals on how good language and usage could be nurtured. He has the Count Lodovico Canossa say that a good speaker and writer should choose beautiful words from the speech current in all parts of Italy, and even, where convention allowed, he might employ French or Spanish terms. The disparity in current usage should not discourage 'men of discernment' from establishing a polished idiom, as the writers of Greece had triumphantly succeeded in doing. Canossa elaborates:

The Greeks selected whatever words, expressions and figures of speech they wished from each of their four languages, and constructed a new so-called common language; and subsequently all five of these dialects were known collectively as the Greek language. Certainly the Attic dialect was more elegant, purer and richer than the rest, but good writers who were not Athenians did not adopt it so slavishly as to destroy the distinctiveness of their own style and, as it were, the accent and savour of their natural dialect.

A little further on Castiglione has the good count express an opinion which was to have wide currency amongst blue blooded intellectuals within and without Italy:

'Thus good usage in speech, so I believe, is established by men of discernment, which enables them to agree amongst themselves and consent to accept those words which commend themselves to them; and these they recognise by means of a certain instinctive judgement and not by any formula or rule.'

This is in keeping with the whole tenor of the *querelle della lingua* as it unfolded in court circles of the late 1520s. The aristocratic and exclusive tenor of Italian theorising about how the language should be shaped and cultivated appropriately led to the objective of these writers being named a *lingua cortigiana*. This is at its most extreme in the esoteric and dogmatic scholarship of Count Gian Giorgio Trissino (1478–1550). In 1529 he rediscovered, translated and published Dante's *De Vulgari eloquentia*, and in the same year his *Ars poetica* appeared in print. The prolific Trissino would certainly comply with all the criteria needed for him to be classed as a man of discernment, and yet most of his theories and conclusions are wholly untenable. He attempted to hellenise Italian spelling and pronunciation, and with a plethora of rules instructs the leaders of society how the national language must be spoken and written. It is an exercise in authoritarian inventiveness, which is at odds with the more general humanist trend exemplified by Pietro Bembo's *De imitatione* of 1512 or Sperone Speroni's *Dialogo della lingue* of 1542, both of which champion the cause of trecento Tuscan as the best foundation for modern Italian. The 'Tuscan School' was convinced of the superiority of modern Italian over Latin, even of that most impeccable model of style, Cicero. Trissino might be best known as the author of the patriotic *L'Italia liberata dai Goti* of 1547, but he also wrote a treatise on architecture in the vernacular, of which only a fragment survives, and it must have been the definitive work, for he complains of Alberti's treatise that it lacks many important things and is full of superfluous matter![14] As with all of Trissino's literary missions, the intention was to interpret Vitruvius faultlessly, to give impetus to a reconstruction of the arts in the land which had the outstanding claim to past eminence. The buildings and writings of Palladio, whose career was launched by Trissino, might be expected to shed light on the supra-regional architecture which he was certainly contemplating, but in print Palladio betrayed nothing of Trissino's brand of artistic nationalism.

The more general humanist trend, to which we have just referred, is little characterised by the ethnocentricity or *italianatà* that fostered the view of Roman traditions being the prerogative of Italians on a geographic and a linguistic basis.[15] Men of discernment learnt from each other. The title of Joachim Du Bellay's famous *Déffence et Illustration de la Langue Françoyse* of 1549 might look like a clarion call to protect the purity of the French language from adulterating influences, but Du Bellay was no *gendarme de la langue française* in the style of the Académie française of later times. Du Bellay (1522?–60) took Sperone Speroni's *Dialogo delle lingue*, published in 1542, as a cue to produce a short manifesto exhorting writers to make more positive, creative and confident use of French. In Du Bellay's eyes the only contemporary language which rivals and might have eclipsed French was Italian, and he plagiarises large parts of Sperone's book so for Italian, read French.[16] Very brief chapters with headings such as 'Why the French Language is not as rich as the Greek and Latin' (I,3), 'That the French Language is not so poor as many esteem' (I,4), and 'That it is impossible to equal the Ancients in their languages' (I,11) give a flavour of the many paradoxical and controversial postures struck by Du Bellay to animate his readers. Grammarians, poets and orators are exhorted to concentrate their minds on the reform, revision and amplification of French to make the language the leader for all intellectual and technical discourse. Du Bellay uses an architectural metaphor in his essay on the impossibility of equalling the ancients in their own languages, to ridicule the absurdity of those who wished to rebuild the achievements of ancient civilisations by using scattered remains. Such an approach to writing or in other liberal arts stultifies, and produces deformed, hybrid work.[17]

Translating great classical works is in itself a far from sufficient means of enriching any language in Du Bellay's view. The real 'grandeur of style, magnificence of words, gravity of sentences, boldness and variety of form' has to remain the preserve of the original, and therefore must be studied. Good creative work in writing as much as in any other art or science is made possible by a thorough analysis of present knowledge and practice. Once needless archaisms and ambiguities are shaken out, the way is clear for French to blossom and outshine all other languages for its purity and versatility. Du Bellay constantly uses the metaphor, lifted from Sperone, of the well-pruned and cultivated plant, to persuade his readers that they live in an age of revitalisation. Cicero in the *De Oratione* (II,23) had warned that an overripe style befits only a luxurious audience. The expansionary rather than introspective tenor of Du Bellay's thesis, with its range of tributes to Greek and Roman authors, makes the *Déffence et Illustration de la Langue Françoyse* agreeable reading for foreigners. From the point of view of architectural history his text is fascinating. When the *Déffence* is read in conjunction with the sonnets of the *Antiquitez de Rome*, the *Songe* and the *Regrets*, all published in 1558, we see that this adept linguist and poet poses pertinent questions about the extension of classical studies into the practice of building. Du Bellay's sojourn in Rome from June 1553 to August 1557 gave authority to his gentle remonstrations to his equals and superiors about the impermanence of fame if earned and expressed in monuments. His cathartic reaction to 'Rome poudreuse' is a potent theme throughout the cycle of two hundred and thirty-eight sonnets, and his casting of the material remains of ancient Rome as a metaphor for decay and chaos was widely influential.

In very crude terms France was much the largest net importer of Italian culture during the sixteenth century, which makes her the richest source for writing on assimilation as a sign of health or sickness in literature, art and architecture. The translation of texts from Latin or Italian generated much discussion about means, methods and aims. Etienne Dolet's *La Manière de bien traduire d'une langue en l'aultre* of 1540 and the *Art poétique* by Jacques Peletier du Mans of 1555 are especially concise and lucid on the subjects of imitation and translation. The eclecticism of Erasmus, which illuminated international humanism of the first quarter of the century, is censured by Dolet. He would not trust one detached from any national affiliation, who felt better living in successive places, where his candour would not be checked. To Dolet such a man would be unable to speak or understand any of the nuances or subtleties in any language. Along with most scholars he took Cicero's Latin as the exemplar for purity and rational structure, and Dolet's mission is to urge his young contemporaries to think in terms of assimilating carefully the 'intention' of a very great author to inspire their writing and speech in the modern vernacular.[18] A condition of good translation is that the preservation of the author's 'intention' goes hand in hand with respect for the 'propriété de l'une et l'aultre langue'. Such a view, which became widely shared inside and outside France, is the basis for an understanding of the conditional and critical assimilation and use of classical texts (including Vitruvius) in different centres of learning and artistic activity.

The classical past is to be refurbished, and this will stimulate the emancipation of modern art and literature. Peletier du Mans assigns separate chapters in his *Art poétique* to imitation and to translation, and one of his summaries of the principles of translation accords well with the outlook of architects and architectural popularisers of different countries of the second half of the sixteenth century, who wrote retrospectively about their sources and practice. In a most conciliatory, universalist spirit Peletier writes:

... word for word translations have no grace. Not that they are contrary to the law of translation, but only because two languages are never uniform in phrasing. Conceptions are common to the understanding of all men: but words and ways of speaking are particular to nations. And let no one come and cite to me the example of Cicero, who gives no praise to the conscientious translator. And I do not understand this in any other way than that the translator should preserve the propriety and the character of the language into which he is translating. But I do say that, in so far as the two languages are in accord, he must lose nothing of the expressions, nor even of the particularity of the words of the author, whose wit and subtlety often consist precisely in that, responding to all the elegance of the first, yet retaining its own. But, as I have said, it cannot be done.[19]

Such reasonableness becomes scarcer in the decade after Peletier published his book, and almost disappears, especially in France and England, under an avalanche of nationalist polemic in which the Italian language and Italianate manners are the objects of both measured and immoderate attack.[20]

The best known of the measured attacks is Henri Estienne's *Deux dialogues du langage françois italianizé et autrement deguizé, principalement entre les courtisans de ce temps* of 1578. The title clearly identifies the ascendancy of Florentines at the French Court as responsible for the corruption of the language. Estienne (1528–98) was deeply imbued with ancient literature and conversant with modern Italian authors, and was a fervent admirer of the Tuscan, but his ire could not be contained at the sound of modish franco-italian jargon. He gives numerous examples of ridiculously affected and congested sentences and expressions, which he had heard uttered by courtiers. This great compendium of linguistic junk was considered highly amusing but also a salutary warning, so much so that Henri III commissioned Estienne to produce the *Précellence du langage françois*, which was written in three months and printed in 1579. In that year Estienne published *L'Introduction du Traité de Conformité des merveilles anciennes avec les modernes, où traité préparatif à l'Apologie pour Hérodote*, which is highly critical of those who presume that all ancient literature and art has to be *exquis*. He ridicules the acquiring at inflated prices of ancient or foreign paintings, a subject to which we shall return. Herodotus is a very interesting author for Estienne to have chosen for his a lengthy commentary. The expatiatory introduction that takes up some two thirds of Herodotus' *History* is a rich source on the geography, antiquities and manners of the nations of the ancient world, and in the course of his account he traces back the enmity between East and West to legendary origins. The acceptance that enmity between nations is long standing and inevitable casts serious doubt on any belief of there being a Western classical tradition in any of the liberal arts, which could be shared and developed communally.

Books on architecture: Manuals and treatises for all nations?

Architecture, amongst the many arts being rejuvenated and reformed on the basis of a clearer reading of ancient literature, was seen by many as the least

106

well-served. The only surviving literary authority from antiquity was Vitruvius.[21] To the annotators Vitruvius was a case of literary archaeology, whose philological difficulties and complexities were such that their efforts were best kept in Latin.[22] The *imitatio* and popularisation of Vitruvius by translation began, gathered momentum and was usurped in the span of the sixteenth century. The prefaces by translators to their editions is where we might expect to find a concise explanation of the value of the book as an inspiration to modern patrons and their builders to excel. The first translation into Italian was accomplished by Cesare Cesariano (1483–1543) in an impressive folio volume published at Como in 1521.[23] Book titles conventionally were lengthy, and served both to identify the work and to advertise it to the well-read and the artisan alike. Cesariano's edition has a title which reads as if in anticipation that any potential buyer would have Vitruvius mentally catalogued as moribund or cocooned, a happy playground for philologists. Cesariano knew that Vitruvius had a reputation for obscurity, and his title sets out to weaken consumer resistance. This magnificent volume was dedicated to the predator of Lombardy, Francis I of France, and the title reads:

Di Lucio Vitruvio Pollione de Architectura Libri dece traducti de Latino in Vulgare affigurati: commentati: et con mirando ordini insigniti: per il quale facilmente potrai trovare la moltitudine de li abstrusi et reconditi vocabuli a li soi loci et in epsa tabula con summo studio exposti et enucleati ad immensa utilitate de ciascuno studioso et benivolo di epsa opera.

The one hundred and fourteen different woodcuts prepared for the edition offer the reader a wonderful gallery of images to explain difficult passages and bring the whole to life (figures 52–5). The architecture and details shown in the woodcuts certainly help to decipher Vitruvius. The style of the buildings used as models is clear testimony of the vigour and individuality of the Milanese architectural milieu that had included Leonardo, Bramante and the mathematician Luca Pacioli amongst Cesariano's friends and acquaintances.[24] The most delightful fancy in Cesariano's architectural gallery is the view of the harbour and city of Halicarnassus with an outlandish version of the Mausoleum in the middle (figure 54). The facade of this whimsy looks like an outline pastiche of the Certosa of Pavia, the richest and biggest church facade being assembled in Lombardy at the time.[25] The image which has attracted the most comment from architectural historians is a section of Milan Cathedral (figure 55). A great Gothic building might seem very incongruous in our only classical architectural text. There are good reasons for its inclusion, none of which would have appeased contemporary or later Italian opinion, which deplored Gothic as 'German', meaning 'barbarian'.[26]

The Latin inscription at the top reads: 'Thorough representation of the elevation raised from the ground plan running forward to the hexastyle facade of the sacred baricephalic temple. According to Germanic symmetry as that which is

52 Table of columns and enrichments.

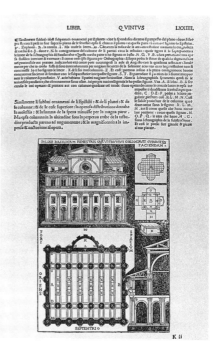

53 Reconstruction of a basilica described by Vitruvius.

54 View of Halicarnassus.

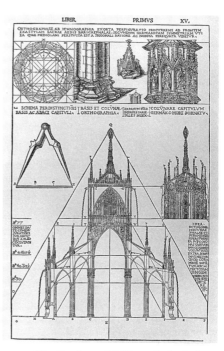

55 Section of Milan Cathedral.

seen to be built at Milan according to the triangular principle and the regular square.'[27] Much ink has been spilt on the subject of the reaction against the Gothic in sixteenth-century Italy, and the nationalist spirit which motivated it. Here, in of all places an edition of Vitruvius, there is a written and visual tribute paid to 'Germanic symmetry'. The Visconti Dukes of Milan were not only the representatives of the German Emperor in Italy at the end of the fourteenth century and early in the fifteenth century, but they also employed German master masons to head the works of Milan Cathedral in key phases of the first building campaigns.[28]

By the time Cesariano came to think of the best building to illustrate triangulation, a succession of Italian, German and Norman master masons had presided over the great project. The result could truly be said to be a building which embodied the technical and decorative genius of the most eminent masters of several nations. It is, and it was well known to be, a giant symbol of Milan's cosmopolitanism and of centripetal political and artistic status.[29] Cesariano would have been well aware of the Florentine brand of racial consciousness, which influenced the architecture of Brunelleschi and the theories of Alberti. He would have been equally well aware of Filarete's petition in his treatise for Francesco Sforza, Duke of Milan, to see the modern (Gothic) and Lombard manners of architecture set aside, and the Florentine manner adopted. Cesariano was unaffected by the *campanilismo* which motivated the most fervent of the Florentines. He was illustrating some principles and procedures with his woodcut, and Peletier du Mans' adage is wholly appropriate for the defence of Cesariano's choice of model – 'conceptions are common to all men; but words and ways of speech are particular to nations'. From Cesariano's edition of Vitruvius onwards the horizons of architectural literature in the vernacular steadily shrink.

Vasari attacks Germany

Vasari's *Lives of the Most Eminent Painters, Sculptors and Architects* of 1550 was so well received that a big printing sold out, requiring by public demand the expanded edition of 1568. Indeed many have searched but none have found an unfavourable contemporary review. It is reasonable to suppose that Vasari's opinions and prejudices were popular and widely held. It is unfortunate that there seems to be no record of any discussion or debate about his most subjective value judgements. Outstanding amongst these is his denunciation of the *maniera tedesca* in architecture, which can be read as racially inspired and historically misguided chauvinism. After a loosely organised discussion of the classical orders he launches his attack on the period and style he most deplores.

We come at last to another sort of work called German, which in both ornament and proportion is very different from both the ancient and modern. Nor is it adopted now by

109

the best architects but is avoided by them as monstrous and barbarous, and lacking everything that can be called order. Nay, it should rather be called confusion and disorder. In their buildings, which are so numerous that they sickened the world, doorways are ornamented with columns which are slender and twisted like a screw, and cannot have the strength to sustain a weight, however light it might be. Also on all the facades, wherever else there is enrichment, they build a malediction of little niches one above the other, with no end of pinnacles and points and leaves, so that, not to speak of the whole erection seeming insecure, it appears impossible that the parts should not topple over at any moment. Indeed they have more the appearance of being made of paper than stone or marble. In these works they made endless projections and breaks and corbellings and flourishes that throw their works out of all proportion; and often, with one thing being put on top of another, they reach such a height that the top of a door touches the roof. This manner was the invention of the Goths, for, after they had ruined the ancient buildings, and killed the architects in the wars, those who were left constructed buildings in this style. They turned the arches with pointed segments, and filled all Italy with these abominations of buildings, so in order not to have any more of them their style has been totally abandoned. May God protect every country from such ideas and styles of buildings! They are such deformities in comparison with the beauty of our buildings that they are not worthy that I should talk more about them, and therefore let us pass on to speak of the vaults.[30]

This is passionate, intoxicating stuff with deformed and abominable architecture having 'sickened the world' ('hanno ammorbato il mondo'): the reader is left with a sense of relief that such artistic damnation is not perpetual. The heroes of Vasari's *Lives* put things to right according to ancient principles, and these saviours of architecture are almost exclusively Florentine, from Brunelleschi to Michelangelo. It would be futile to try to play down the bias of Vasari, but there are places in his writings where there is a strong hint of the plurality found in Vitruvius or Alberti. In his biography of Brunelleschi Vasari reports the great debate which preceded the nomination for the seemingly impossible task of designing a dome for Florence Cathedral. 'Florentine merchants living in Germany, France, England and Spain were instructed to spare no expense in securing from the rulers of those countries the services of the most skilled and intelligent artists and sending them to Florence.' Such congresses are known to have served as a preliminary for other major building works. This anecdote reveals that in the Florence of 1420 questions of engineering and structure were deemed matters in which no one people had absolute mastery. The fact that Brunelleschi won the argument over what should be done is to his credit as an innovator, and not to the detriment of the talented men from abroad, who learnt something from their expedition. The unidentified deformed buildings to which Vasari alludes look as if they should fall down, but they had not. His invective concerns proportion and style: there is no mention of structure.

The obvious place to look for a modification of the pejorative use of the word German, or even for a retraction, is where he writes of Dürer. Vasari blatantly cheats to appear consistent, by denying Dürer's German nationality and his proud citizenship of Nuremberg, calling him Flemish and active at Antwerp. Dürer is not accorded the distinction of having a biography to himself, for Vasari squeezes his lengthy discussion of Dürer into the biography of the engraver Marcantonio Raimondi. Dürer's technical skill as an engraver was too widely and greatly admired in Italy for him to be ignored, and Vasari knew that he had to be taken into account and evaluated as an influence on Italian art. He did not shrink from casting Dürer as a major contributor to the evolution of art and its techniques.

In writing of Dürer's print of St Jerome he is unrestrained in his praise: '... nothing more and nothing better could be done in this field of art'. But he quickly forgets his superlative statement. A little further on we read: '... more and better could be done in that field'. The heart of the problem of Dürer for Vasari is quite simply that he was foreign, and he admits to his true feelings with the observation: '[if this man] ... had had Tuscany instead of Flanders for his country, and he had been able to study the treasures of Rome as we ourselves have done, he would have been the best painter of our land ...' Only once does the word 'German' crop up in the account of Dürer's work, in his praise of the engraving of the Prodigal Son of about 1496 (figure 56). He remarks that '... in this work are some beautiful huts after the manner of German cottages'. This might be read as deeply ironic. He admires the ability of Dürer to make a beautiful passage of engraving out of a subject which is inherently ugly. Such skill as Dürer's is evidence of misplaced natural, not national talent.[31]

Germany's Renaissance

In the case of no other country was the name of a contemporary people used as a term for the debasement of art. We can trust Vasari, when he reports that to call something 'German' was well understood by all Italians as being the ultimate insult, but there are good reasons for believing that this was a comparatively recent development. A hundred years earlier the future Pope Pius II, Aeneas Silvius Piccolomini, wrote admiringly of what he had seen in his travels '... in my opinion the Germans are wonderful mathematicians and in architecture they surpass all peoples'.[32] German writers of the sixteenth century were especially pleased by this compliment and liked to quote it.

As early as 1492, in an address at Ingolstadt, the German 'arch-humanist' Konrad Celtis was incensed and impressed by Italian superiority. He was intent on activating a mission to arouse fellow German-speakers, and it worked. Foreigners during the early sixteenth century were generally favourably impressed by the orderliness of Germany, the skill of her people, and their inventions, above all printing. The acrimony between Italian and German scholars begins on the issue of language, with Italian claims to primacy as direct heirs of Latin. One

56 Albrecht Dürer. *The Prodigal Son.*

early example of the hurt and irritation felt amongst German intellectuals is Franz Irenicus' *Germaniae exegeseos* of 1518, in which there is a lengthy refutation of recent libels emanating from Italy. The destroyers of ancient Rome were the ancestors of modern Germans and, so the argument goes, it is the destiny of the true descendants of ancient civilisation to lead in the renewed quest for perfection in the arts and sciences. One of the real surprises in wading through some of this mindlessly partisan material is to find Frenchmen concerned with their language joining the German cause. Etienne Dolet (1509–46) and Pélétier du Mans ranked Germany, not France, directly after Italy in importance in the process of re-awakening the arts and sciences, and the 1574 book fair at Frankfurt was the occasion to inspire a lofty eulogy by Henri Estienne (1528–98) on German culture in general.[33]

Parallels in France

Such fraternal feeling might have found some expression in architectural literature. The move to use ancient literature as a transfusion to invigorate the vernacular saw the translation of Vitruvius into French in 1547 and into German in 1548. The *Architecture où Art de bien bastir de Marc Vitruve Pollion* translated by Jean Martin and the *Vitruvius Teutsch* by Walther Ryff have much in common. Both are abundantly illustrated with 151 woodblocks cut for the French edition and 190 for the German, many of the plates having been cribbed from earlier Italian editions of Vitruvius as well as from Serlio (figures 57–60).[34] Martin and Ryff emphasise the labour of the translation in their prefaces, both stressing how it has been a hard task to make sense of a text which is so frequently obscure. Martin writes of the 'vulgar herd of artisans' (*la tourbe des artisans*) who can now make use of the book. Ryff enumerates the 'artisans, master builders, stone masons, foremen, masters of ordnance, painters, sculptors, goldsmiths, joiners' who now can benefit. Although both translators knew Cesariano's edition, for they lifted illustrations from it, neither was concerned, as had been the conscientious Italian, to make known to their readers the Greek names of the ornamental forms which occur in Vitruvius. Often Vitruvius does not explain important matters because the appearance, meaning and associations of an architectural form or detail would be very well-known to his compatriots.[35] In both French and German the architectural language of Vitruvius almost totally loses its implied meanings and unspecified associations. The tropes from the Greek which can reveal the significance in myth and ritual sacrifice of every major form and minor ornamental detail of columnar architecture are not discussed. The Martin and Ryff translations are not architectural Rosetta stones. The utility of the book, which both translators stress, has to be in the illustrations. There is not a scrap of evidence in building contracts, letters or diaries that either the French or German language Vitruvius was consulted to resolve any

57   Jean Martin's Vitruvius. Caryatids.

58   Jean Martin's Vitruvius. Plate illustrating the adjustments in scale required for the upper portions of a portico.

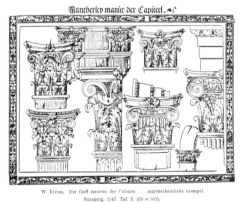

59   The *Vitruvius Teutsch.*

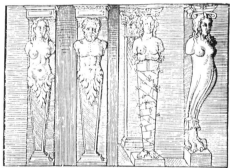

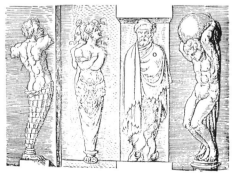

60   The *Vitruvius Teutsch.*

question of actual building procedure. This is no denial of the avid interest felt in the book as an authentic ancient text, but no assimilation of any of its theoretical propositions or stylistic principles can be traced in a single French or German town or country house, that might not have arrived by another route. National feeling and practical sense combined to make a market for books which dealt with building and style in terms of the present. This led to the appearance of building manuals and pattern books for different peoples and places. It is noteworthy that, in the course of the first half of the sixteenth century the full text of Vitruvius was translated only into Italian, French and German.

The humanity of Spanish Humanism

In Spain, where there was very considerable enthusiasm for adapting ancient Roman and modern Italian stylistic fashions, Vitruvius was left in the Latin, for clerics and scholars, until 1582.[36] By that date there were over seven hundred 'Renaissance' structures standing in Spain in the so-called Plateresque style, which is abundant testimony to the vigour and independent spirit of Spanish patrons and master crafts-men keen to build rather than to read and worry about rules.[37] Diego da Sagredo's short treatise *Medidas del Romano,* first published at Toledo in 1526, was a very selective architectural digest. It achieved considerable popularity, if one is to judge by the frequency of its reprinting in Spanish, and its translation into and no fewer than six editions in French from 1537 to 1555 (figure 61).[38] It was the first book on architecture to be published by a non-Italian. The aim of the work is stated succinctly in the title *Medidas del Romano necessarias a los oficiales que quieren seguir las formaciones de las basas, colunas, capiteles y otras pieças de los edificios antiguos.* More than any other architectural book of the sixteenth century Sagredo's text, much of which is written in the form of a dialogue between a clergyman and a painter, reads like a no-nonsense guide to some of the intricacies of composing a well-proportioned facade in the Roman manner. There is nothing on plans or interiors, nor is there any discussion of any Roman remains in Spain or elsewhere. Sagredo even leaves in suspense the whole issue of whether the various orders of columns, cornices and pediments the architectural apparatus of temples are appropriate for private houses. He lived in times, as he says, when elements of the style were proliferating on many classes of building, and his aim was to improve know-ledge of the form, proportion and nomenclature of the orders and their many ap-purtenances. Keenness to build *a lo romano* had preceded elementary knowledge, and patrons and masons should at least know the proper names for the components.

In this congenial book there is not a hint of the almost freemasonic exclusiveness of the scholarship which was investing so much effort in the elucidation of Vitruvius. There are no diversions into aesthetic or philosophical matters. It was Sagredo who told several generations of builders in Spain the rudiments of classical

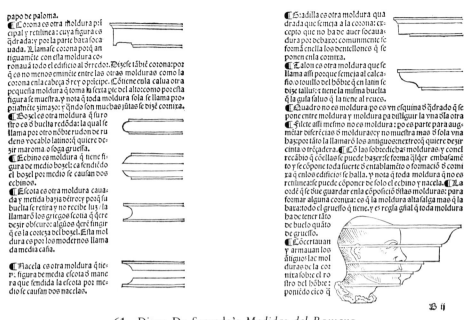

papo de paloma.
¶Corona es otra moldura prí
cipal y rectilinea: cuya figura es
qdrada: y por la parte baxa soca
uada. Llamase corona porq an
tiguamête con esta moldura co
ronaua â todo el edificio al ôrredor. Dizese tâbiê corona: por
q es no menos eminête entre las otras molduras como la
corona en la cabeça ô rey o prîcipe. Côtiene en la calua otra
pequeña moldura q toma la sexta pte del alto: como por esta
figura se muestra. y nota q toda moldura sola se llama pro-
priamête zimaso: y qndo son muchas jûtas se dizê cornixa.
¶Bozel es otra moldura q su ro
stro es ô buelta redôda: la qual se
llama por otro nôbre rudon de ru
dens vocablo latino: q quiere dezir maroma.o soga gruessa.
¶Echino es moldura q tiene figura de medio bozel: ca fendiêdo
el bozel por medio se causan dos
echinos.
¶Escota es otra moldura caua
da y metida hazia dêtro: y porq su
buelta se retira y no recibe luz / la
llamarô los griegos scotia q qere
dezir obscuro: algûos qerê fingir
q es la cortexa del bozel. Esta mol
dura es por los modernos llama
da media caña.

¶Nacela es otra moldura q tie
nê figura de media escota ô mane
ra que fendida la escota por medio se causan dos nacelas.

¶Gradilla es otra moldura qua
drada que semeja a la corona: ex-
cepto que no ha de auer socaua-
dura por debaxo: comunmente se
formâ en ella los dentellones q se
ponen en la cornixa.
¶Talon es otra moldura que se
llama assi porque semeja al calca-
ño o toutllo del hôbre q en latin se
dize tallus: y tiene la misma buelta
q la gula saluo q la tiene al reues.
¶Quadro no es moldura/po es vn esquina ô qdrado q se
pone entre moldura y moldura pa distiguir la vna ôla otra
¶Filete assi mesmo no es moldura: po es parte para aug-
mêtar diferêcias ô molduras: y no muestra mas ô sola vna
baxa: por tâto la llamarô los antiguos: nextro: q quiere dezir
cinta/o trêçadera.¶Cô las sobredichas molduras/y conel
recâbio q ô ellas se puede hazer: se forma qlqer embasamê
to y se côpone toda suerte ô entablamêto o formaciô ô corni
xa q enlos edificios se halla. y nota q toda moldura q no es
rectilinea: se puede côponer de solo el echino y nacela.¶La
ordê q ôue guardar en la côposiciô ôstas molduras: para
formar alguna cornixa: es q la moldura alta salga mas q la
baxa: todo el gruesso q tiene y es regla gñal q toda moldura
ha de tener tâto
de buelo quâto
de gruesso.
¶Côcertauan
y armauan los
âtiguos las mol
duras de la cor
nixa sobre el ro
stro del hôbre:
poniêdo cico q

B ij

61 Diego Da Sagredo's *Medidas del Romano*.

proportion based on 'our Vitruvius', and with such an assurance patrons and master masons could find plenty of scope for invention and individualism. The only note of caution sounded by Sagredo comes at the beginning of his book, with what amounts to a moral apology for the greater financial expenditure which must be incurred if embarking on building with antique features. He does not say that building *a lo romano* is a luxury for a very few in order to discourage enthusiasm for the style, but he is concerned and conscious of the fact that all the ornamentation which he describes will be expense on top of the essential fabric of any house. Such embellishments must be modest or great according to means.

Sagredo's book is sparsely illustrated with serviceable but very crude woodcuts, and to give the Spanish public the best complement to it Francisco de Villalpando published free translations of Serlio's third and fourth books at Toledo in 1552. These are the books on Roman monuments and some of their details, and that which deals with the orders of the columns and their use and adaptation in secular building (figure 62). They ran through no less than three editions in that year, and their popularity justified reprints in 1563 and 1574. It is significant that just these two of Serlio's six published books were then thought to be of special value to the Spanish public. The books on geometry, perspective, temples and gates and doorways were not thought to be of enough popular interest to be brought out in Spanish. The real appeal of Serlio's work was his offering of a sample of major antique Roman monuments in Italy which, along with the major

116

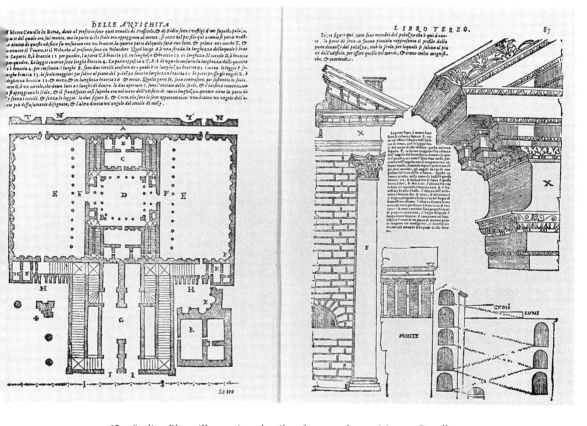

62   Serlio. Plate illustrating details of a temple on Monte Cavallo.

117

Roman remains of Spain, gave Spaniards a real sense of familiarity and continuity. A most endearing discussion of this genuine sense of kinship with the Roman world is Cristobal de Villalon's *Ingeniosa comparación entre lo antiguo y lo presente* of 1539, of which only one copy survives.[39] This is a rare work in another sense too; in the extraordinary picture it paints of a general, international, cultural renewal. His interest was not so much in architecture as in the engineering achievements of the ancients, which contemporaries had equalled, as can be seen in the cathedrals of Spain. Part of his thesis is that the ancients had exaggerated their accomplishments in both the arts and the sciences. In his summary of the measure of success now seen in the arts he lists France, Germany, Flanders, England and Holland along with Italy and Spain as making major contributions to progress.[40] In all this ferment of creativity the Spanish are amongst the most eager to contribute, according to Villalon. This keen sense of the past providing some models, but not necessarily the methods, might help to explain why Serlio's Books III and IV were welcomed in Spain as of interest and value to the public in their own language.

It would be very interesting to know if the translator of Serlio, Francisco da Villalpando, a scholar of considerable standing at the Court of Philip II, knew Torello Sarayna's *De origine et amplitudine civitatis Veronae*, an illustrated survey of the Roman antiquities of Verona published in 1540. In it he would have seen a woodcut portrait of the author (figure 63), with the following astonishing inscription beneath it:

Here we thought to warn you, [dear] reader, [about] what previous to this publication of ours, a certain Sebastiano Serlio from Bologna put out on the antiquities of many places. He claimed to be an antiquarian also of some monuments in Verona, which, because he himself had not seen them, unwisely perhaps taking from the carelessness of another, either he did not draw properly, or [because they were] unknown to him, he passed over in silence. And therefore, if anything is found in this book which differs from [that found] in his book, you should know that in our chapters what is true and exact is reproduced, as you as an inhabitant of Verona will ascertain, or as a traveller, if it ever happens that you go to the antiquities of Verona.[41]

Serlio

Serlio (1475–1553?) was the major sixteenth-century populariser of ancient Roman and modern Italian architecture; his books were a prodigious international publishing success. This is witnessed by the number of reprints in the original Italian and the translations into French, Flemish (unauthorised) and German.[42] Serlio's claims as a teacher and an authority are consistently modest, and Sarayna may well be reporting the truth, based on hearsay, when he states that Serlio used second-hand sources for his woodcuts, and did not survey the monuments himself. Serlio's achievement in publishing such an impressive quantity of ancient architecture in the *Libro Terzo*,

63 Torello Sarayna.

the first edition of which appeared in March 1540 at Venice, is not readily perceived in the twentieth century, when the general appearance of the Colosseum or of the Pantheon is part of the common knowledge of schoolchildren anywhere in the Western world. Sarayna's illustrations of Verona's Roman monuments are without doubt superior to Serlio's, but he has not understood either the public or the needs which Serlio's book satisfied. Up to 1540 not a single ancient Roman building had been published, and suddenly, with the appearance of the *Libro Terzo*, over fifty monuments were accessible to those who had never travelled. The temples, baths, theatres and triumphal arches in the *Libro Terzo* became the common property of all concerned with an informed and selective assimilation of ancient architecture into the architectures of their own nation or region. Praise for Serlio for making known and available a corpus of ancient monuments came from many parts of Europe throughout the rest of the sixteenth and well into the seventeenth century.

When the *Libro Terzo* was published Serlio was sixty-five and anxious about money and his future. His reputation made, he should have found an honourable post somewhere, but none was to be found in Italy. After many machinations he left Venice late in December 1540 to enter the service of Francis I. His *Libri I–II* on geometry and perspective were published in Italian and in French at Paris in 1545, which further shows that the brevity and clarity of his writing, coupled with an abundance of illustration, had made his work the best elementary material available on either side of the Alps. As a teacher and as a practising architect he expected to do much to influence the course of French architecture by his knowledge and understanding of recent creative design *a l'antica* at Rome or Venice. He ardently desired to see innovations from the south blended with the best qualities of the French tradition, but he had few disciples. The story of Serlio in France is complex, but very revealing. His frustration demonstrates that at this period books and architects might travel, but architecture did not.

Amongst the many things which Serlio tried but failed to achieve in France was to publish his 'true' *Libro VI*, a pattern book of house plans and elevations 'from the meanest hovel to the most ornate palace'. He produced two full manuscript copies in the course of the mid and late 1540s.[43] Although the *Libro VI* languished in manuscript, and therefore had no direct influence on the course of the history of planning and style anywhere in Europe, it is a document of the greatest value. The summer of his life had been in Rome watching and playing a minor role in the architectural revolution effected by Bramante and Raphael. A fruitful autumn was spent in Venice in the circles of Sansovino, Titian and Aretino. The winter of his life in France allowed him, if it did not force him, to look back with a view to making such privileged experience the basis for a book on domestic architecture. This he expected would be his most useful legacy to the future. The 'true' sixth book by Serlio is the only instance of an honest and detailed attempt to transcend national traditions of ideology or cultural fantasy, in order to produce a creditable pattern book of secular design. From the humblest to the richest, here are buildings which correspond to means, and set standards of modernity *a l'antica* by which the book might have changed the course of the architectural histories of many countries had it been printed and circulated.

The progression from the 'meanest hovel to the most ornate palace' involves over sixty designs; first there is a sequence of designs of country dwellings, houses and palaces followed by a set of designs appropriate to a city. All those who had attacked and were to attack the new style because it was foreign, costly and liable to make the newly rich the envy of the established order would have found Serlio conscious of their concerns. The humblest building is very humble, and there is a very great distance from the bottom of Serlio's socio-architectural hierarchy to its top (figures 64–71). At the bottom of the ladder in the polished version of the book, which was completed about 1550, there are dwellings for peasants of four *gradi di poverta* followed by designs for peasants or farmers of three *gradi di richezza*. Exactly how to measure or distinguish one grade or level of poverty or wealth from another is not discussed, but inferiors, peers and superiors are understood as accepting their place. In the text accompanying the third sheet, which has schemes for houses of poor artisans of three levels of poverty, Serlio summarises one of the themes of the work as the adaptable manner, which is the *costume italiano*. This he follows methodically in the first eight folios of country cottages and houses, and in the first seven folios of designs appropriate to a city, the grandest of which, for a rich citizen or merchant, is labelled *alla parisiana* (figure 66). Amongst the many implications of these juxtapositions is that Serlio viewed the lower and middle classes as best suited to remain within the established tradition of their own country or city, as befitted their rank in a static society. Over two-thirds of the book is devoted to projects for nobles, princes and the king, and these in plan and elevation are wholly in *la buona Architettura*, a term coined by Serlio in his introduction to describe the synthesis of Italian style. He hoped and believed *la buona Architettura* would become the basis of building for the upper classes in France and elsewhere. Italian achievement in many arts and sciences was known and appreciated by the discerning without prejudice, so he saw no reasonable obstacle to a dissemination of Italian architectural style, if a workable repertoire of models was put before the public. This was his big mistake.

A Serlio for France: Jacques Androuet du Cerceau

In 1559, some five or six years after Serlio's death, Jacques Androuet du Cerceau (1515?–85/6) published at Paris his first *Livre d'Architecture*, a collection of fifty projects beginning with some for those of the *moyen estat* and ending with large complexes of buildings (figures 72–5). The needs of the lower orders are not given any consideration. The Frenchman was a gifted stylist and a skilled parodist. He owned or had borrowed the earlier manuscript of Serlio's 'true' sixth book, which served as the unacknowledged inspiration for the form of his publication.[44] In his dedication to the King, du Cerceau immodestly pronounces that his subjects had no need to travel to other countries to see better composed buildings, than those being built in the kingdom at the time, and those in his pattern book. Serlio's idea has been hijacked in the name of the French manner.

The most marked differences between Serlio's Italian and his French country houses are in the elevations rather than the plans. The Italian houses tend to have open loggias on the ground floor at the front and comparatively low-pitched roofs; equally consistent are the French houses with closed fronts, a central front door and a roof of high enough pitch to contain a sequence of rooms not much smaller than on the main floor. The same is the case with the first of the collections of town houses, where the Italian examples tend to be open at the front at ground floor level, with low-pitched roofs, whilst the French examples have no ground floor arcades and make full use of the space afforded in a high-pitched roof. Custom and climate are the simple reasons given by Serlio for these obvious differences.

Androuet du Cerceau most probably never had set foot in Italy, and it was no part of his purpose to dwell on how others live. It was a book first and foremost

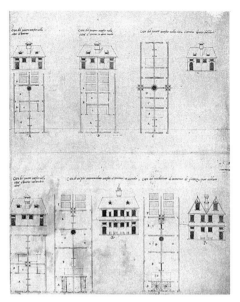

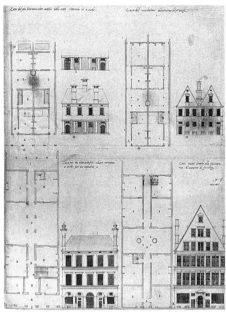

64 Serlio. Manuscript for the true Book VI.　**65** Serlio. Manuscript for the true Book VI.

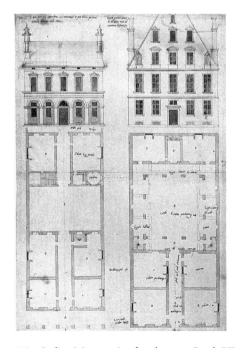

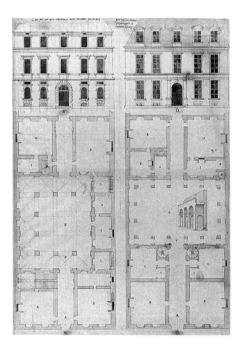

66 Serlio. Manuscript for the true Book VI.　**67** Serlio. Manuscript for the true Book VI.

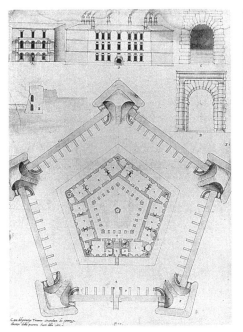

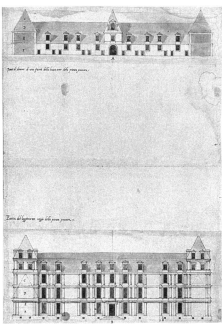

68 Serlio. Manuscript for the true Book VI. 69 Serlio. Manuscript for the true Book VI.

70 Serlio. Manuscript for the true Book VI. 71 Serlio. Manuscript for the true Book VI.

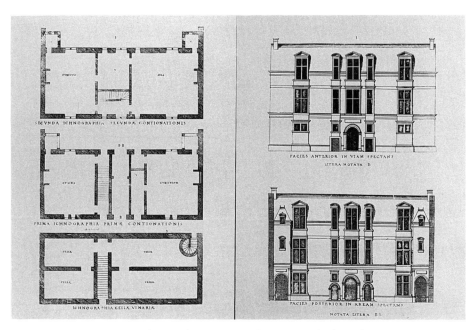

72 Jacques Androuet du Cerceau. Elevation and plan of project I.

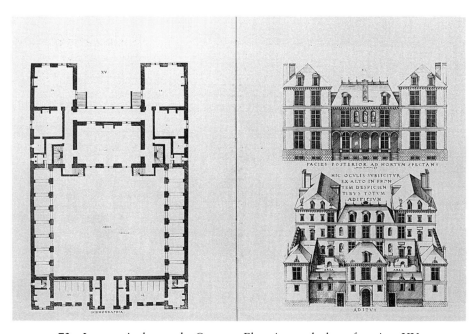

73 Jacques Androuet du Cerceau. Elevation and plan of project XV.

for a French audience, as the tone of the dedication to Henri II makes plain, but to a Parisian or a country landowner who opened a new copy of the book, the great majority of the designs would have looked innovative and radical. Here are symmetrical and carefully balanced houses rectangular in plan, houses built around a court, as well as some remarkable and apparently eccentric ideas for houses. One of these is planned within the shape of a circle, another is triangular and the penultimate has a decagonal main courtyard surrounded by five very substantial pavilions (figures 74–5). At first sight the inducement to build seems responsive to the needs of men of very different means. The descriptive notices for each 'project' attempt to give sufficiently accurate information on dimensions for the interested reader to estimate cost. However, such a pattern book appealed to ambition and not to economy. Would any be enticed by a design below his own estimate of his local rank? In the terms of the moralists, pattern books are inducements to luxury.

The influence of Serlio is apparent throughout du Cerceau's book, but only once (in project XXVI) does he plagiarise in a pastiche a scheme shown by the Italian. That unique case was the substantial country house of Ancy-le-Franc in Burgundy designed by Serlio for Antoine de Clermont-Tonnerre.[45] The patron, he tells us, wanted a distinctively Italianate building, but somehow the clear and beautifully balanced designs devised by Serlio were gallicised for the house as built. This is the closest we ever get to a real and unconditioned architectural import from Italy in northern Europe during the sixteenth century.

The impetus for du Cerceau's book was brought about by Serlio. Whether it was du Cerceau alone or in company with friends or superiors who wanted to take the initiative in the name of France, we do not know. The influence of Serlio on the book is both positive and negative. Set pieces such as loggias and arcades, which Serlio does not associate with the *modo di Franza*, are introduced by du Cerceau. The Frenchman made the attic storey tall enough to be used for accomodation from the smallest to the largest scheme. In the deployment of features which Serlio would have thought characteristically Italian in very French-looking buildings, du Cerceau produced a patchwork of quotations from the two manners. As far as he was concerned these should satisfy any who wanted to have a modern building in a suitable form. The question of the assimilation of Italian with French was settled; he had adapted for integration some planning formulae and a number of compositional and decorative exterior features, but this was to be seen in no sense as imitation.

The text of the book consists merely of matter-of-fact notices setting down the dimensions of the whole and parts of the schemes, in order that anyone contemplating following one of the designs might be able to calculate the cost of building, and above all estimate whether such work is within his means. In the foreword du Cerceau ends with a censure of the many who are often fooled or deceived,

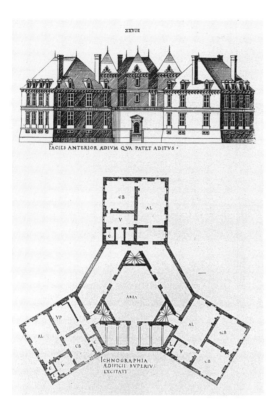

74 *left* Jacques Androuet du Cerceau. Elevation and plan of project XXVIII.

75 *below* Jacques Androuet du Cerceau. Elevation and plan of project XLIX.

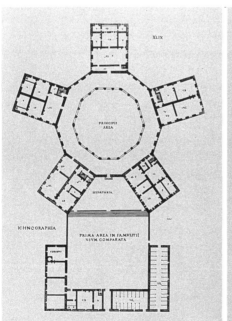

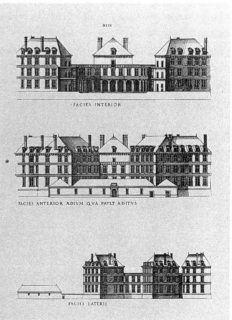

and who do make these estimates and calculations correctly. Embellishments and enrichments for a new house, such as fancy dormers, doorways and fireplaces are treated by du Cerceau as a matter apart, which he treats in his *Second Livre d'Architecture* of 1561. This miscellany of ornate architectural accessories is for the person whose house is built, and who has the means to add to it. These are architectural accessories or options for expenditure.

Latin editions of the first *Livre d'Architecture* of 1559 as well as of the *Second Livre* of 1561 were issued concurrently, which might seem surprising if these books were seen as wholly tailored to French practice and requirements. Our retrospective view of the significance of pattern books reveals illustrated and unillustrated builders' and decorators' manuals of many kinds and qualities. These books of 1559 and 1561 were the first of their kind published anywhere, and they were intended as both an invitation and a stimulus to foreigners to think of changes and improvements to their own ways of planning, building and ornamentation.

Androuet du Cerceau never acted as an architect in the conventional sense. He did not design a single building on commission which was then built. He had no training in technical matters of construction nor first-hand knowledge of anti-quity.[46] Illustrated books on architecture and design of the sixteenth century, leaving aside publications on antique monuments and editions or erudite collections of annotations of Vitruvius, may be divided into two categories. The first is the pattern book invented by Serlio and realised to his immense profit by Androuet du Cerceau. The second category is the technical, theoretical and historically-minded architecture book written by practised and experienced architects, of which the sixteenth century produced only two true examples in the publications of the Frenchman Philibert de l'Orme (1510?–70) of 1561 and 1567 and of the very famous Andrea Palladio (1518–80) of 1570 (figures 83–90).

Antwerp

The most spectacular production of the pattern book genre by far is Hans Vredeman de Vries' *Architectura* of 1565 (reprinted in 1577, 1581, 1587, 1597 &c.), in which there is a set of twenty-three lavishly columned and pilastered buildings, whose obvious parentage was the new town halls of the Low Countries (figures 76–7).[47] The most prestigious of all of these was Antwerp Town Hall, in whose design de Vries had played an important secondary role during the 1560s (figure 78). They are ostentatious buildings to tempt only the richest burgher or town council with well stocked coffers and a sense of civic competitiveness. Just as du Cerceau had dismantled and rebuilt the projects he found in Serlio's manuscript the better to conform to French building practice, de Vries (1527?–1604) justified the thoroughly Flemish mode of forms and decorative systems developed in his publication. In

76 Hans Vriedeman de Vries. Alternative designs for town halls.

77   Hans Vriedeman de Vries. Alternative designs for mansions with towers.

129

78 Antwerp Town Hall. Architects Cornelis Floris and others.

a short French introduction to the book he tells readers not familiar with his home country that:

... here in the Low Countries conditions are different, above all in the centres of commerce where plots are cramped and costly ... which means that one must build tall and light the floors with as great an opening as possible. This is why we have to honour those masters who have ingeniously sustained amongst us the native tradition such as Maître N. Floris, the father of Corneil Floris, Maître Jacques van Berghen, Maître Ian Gilgo, Maître Anthonis Mockaert, Maître Jan de Heere above all must rank Corneil Floris [the head architect of Antwerp Town Hall], at Liège Maîtres Thomas Voor and Guillaume Paludani stand out ...

His roll call of eminent men is completed by an acrostic poem in which Serlio, Jacques Androuet du Cerceau and Pieter Coecke van Aelst (author of an abridged translation of Vitruvius and of unauthorised translations of Serlio) are credited as the authors to whom he is most indebted.[48] A highly developed sense of regional distinctions within the Low Countries themselves shows at certain points in the book, for example where he suggests that walls should be of brick to contrast and set off the mouldings, which should be in stone. Such 'decorative and gay' effects are seen to best advantage in the provinces of Holland and Flanders principally at Bruges. The polychromy of brick with stone is not only attractive, but allows builders the flexibility to use more or less of each material according to cost, availability and taste. Some fifty years later we find Philippe de Béthune, the brother of Sully, the great reforming first minister of France under Henri IV, writing an appreciation of the orderliness and proportion of town houses in Flanders. Conformity to tradition, careful economy in building and regard to the form and scale of the houses of neighbours are qualities he admired and commended to his compatriots for emulation.[49] In such a spirit pattern books and the benefits of travel might combine to blur regional or national distinctions in architecture, but such cases are very rare in literature and reality. Architects who turned to writing were not inclined towards such supra-regional or supra-national sentiments.

De l'Orme and Palladio

Philibert de l'Orme and Andrea Palladio have never been thought of as having much in common other than as being devoted and expert students of ancient architecture, and as the most eminent and successful architects in their native lands. Both of their publications are in significant part illustrated architectural autobiographies. De l'Orme, in his *Architecture* of 1567, writes in the first person and offers his readers a portrait of himself and woodcuts of the plans, elevations and details of some of his major commissions of the previous twenty years (figures 83–6). His sojourn in Rome between 1534 and 1536 is given prominence to give weight to his account of the orders and their proportions, in whole and in detail, based on first-hand experience. However, his presentation of the ins and outs of ancient Roman architecture is neither systematic nor comprehensive. The process he set in motion, and which he led from his powerful position as royal architect, was one of a most thorough, yet empirical assimilation of correct Roman detail into pure prestige French architecture.

De l'Orme was the first Frenchman to claim in print and to deserve the title of professional architect. All the royal and aristocratic châteaux, the Tuileries palace in Paris and the other work that he described as his architectural revolution, not least of which was his own Parisian town house, were quintessentially *à la française* (figures 81–2). This was new blood pumped into revered but dry bodies. Inside the spirit was different and distinct from old values, and outside the intention was to show much more than a re-enactment of the iconography and the show of the grand piles of *Rome poudreuse*. Throughout his long monologue De l'Orme makes no reference to contemporary Italian architecture, and the uses and abuses he must have seen of ancient forms. His purpose is 'de faire profit au bien public et signamment [avant tout] à ma Patrie' with special care taken to show how ancient models might be adapted 'à l'usage et pratique de notre architecture'.[50] The sample of his executed work illustrated in the *Architecture* underscores his point. The woodcuts showing his own house should have made the reader of solid but average means wonder why he should bother with antiquity at all.

The seriousness with which de l'Orme set about his self-appointed mission is seen in the amount of space devoted to technical matters. Six books out of the

79 Philibert De l'Orme. Allegory of the Bad Architect. Eyeless, earless and surrounded by desolation and ugliness, the Bad Architect is a charlatan and an ogre.

80 Philibert De l'Orme. Allegory of the Good Architect. with three eyes, one to contemplate God, four ears and four hands, the Good Architect instructs in surroundings of buildings dedicated to wisdom and piety.

81 Philibert De l'Orme. His own house on the rue de la Cerisaie, Paris. Courtyard elevation. A model for the reader of stylistic restraint and economy.

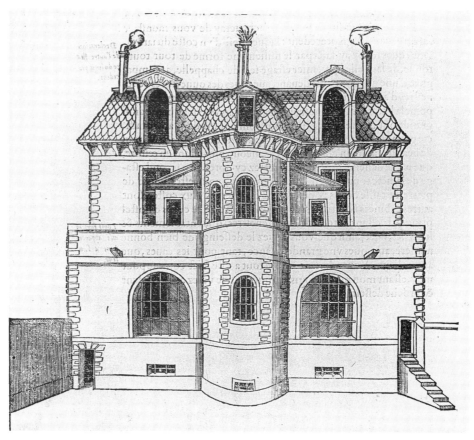

82 Philibert De l'Orme. His own house on the rue de la Cerisaie, Paris. Garden front elevation.

eleven of the *Architecture*, or a hundred and fifty-six folios out of the three hundred and thirty of the whole book, are taken up with analytical descriptions of foundations (*livre II*), vaults (*livres III & IV*), the structure of chimney stacks (*livre IX*), and joinery (*livres X & XI*).[51] The pattern books of architectural designs *à la française* by Androuet du Cerceau, of which de l'Orme wholeheartedly disapproved, would give the public a fair but not exact idea of the costs involved by listing the measurements in order to arrive at a round total for materials and labour. There is not a word on how work should begin or proceed, a shortcoming amply remedied by de l'Orme, to whom practical amateurism and technical ineptitude were sins bound to result in waste and bad architecture.

Architecture à la française for de l'Orme was the science of the use of materials coupled with the art of the use of decorative components. Three elements might be singled out from his writings to highlight his fundamental approach, which was to take his readers from sound basics to intricate questions of style. They are his *nouvelles inventions* for joinery, the *stéréotomie*, for understanding complex stone vaults and his invention of a sixth order of column, the *ordre françois* (figures 83–6). The first book issued by him in 1561 on large-scale joinery has a characteristically pithy title, *Nouvelles Inventions pour bien bastir à petits fraiz*. The *petits fraiz* is probably better understood and translated as meaning 'at reasonable cost' rather than 'at small cost', for the roof and floor structures he describes and illustrates are mostly for houses for the prosperous, at the very least. De l'Orme's aim with this wholly utilitarian book was to inspire craftsmen and builders to make more imaginative and ambitious use of wood. God and gallic ingenuity could produce amazing results with timber, whose potential had not been realised to date. Wide spaces could be roofed or vaulted with ribs made up of cleverly designed interlocking pieces, whose joins should need no gluing or metal bolts if correctly cut.

Stéréotomie is a geometric procedure and manual art for the cutting of stone of equal if not greater complexity, which de l'Orme developed into the trademark of much that was exclusive to *architecture à la française*.[52] His diagrams of vaults, especially those for the *trompe* or projecting angle cabinet of the château of Anet designed by him, is a display of technical virtuosity not on a grand scale, indeed, but he calculates to impress by the exactitude with which the blocks of very gradually changing shape have to be cut. In two dimensions he provides all the information required by a top quality mason to prepare a complicated convex squinch (figures 83–4). If he betrayed some of the secrets of the masons' lodge, his defence is that such techniques exist to be developed and improved, and that since there is no such thing as a static tradition for masons, far less can there be one for architects.

With such inventive enthusiasm, it was logical, that he should regard the canonical orders of columns as needing a further order for France (figures 85–6). His argument for the desirability, if not the necessity, for such bold and unconventional stylistic innovation is persuasive. He tells his readers that the stone available in France was not suitable for the cutting of monolithic columns, as could be done by the Italians, who had marble of suitable quality. This he does not deem a shortcoming, but a condition which called for the creation of an order of a form which would use the indigenous sandstone or limestone of France to the best effect. The shaft of de l'Orme's sixth, French order is made up of drums with foliated bands or a torus sandwiched between them. Thus the apparent disadvantage of a light stone is circumvented and turned to decorative effect while the assemblage of parts remains undisguised. Although de l'Orme does not discuss fully how he devised his French order, he does insist that as the ancients invented orders, so must we. The adherence to tradition in his sequence of orders is a paradox, for he retains the distinctive succession of Tuscan, Doric, Ionic,

P

83 *left* Philibert De l'Orme. Anet, the suspended angle cabinet or *trompe*.

84 *below* Philibert De l'Orme. Anet, plan and projection of the masonry of the *trompe*.

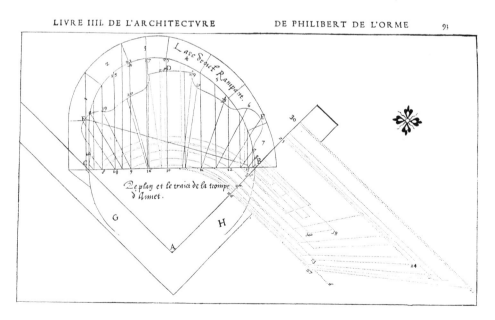

L'arc droict Rampant.

Le plan et le traict de la trompe d'Anet.

85 Philibert De l'Orme. French Doric Order.

Corinthian and Composite for the capitals of his column shafts dressed *à la française*. It would have helped if he had explained his thinking in producing just a new wrapping for the old, but what is strongly suggested is a subtle architectural patriotism, which has usurped antique forms in a forced adoption. Tuscan, Doric, Ionic and Corinthian are now all French.

Andrea Palladio's *Quattro Libri dell'Architettura* of 1570 is a book whose fame far exceeds de l'Orme's *Architecture*. The fame of Palladio has obscured many areas of common purpose shared by the two men. The first of Palladio's four books deals with the fundamentals of architecture and the orders; the second book covers domestic design, almost all of which is his own past work; the third book deals with public works such as roads, bridges and basilicas; the fourth is a succinct compendium of choice ancient Roman buildings. It is the second book which has attracted much the most interest and comment from later patrons, architects and writers. The *Libro Secondo* might be called Palladio's architectural autobiography, in which he illustrates his major palace and villa commissions, with the briefest of texts (figures 87–90). Here is where we would expect to find the distilled opinions of a man with unparalled experience, after thirty or more

137

86 Philibert De l'Orme. French Ionic Order, the Tuileries Palace, Paris. Built 1566–72. Burnt and dismantled May 1871.

years of designing buildings for very discriminating patrons, both men and women, whom he described as 'subtle and imaginative'.

The *Libro Secondo* is anything but an abrasive or boastful advertisement 'à la Philibert' for the architectural style developed by Palladio. Everything that we know of his personality paints a picture of a man who was persuasive, eloquent and much liked by his noble patrons as well as the labourers whom he instructed on site. The Vicentine nobility, for whom he designed so many palaces and villas, were rightly proud of their greatest artistic servant, and collectively welcomed the *Libro Secondo* as a testament for the outside world to their status and taste, which tactfully avoids any allusion to the many schisms amongst them or mention that few of the town palaces were complete. There are two levels of persuasion in the *Libro Secondo* for potential builders in other parts of Italy and abroad. The first is Palladio's advice to the leading families of Vicenza to dispel any reserve which might be caused by the unfamiliarity of the architecture. If such things can be achieved in a town of Vicenza's size, then the reader is bound to wonder what can and might be done by grander nobles, cardinals and princes elsewhere. A second level of persuasion is the way in which Palladio offers descriptions, plans and elevations of palaces and villas as work which has been satisfactorily completed. He created the impression that all such enterprises are affordable and are a natural expression of personal and civic pride for members of a model oligarchy. Palladio illustrates the Basilica, but omits the wonderful and as yet unbuilt Teatro Olimpico of Vicenza, both of which he designed and were built out of the commune's purse, as if to sharpen the image of Vicenza as a centre of architectural perfection. It is beyond dispute that, thanks to Palladio's *Libro Secondo*, Vicenza was the first town in Europe to be internationally known for its most modern buildings.

To commend himself and the architectural subjects which he offers his readers whoever they may be, Palladio says in his *proemio ai lettori* that he has undertaken to write clearly and simply

... to discuss architecture in as orderly and clear a fashion which I can ... And in all these books I shall avoid long windedness [*lunghezza delle parole*], and will simply provide the comments which I think most necessary, and I shall use those terms which craftsmen normally use today.

In a similar vein he writes of his amenability, when he reassures his unseen social superiors that '... often it is necessary for the architect to fit in with the views of those who are spending, rather than with that which one should observe' [i.e. the rules]. His affability might have been the root cause of one of the deadliest of sins for an architect underestimating costs. His failing in such matters was for all to see close to the end of his life in 1577, when after the fire which burnt out much of the Doge's palace he submitted a spectacular new design (figure 91). This, he calculated, would cost the absurdly small sum of 42,000 ducats.[53] Most

87 Andrea Palladio. Palazzo Thiene, Vicenza. Elevations.

LA SEGVENTE fabrica è del Magnifico Signor Francesco Badoero nel Polesine ad vn luo go detto la Frata, in vn sito alquanto rileuato, e bagnato da vn ramo dell'Adige, oue era antica mente vn Castello di Salinguerra da Este cognato di Ezzelino da Romano. Fa basa à tutta la fabrica vn piedestilo alto cinque piedi : à questa altezza è il pauimento delle stanze : lequali tutte sono in so laro, e sono state ornate di Grottesche di bellissima inuentione dal Giallo Fiorentino. Di sopra hanno il granaro, e di sotto la cucina, le cantine, & altri luoghi alla commodità pertinenti : Le colon ne delle Loggie della casa del padrone sono Ioniche : La Cornice come corona circonda tutta la ca sa. Il frontespicio sopra loggie fa vna bellissima vista : perche rende la parte di mezo più eminente de i fianchi. Discendendo poi al piano si ritrouano luoghi da Fattore, Gastaldo, stalle, & al ri alla Villa conueneuoli.

IL MAGNIFICO Signor Marco Zeno ha fabricato secondo la inuentione, che segue in Ce falto lu ogo propinquo alla Motta, Castello del Triuigiano. Sopra vn basamento, il quale circonda tutta la fabrica, è il pauimento delle stanze : lequali tutte sono fatte in uolto : l'altezza de i uolti delle maggiori è secondo il modo secondo delle altezze de' volti. Le quadre hanno le lunette ne gli an goli, al diritto delle finestre : i camerini appresso la loggia, hanno i uolti à fascia, e così ancho la sala : il volto della loggia è alto quanto quello della sala, e superano tutti due l'altezza delle stanze. Ha que sta fabrica Giardini, Cortile, Colombara, e tutto quello, che fa bisogno all'uso di Villa.

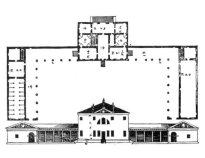

, IL MAGNIFICO   GG   NON MOLTO

88 Andrea Palladio. The Villas Badoer and Zen. Plans and elevations.

LA SEGVENTE fabrica è stata cominciata dal Conte Francesco, e Conte Lodouico fratelli de' Trissini à Meledo Villa del Vicentino. Il sito è bellissimo; percioche è sopra vn colle, il quale è bagnato da vn piacuole fiumicello, & è nel mezo di vna molto spaciosa pianura, & à canto hà vna assai frequente strada. Nella sommità del colle hà da esserui la Sala ritonda, circondata dalle stanze, e però tanto alta che pigli il lume sopra di quelle. Sono nella Sala alcune mezze colonne, che reggono vn solo vn poggiuolo, nel quale si entra per le stanze di sopra; lequali perche sono alte sotto sette piedi, seruono per mezati. Sotto il piano delle prime stanze vi sono le cucine, i tinelli, & altri luoghi. E perche ciascuna faccia hà bellissime viste; vi uanno quattro loggie di ordine Corinthio: sopra i frontespicij delle quali sorge la cupola della Sala. Le loggie, che rendono alla circonferenza d'anno vn gratissimo aspetto: più presso al piano sono i fenili, le cantine, le stalle, i granari, luoghi da Gastaldo, & altre stanze per vso di Villa: le colonne di questi portici sono di ordine Toscano: sopra il fiume ne gli angoli del cortile vi sono due colombare.

LA FABRICA sottoposta è in Campiglia luogo del Vicentino, & è del Signor Mario Repeta, ilquale hà eseguito in questa fabrica l'animo della felice memoria del Signor Francesco suo padre. Le colonne de i portici sono di ordine Dorico: gli intercolunnij sono quattro diametri di colonna: Ne gli estremi angoli del coperto, oue si ueggono le loggie fuori di tutto il corpo della casa, vi uanno due colombare, & le loggie. Nel fianco rincontro alle stalle vi sono stanze, delle quali altre sono dedicare alla Continenza, altre alla Giustitia, & altre ad altre Virtù con gli Elogij, e l'Pitture, che ciò dimostrano, parte delle quali è opera di Messer Battista Maganza Vicentino Pittore, e Poeta singolare: il che è stato fatto affine che questo Gentil huomo, il quale riceue molto uolentieri tutti quelli, che vanno à ritrouarlo; possa alloggiare i suoi forestieri, & amici nella camera di quella Virtù, alla quale essi gli pareranno hauer più inchinato l'animo. Hà questa fabrica la commodità di potere andare per tutto al coperto, e perche la parte per l'habitatione del padrone, e quella per l'vso di Villa sono di vno istesso ordine; quanto quella perde di grandezza per non essere più eminente di quella; tanto questa di Villa accresce del suo debito ornamento, e dignità, facendoli vguale à quella del Padrone con bellezza di tutta l'opera.

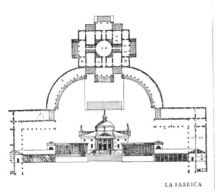

LA FABRICA

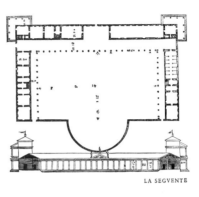

LA SEGVENTE

89   Andrea Palladio. The Villas Trissino and Repeta. Plans and elevations.

I DISEGNI, che seguono sono della fabrica del Conte Ottauio Thiene à Quinto sua Villa. Fù cominciata dalla felice memoria del Conte Marc'Antonio suo padre, e dal Conte Adriano suo Zio: il sito è molto bello per hauer da una parte la Tesina, e dall'altra vn ramo di detto fiume assai grande: Hà questo palagio vna loggia auanti la porta di ordine Dorico: per questa si passa in vn'altra loggia, e di quella in vn cortile: i lati hanno i fianchi due loggie: dall'vna, e l'altra testa di queste loggie sono gli appartamenti delle stanze, delle quali alcune sono state ornate da pitture da Messer Giouanni Indemio Vicentino huomo di bellissimo ingegno. Rincontro all'entrata si troua vna loggia simile à quella dell'entrata, dalla quale si entra in vn'Atrio di quattro colonne, e da quelle nel cortile, il quale hà i portici di ordine Dorico, e serue per l'vso di Villa. Non vi è alcuna scala principale corrispondente à tutta la fabrica: percioche la parte di sopra non hà da seruire, se non per sala uaroba, e per luoghi da seruitori.

IN LONEDO luogo del Vicentino è la seguente fabrica del Signor Girolamo de' Godi posta sopra vn colle di bellissima uista, & à canto vn fiume, che serue per Peschiera. Per rendere questo sito commodo per l'vso di Villa si sono fatti tutti i cortili, & strade sopra uolti con non picciola spesa: La fabrica di mezo è per l'habitatione del padrone, & della famiglia. Le stanze del padrone hanno il piano loro alto da terra tredici piedi, e sono in solaro, sopra quelle vi sono i granari, & nella parte di sotto, cioè nell'altezza de i tredici piedi in solaro sono disposte le cantine, luoghi da fare i uini, la cucina, & altri luoghi simili. La Sala giunge con la sua altezza fin sotto il tetto, & hà due ordini di finestre. Dall'vno e l'altro lato di questo corpo di fabrica vi sono i cortili, & i coperti per le cose di Villa. E' stata questa fabrica ornata di pitture di bellissima inuentione da Messer Gualtiero Padouano, da Messer Battista del Moro Veronese, e da Messer Battista Venetiano: perche questo Gentil huomo, il quale è giudiciosissimo, per ridurla à quella eccellenza & perfettione, che sia possibile, non hà guardato à spesa alcuna, & hà scelto i più singolari, & eccellenti Pittori de' nostri tempi.

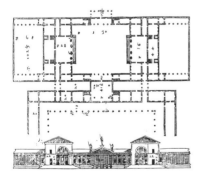

IN LONEDO

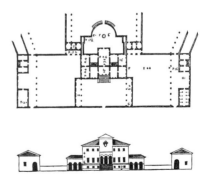

II   A SANTA

90   Andrea Palladio. The Villas Thiene and Godi. Plans and elevations.

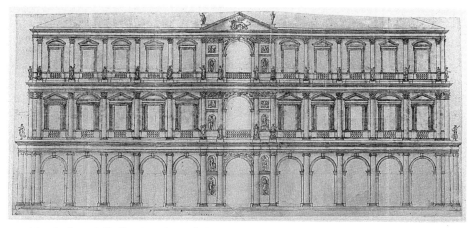

91 Andrea Palladio. Unadopted design (1577–8) for the Doge's Palace, Venice.

interestingly for the theme of nationalism or patriotism in the context of architecture, the project was turned down, because the great majority of those with power in this matter wanted to see it rebuilt as before. This was a gesture which must have sent a clear signal to contemporaries and later generations, that some buildings are too symbolically important to be changed. Vasari's message had not been received and understood in Venice. Venetian-ness, however it had evolved, had priority.

Some of Palladio's most interesting observations about style, building and related matters are to be found in documents such as the opinion solicited from him on a model for the new Cathedral at Brescia. His report of 1567 begins with fulsome praise of the local man Lodovico Beretta's design, but by gradual steps and in the most diplomatic terms he undermines it by verbally redesigning it, offering to provide Beretta with '... all the profiles of the bases, capitals, cornices, and the measurements of all the parts of the building which will be noted in the design'.[54] In this same document is a most revealing statement prompted by the use of columns and the expensive materials proposed by Beretta. Palladio insists that '... buildings are esteemed more for their form than for their materials ...', and to justify his view he calls attention to his own way of doing things at one of his great Venetian commissions, the church of San Giorgio Maggiore. There the humble brick has been used in no sense as a poor relation to stone or marble to form the body of even the great columns of the nave. The finish of a building was a matter of great importance to Palladio, and he must have made the case over and over again, in the course of numerous discussions with patrons and builders, that building or facing interior or exterior walls in stone was not the only way to achieve a truly satisfying result. In the same vein he talks enthusiastically, in the *Quattro Libri*, of brick being more fire-resistant than stone, and that, with a coating of stucco, it will harmonise perfectly with any stone features. From an architect who was by training a stone mason, and in the years when he was personally supervising every stage of the building of the Basilica of Vicenza from the quarrying of the stone, the cutting and carving of blocks and their setting in place, such enthusiasm for the humble brick might seem a little paradoxical. In making such comments he had the authority of the ancients and the building world of Venice, where by this time he was established full-time. Stone was neither indigenous to Venice nor usually a suitable material used in large quantities because of the dangers of subsidence. Like de l'Orme, Palladio sought to persuade his readers and patrons that the natural was always preferable to the artificial. Good architecture must be created from the skilful use of the material resources of the place. Such an outlook has both artistic consequences and ethical connotations, which fortify any arguments detailing how and why distinctions must exist between the form and appearance of the buildings of different classes, regions and nations.

Roads from Rome

When the study of Renaissance architecture across Europe is approached not from the point of view of the primacy and diffusion of Italian style, but from a pluralist standpoint, major centres of architectural activity are not seen simply as outstations of a never-existent consortium of Italian centres of excellence. This is not to overlook the importance of Italian artists and craftsmen who travelled or settled abroad. Giuliano da Sangallo designed a palace for the king of France, and a four-towered residence was planned by Andrea Sansovino for the king of Portugal, according to Vasari, but of them there is no known record. It is most likely that no action was taken to set any building in motion.[54] My aim here is to take some account of the known and understood differences between peoples and places, that have made the idea of a pan-European or supra-national manner in architecture a notion only to be entertained in the wake of the invention of the Renaissance by historians in later centuries. From the evidence of many types of sixteenth-century literature it is clear that peoples are more likely to agree on the differences between themselves than on their similarities. Likewise native or national tradition is understood in positive, not negative terms. A vigorous tradition in literature, art or architecture is one that has the will to assimilate and emulate, and a weak tradition is one which succumbs to mere imitation.

There is no more apt or spectacular testimony for the pluralist approach than the flagship building programmes of the crowned heads. To sixteenth-century kings of France, Spain and England architectural magnificence could be as important as treasure or victories. The person of the sovereign is the only embodiment of the achievement of the nation, according to every piece of monarchical panegyric and propaganda. Thus their buildings had to be unprecedented. In both style and function Francis I's Chambord, Charles V's Alhambra palace, Henry VIII's Nonsuch, the Louvre as built for the last of the Valois kings and Philip II's Escorial are not a heterogeneous group of monuments (figures 92–7).[55] Nevertheless, all stood or stand for the justice and morality of might in seemingly Roman or Italiate architectural and decorative language. No bourgeois, aristocratic or least of all royal architecture is innocent of boastfulness at the least, and for the mightiest the message is unfettered propaganda. The dissimilarity in appearance amongst this group of flagship buildings should not be surprising, for if the theorists of translation, the concocters of pattern books and the architects speak with the same voice, it is to say that the past is the servant of the present. Antiquity is a quarry for writers, painters, sculptors and architects, whose resources are to be used with care, discrimination and in a mind not to seem to copy the doings of neighbours and rivals Henry VIII and Philip II who were keen for intelligence on French royal building like Chambord and Fontainebleau, to which particular prestige was attached.[56] It was natural for monarchs to be curious about what their cousins or in-laws were commissioning, but visible evidence of artistic information or even of artists circulating between one court atelier and another are very scarce. In the cases of these five very special edifices, they are very clear and cerebral expressions of dynastic and national character and of self-determination in architecture.

France

The early history of Chambord has not and probably cannot be fully explained. Francis I directed Leonardo da Vinci to spend some of his time on architectural ideas for his proposed palace at Romorantin, and in the year before the great man's death in 1519 the king resolved to shift his major building initiative to Chambord, close to Blois. Amongst Leonardo's sketchbooks are plans for great keep-houses with a Greek cross of halls or corridors with a central spiral staircase, as came to be built on the grandest scale at Chambord. The wooden model of the project, which survived into the seventeenth century to be recorded in drawings, was a large and expensive work of art in itself, and was made by Domenico da Cortona. As built, the central *donjon* of Chambord inside and out betrays little of the Italian origins of its form because it wears a disguise of rich and complicated architectural decoration that is entirely Ecole de la Loire. The pedigree of the initial ideas has been submerged, and to none in the sixteenth century did the role of Leonardo or any other Italian seem to matter, for all reports of the building, whether French or foreign, speak of it as the product of the king's passion for building. In such terms a building is seen as a metaphor for royal government, in which much is said, submitted and considered for policy, but the decision on what is done and how it

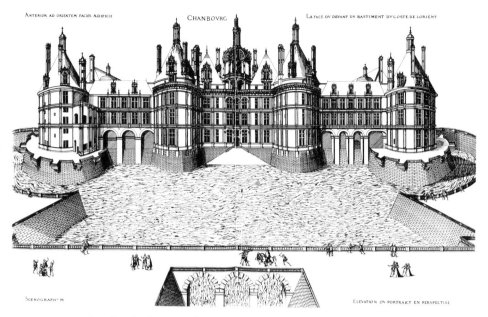

Scenographvm   Elevation ov portraict en perspective

92   Chambord, showing the grandiose, unexecuted scheme for a moat.

is done is the sole prerogative of the monarch. The energy and resources poured into Chambord did not result in the house becoming a main stage for the rituals and pleasures of the Court, and critics of 'vain expenditure' on architecture would have delighted in the case of Chambord had they known how very infrequently it was used by its proud builder.

Spain

Francis' lifelong adversary, the Emperor Charles V, only took the decision to build something of originality and distinction once. Of all the cities of his Spanish domains which he saw in 1526 he liked Granada best. The Alhambra and its famous Nazaride palaces, with their cool and exotic interiors surrounded by verdant countryside, were prizes after the surrender of Granada to the Catholic Monarchs in 1492, which symbolised final victory. Charles was admonished by his mother and grandparents to preserve them, but it seems that the Imperial Court needed to be housed in the European manner. In its setting on the Alhambra Charles V's square building, with its massive exterior of rustication and pilasters and its central circular peristyle of Doric and Ionic columns, is a forceful statement of the new regime. The architectural language of this statement is immediately read as imperial in meaning and Roman in origin, which is not to say that contemporary Spaniards perceived such forms as Italian. Indeed there is evidence to show that the generation of Diego

93 Granada. The Emperor Charles V's palace. Begun 1527, left unroofed in 1557. Architect Pedro Machuca.

Sagredo, or of the official to whom Charles entrusted the project, the governor of the Alhambra, Luis Hurtado da Mendoza, with the Italian-trained painter and architect Pedro Machuca, scorned the idea of Italian hegemony in the classical inheritance. As if to demonstrate this genuine disbelief the emperor was to be celebrated in architectural terms which were universal and especially valid for one so titled. This choice of a rigorously Roman architectural repertoire, to which Charles was without doubt a party, might seem to be at odds with the stormy events of the late 1520s, not least of which was the sack of Rome by imperial troops in 1527. At his court Charles regarded most of the ambassadors as representatives of enemies, especially the Italians, and his expulsion of the representatives of both Venice and Florence the year before the sack is sometimes quoted as proof positive of a deep personal racial animosity. Coming in the first years of his reign over his extraordinary accumulated inheritances of the Burgundian Netherlands and of Spain, the choice of site and of style for this building is intriguing. It was to be the first and last major creative architectural enterprise in his name and, as Earl Rosenthal has so justly concluded, the palace was 'great in conception and impotent in conclusion'.[57] This stylistic 'caesura' amongst the architectural luxuries of the conquered Moors on the Alhambra was built but never roofed and therefore never used during Charles' reign. The theatres of war and the centres for the brokerage of power kept the Emperor for the duration of his reign away from Granada, or from anywhere else that he might have liked to have settled and developed with buildings.

Southern England

If we shift our attention to England, Henry VIII's Nonsuch fits into a class of distinction, which even from the scanty records of the exterior is instantly recognisable as an epitome of Tudor *Romanitas*. The painted view of the house approached by road from London shows the front of the outer court of a grand country mansion built of brick in the manner current in the south-east of England (figure 94). It betrays nothing of the amazing display of sculpture on the inner and outer elevations of the inner court. The views of Hoefenagel and Speed tantalise, which sensation becomes more acute when it emerges from the building accounts that the decoration of the house covered some 2,055 square metres with probably seven or eight hundred high-relief, figurative panels in *stucco duro* (figures 16–17).[58] The inner court was built of stone at ground level, but the floors above were of timber-frame construction with the timbers encrusted with plaques of carved and gilded slate. There were three registers of panels on the inner-facing walls of the inner court, the uppermost of which presented figures of the Roman emperors from Julius Caesar to Aemilianus. The middle register on the king's side of the court showed the gods of the ancient world and on the queen's side, appropriately, the goddesses. The lower register on the king's side displayed scenes from the life of Hercules from the cradle to his death on Mount Oeta, with personifications of the liberal arts and virtues opposite, all of which were identified with mottoes imperative and admonitory in letters of gilded lead. From the centre of the south side, amongst the gods, were figures of Henry VIII with Prince Edward surveying these scenes, which were didactic and tutelary. From this wealth of allegory, which was surely the product of Henry's mind, the boy could be taught the duties of a Christian prince.

The style and quality of the stucco work show Nonsuch to have borne no empty name. The decorative work was as up to date as anything in Europe of the 1540s. The one panel which can be reconstructed, showing a soldier sitting on a shield, is the work of an artist fully conversant with the conventions of imperial Roman relief sculpture. Nicolas Bellin of Modena is the artist credited with the design and technical supervision of the stucco work, which was actually carried out by an English artificer called Kendall and subsequently by an otherwise unknown foreigner called Giles Geringe. Bellin had worked under Primaticcio at Fontainebleau from 1532, and his move to England brought Henry not just a

94 Nonsuch, Surrey, seen from the north-west.

technical expert, but a man fully conversant with all that was said and done by artists at the Court of Francis I. Given the scale and sophistication of the works at Nonsuch, it is easy to imagine that his defection was a considerable loss to the French, but Henry was only behaving like Francis in offering experienced Italian practitioners commissions for work on a scale they could hardly hope for at home.

Blocked roads

A conventional or traditional policy in France excluded foreigners from key positions in the royal building works. Primaticcio did indeed carry the title of royal architect, but his role as designer and superintendent of any building is problematic. The planning of the new Louvre might have been expected to be the occasion for the employment of Italian architectural talent already in the royal service, most obviously Sebastiano Serlio. His ardent desire for an executive role in a major royal commission is well attested in his writings, but nothing designed by him during his years at Paris or Fontainebleau for the king or any lesser Frenchman was built as he designed it. The full story of how and why Pierre Lescot (1510?–76), a cleric from the lesser nobility, was awarded this key commission will never be known. Laudatory verse addressed to him by several of the leading court poets, especially Ronsard and Du Bellay, leave no doubt that he was a man of many parts. He could impress even the most jealous rival in the clamour for preference at Court. The range of Lescot's accomplishments, which are lost to us today, included being a supreme painter, a persuasive speaker and being consummate also in a range of

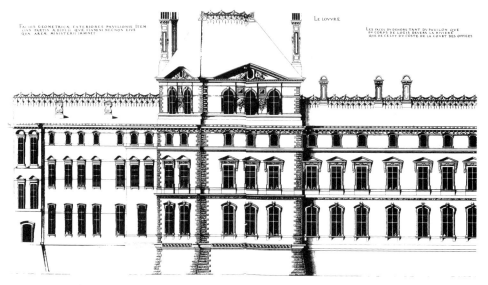

Faces geometricae, exteriores pavilionis item eivs partis aedifici qva flvmini necnon eivs qva area ministerii imminet

Le Lovvre

Les faces dv dehors tant dv pavillon qve dv corps de logis devers la riviere qve de celvy dv coste de la covrt des offices

95   Paris. The Louvre, showing the west exterior front (left), the 'pavillon du roi' (centre) and the south front.

other accomplishments.[59] As built according to contracts of 1551 and 1556 the 'Lescot' wing of the Louvre on its outward- and inward-facing elevations is the most concentrated demonstration of French architectural emulation of the antique and critique of the modern Italian imaginable. The original south and west fronts shown in du Cerceau's engraving are of plain, dressed stone with fine detail confined to the window surrounds and the belvedere chamber at the top of the angle pavilion – the *pavillon du roi* (figure 95). To the outside world the Louvre was to appear plain, statuesque and much greater than its surroundings. This is just the sort of distinction and *gravitas* insisted upon by Italian or French writers, who were pre-occupied with the public face of princes. The reverse is true of the inner face, which at first sight is a clamour of architectural forms and relief sculpture (figure 96).

All this is calculated to astound the foreigner and cheer the Frenchman who peels away the layers of meaning of this very expensive and exceptionally finely built facade. The three frontispieces are vertical displays of triumphal arches taken from their true free-standing context, and hung like trophies or escutcheons a most felicitous architectural expression of contemporary French *imperium*. Here impeccably carved Roman arches are seconded, just as the Romans themselves had adopted Egyptian obelisks. Their transfer to the capital of Empire was a symbol of their subjugation. If the symbolism of the architectural language of the court facade of the Louvre is not obvious to the onlooker, the purpose of the relief sculpture by Jean Goujon could hardly be mistaken. These allegories are a

96   Paris. The Louvre. West wing, courtyard facade. Built 1551–6. Architect Pierre Lescot, sieur de Clagny. Sculptor Jean Goujon.

paean of praise to monarchical government, its pretensions, prerogatives and obligations, as well as of the blessings it assures. The achievements conveyed by the figures in the attic from left to right are Abundance, personified by Neptune and Ceres below, Victories with the royal escutcheon fill the central attic pediment with Mars and Bellona below, and lastly Science celebrates the intellectual prowess of the French, personified by Archimedes and Euclid accompanied by a Genius reading and a Genius writing. Whether the message of all this is received in full or in part, the assertiveness of the sculptural and architectural ensemble is impossible to deny. Amongst secular buildings of the period only Nonsuch could have competed with the Louvre as designed by Lescot as a showcase for didactic, nationalistic allegory expressed in a grandiose cycle of sculpture.

The mentality which brought Nonsuch and the Louvre into being was the same. Architecture even in a developed and elaborated national manner was not enough; to deliver the full charge of historical and cultural propaganda a lot of figurative sculpture was required. Buildings as political, dynastic and national emblems needed an allegorised heroic personality for which mere inscriptions would not suffice. If Nonsuch and the Louvre have substantial affinities in purpose, and their contrasting appearances can be understood as underlining their common aim of distinction nationally and internationally, the appearance of the Escorial,

97 The Escorial. Begun 1562, completed 1586. Architects Juan Bautista de Toledo, succeeded by Juan de Herrera.

built between 1562 and 1584, helps to develop and complete the theme in the realm of sixteenth-century royal monuments (figure 97). This massive and relentlessly austere building might be taken as a Habsburg antitype to Tudor or Valois architectural self-glorification.

An anonymous treatise on architecture, written at the request of Philip II in the years before he began building the Escorial, opens with a lengthy analogy between good government and restrained architecture.[60] The author argued that greed was the greatest social evil, and a consequence of it was wasteful buildings. The chief aim of this text was to demonstrate to the king connexions between morality and an acceptable classical style; there is hardly a mention of ornament or of beauty, with terms such as 'magnificent' and 'full of authority' being preferred. The pagan connotations of the orders, which were the only elements of ornament and articulation admitted by the writer, are played down. Every direct reference to classical antiquity introduced by his main source Alberti is removed, as the reform of Spanish architecture envisioned is one which will metamorphose the pagan into the Christian and Catholic. It is a reductive process, which sets out to dissociate classicism in architecture from revivals of antiquity in other spheres, which must portend corruption. The whole argument and conclusion of the text must have been to the liking of the ascetic Philip. The triple role of the Escorial as Jeronymite monastery, Spanish-Habsburg mausoleum and royal palace, made the resolution of an ethical style for it the more imperative at the earliest stage of planning. The result is a massive building, which every later description sees as a quintessence of Counter-Reformation Spanish Catholicism in architecture, but none have seen luxury in such grandeur.

Ring roads and bypasses

All theories and arguments about imitation, assimilation or emulation of antiquity take the differences between present and past, and between peoples very seriously. The erudition of a poet and of a learned architect would be based on very dissimilar sources and skills. Many developments in literature and the visual arts during the fifteenth and sixteenth centuries in centres across Europe point to a common purpose, that is the emulation of the Latin language and of classical art by the study and judicious reform of the vernacular. Alberti, who is often mistakenly pigeon-holed as an elitist, humanist Latinist, wrote in the 1430s that the *volgare* (i.e. Tuscan) might attain 'the authority of Latin if only learned men would try to make it refined and polished'.[61] There are strong Portuguese, Spanish, French, German and English echoes of this proposition in the course of the following two hundred years. The association of language and tradition with architecture and its sources is common throughout Europe, where writers concerned themselves with a reappraisal of their past. The Renaissance in its multifarious forms is sometimes subtitled or renamed 'The Age of Humanism'.[62] From the late fourteenth century onwards, beginning in northern Italy, there were small groups of scholars and detached individuals for whom a fully fledged revival of the Latin language, literary forms and even institutions was a prime concern. Highly educated men who liked to communicate with each other in a dead language were always exclusive if not isolated from their fellow citizens. In quantitative terms there is much more written about the antique as a means of improving the vernacular. Thus when we read of building or decorative work, which was to be *all'antica*, *ao bom romano, a lo romano, selon l'antique, antieksnyders* or *Romaigne work*, we can be certain that such suffixes in the vernacular meant 'in our fashion'.

Exceptions to the pluralist argument

To escape desecration by heathens the *Santa Casa* of the Virgin Mary lifted off from Palestine and flew to Loreto for sanctuary. This may be the most spectacular case of architectural avionics in the history of the world, but there are some less spectacular examples of architecture crossing borders from the Renaissance period. North Italian architects and masons found sympathetic patronage and employment in limited numbers in Poland, Moravia and Bohemia in the third quarter of the sixteenth century (figures 98–9).[63] Unfortunately, not enough is known of their lives to know if they became naturalised or assimilated into the building trades. Nor is there any literary evidence of favourable or unfavourable reaction to these developments. Language may not have been a real obstruction to carrying architectural fashions long distances. Nicholas Chanterene (*c.*1516–50) had a long

98 Prague. The Belvedere. Built between 1538 and 1563. Architects Paolo della Stella and Bonifaz Wolmut.

99 Bucovice. Begun 1567, completed *c.*1582. Architect Pietro Ferrabosco, entrepreneur Pietro Gabri.

and successful career in Portugal as an ornamental mason, working in the *Ecole de la Loire* style well after its eclipse in France. He surely learnt Portuguese, and his patrons in his later years must have been little curious about contemporary developments in France or Italy.[64] Alien ornamental masons and craftsmen in wood or plaster flourished in markets more fluid than those which existed for architects.[65]

In all western European secular architecture north of the Alps the palace built in Brussels for Nicolas Perronet de Granvelle, first minister to the Emperor Charles V, was the only true Italian import. The engravings from Pierre-Jacques Goetghebuer: *Choix des monuments, édifices et maisons les plus remarquables du royaume des Pays-Bas*, published in Ghent in 1827 deserve more attention (figures 100–2). The first-floor arcade facing the courtyard might have been designed by Palladio, whose Basilica at Vicenza, designed between 1546 and 1549, cannot predate Granvelle's palace by more than a few years. Here the imperial message is the motive, just as with Charles V's palace at Granada. Granvelle's palace had no known progeny, which need not be surprising. It was a building for a supra-national figure, whose distinction and exclusiveness the architecture perfectly exemplified.

The story of the building of the Royal Exchange of London brings to mind the myth of the *Santa Casa*. Sir Thomas Gresham (1519?–79), the Queen's agent at the all- important bourse of Antwerp, who paid for it, 'bargained for the whole mould and substance of his workmanship in Flanders' (figures 103–4).[66] Hendrick van Passe was the master of works employed, and we should think of him as the architect. He supplied all the glass, slate and stone ready-carved from the yards of Antwerp. Between 1566 and 1570 Gresham's Exchange was largely prefabricated, shipped and assembled in London under van Passe's supervision.[67] At a stroke the restrictive City of London acquired a monument to free trade from Antwerp to rival Antwerp by making her bourse look stylistically old-fashioned. Gresham's Exchange was a utility long overdue. Formerly traders and merchants had to assemble at appointed times in the street, and so the import need not be deemed a luxury. His building was immodestly festooned with his personal emblem of the grasshopper, and the style and manner of its building must have been seen as a considerable affrontery by established figures in the building trades. Clearly Gresham could not get what he wanted in London, and his strategy was as radical as his solution was unique in the history of Renaissance architecture. Carriage was relatively easy between the ports of Antwerp and London, but Gresham attempted to break down barriers, which were more in the mind. As early as 1581 there were complaints amongst aldermen that the workmanship was shoddy and the building positively dangerous, because stones were dropping from the arches of the arcade.[68] They had got the Exchange at no cost to themselves, but this 'crazie and ruinous' building was not of their own making nor was it their responsibility.[69] In this first fully-fledged appearance Italianate Flemish architecture did not register as an appropriate use for wealth. The style had not had time to become English. It had been adopted, not fostered.

'Out of Italy'

Amongst the last published writings of the eminent French historian Fernand Braudel (1902–85) is a work of brilliant illusionism. *Il Secondo Rinascimento. Due Secoli e tre Italie* appeared in 1986, the original French text as *Le Modèle italien* in 1989 and in English it was published in 1991 as *Out of Italy, 1450–1650*. The great man would have been pained to read this essay. The cultural 'greatness' of Italy dazzled foreign rulers, and likewise aristocratic circles in cities extended a warm welcome to an art and way of life whose refinement no one could deny. 'Reception committees' from royalty to their literary and artisanal servants had to meet a challenge. Italy's achievements were a resource which could uniquely invigorate all other European cultural traditions. 'The Italian Renaissance was a continuous, moveable feast.' Braudel contends that Italian luxury (actual or imagined?) was irresistible. 'Braudel's Pendulum' swings through time and space with such a smooth motion that it would be small-minded not to enjoy the spectacle. However, Italian architectures, Florentine, Roman, or Venetian remained the intellectual and artistic property of Italy. Borrowings were changed into local currencies. Only with the illusory concept of luxury applied in the modern sense is there real historical validity, and with luxury Braudel's approach can be reconciled with the arguments promoted here. Without irreverence we might lift a quotation from the middle of his book; it is from an Italian poem mocking the defeat of the French at Pavia in 1525.

> Son confusi li Francios; O Nostre Dame, O bon Jesus
> A st'ur nous sommes tous perdus.

'Quo vadis'?

Architecture, or building on a grand scale, has always been amongst the most expensive forms of personal gratification. If peoples could not reconcile their differences on issues of language or history or how to build, it is inevitable, that there would be arguments within societies about the best uses of wealth. Nothing has changed. Major new buildings of any period make contemporaries think about their value and cost for their own times and for future generations.

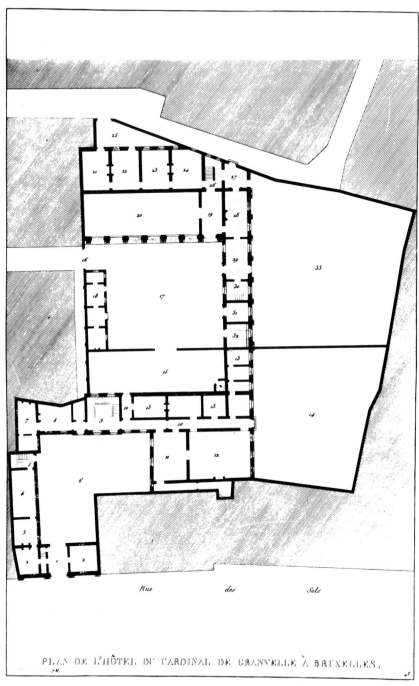

PLAN DE L'HÔTEL DU CARDINAL DE GRANVELLE À BRUXELLES.

100 Brussels. The Palais Granvelle, plan. Built in the 1550s? Architect uncertain.

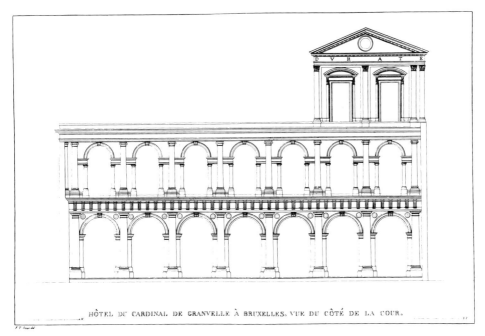

HÔTEL DU CARDINAL DE GRANVELLE À BRUXELLES, VUE DU CÔTÉ DE LA COUR,

101 Brussels. The Palais Granvelle, elevation of the courtyard arcades.

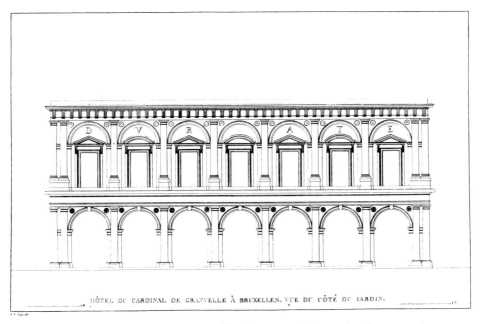

HÔTEL DU CARDINAL DE GRANVELLE À BRUXELLES, VUE DU CÔTÉ DU JARDIN,

102 Brussels. The Palais Granvelle, elevation of the garden front arcades.

157

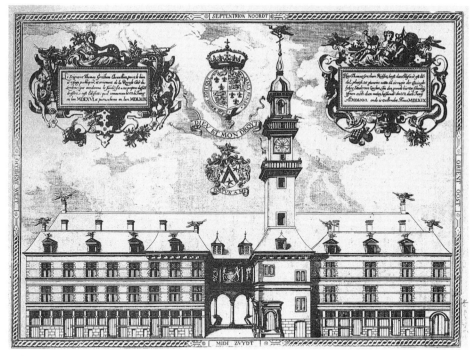

103 London. Royal Exchange, southern street facade. Begun 1566, completed 1569. Acting architect Hendrick De Passe. The entrepreneur Sir Thomas Gresham's emblem, the grasshopper, is seen on dormers, the pitches of roofs, and atop the clock tower.

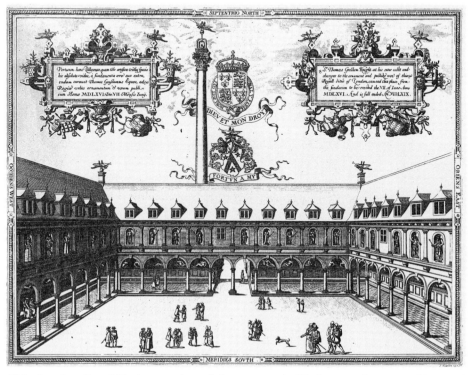

104 London. Royal Exchange, view of the courtyard. All the carved stone architectural set pieces were imported ready-made from Antwerp.

4

USES OF WEALTH

The admirable wealthy

As if the Bible did not exist, and the writings of Roman Stoics were unknown, the Florentine Poggio Bracciolini (1380–1459) wrote his treatise *On Avarice and Luxury*, in 1428 or 1429. It is obvious that his intended audience was in need of an unashamed theory of capitalism. With considerable polemical emphasis he attacks all philosophies in which men are exhorted to strive for a life of virtue through frugality. If men acted with a common will for the common good the result would be a vegetative society.

All splendour, all beauty, all charm would disappear from our cities. There would be no more temples, no more monuments and no more art . . . Our whole existence, as well as that of the state would be disrupted, if everyone endeavoured solely to provide for his own necessities . . . For the commonwealth money is the nerve of life, and those who love money are its foundation.[1]

Quattrocento Florentine 'civic humanists' did not invent the idea that increasing private wealth could serve as a positive blessing. However, it is the emphasis which they give to their justifications and their accounts of the benefits which is novel. If there were any sin associable with wealth, it is not Biblical usury but avarice. It is the avaricious poor he deplores, not the rich. He leaves the reader wondering if the only real danger of luxury is that it might sap the strength of the lover of money for making greater gains.

A more cautious approach is found in the ever helpful Alberti's *Della Famiglia*, written in the early 1430s. Here avarice is properly condemned as being 'detrimental to our gaining fame and honour', and private wealth is commended as being particularly conducive to 'gaining and preserving happiness'. During the second and third quarters of the fifteenth century Florence must have been fostering some determined and potent opposition to the building ambitions and pretensions amongst the leading patricians. Very regrettably, we have no significant record of such machinations. Bracciolini, Alberti and the panegyric on Cosimo de' Medici's buildings by Timoteo Maffei, which we have quoted, develop in very different ways the argument that architecture is a natural consequence and common benefit of wealth. If the prestige of some attaches to all, so the anti-stoic case goes, then wealth is the means by which the temples, monuments and art, for which all are said to crave, can be created.

Machiavelli and Guicciardini in the next century were not noted as critics of any ethos which defended private wealth in this way, but their concerns for their beloved city extended to reminding fellow citizens of historic warnings about 'wealth without worth'. Salutary lessons could be gleaned from a reading of Sallust on the collapse of the Roman Republic into the despotism of Empire, and of Juvenal, to name just two of the pre-Christian writers most frequently quoted in this debate. The 'civic humanists' who smiled on the motives of merchants and princes who were building in a grand manner, could not find immunity in Aristotle from objectors to the obvious denial of early Christian doctrine involved in such use of wealth. The very familiar divine insistence on poverty as a prerequisite of the devout life, as well as the absolute exclusion of the rich from heaven (e.g. Matthew XIX, 21, 24; Luke XVIII, 22, 25), leaves no room for manoeuvre or negotation. In the context of the sixteenth century, the 'economic case for building' was a subtle ploy which wholly contradicted the ethical fundaments of Renaissance Europe's one but divided religion. Secular building of any degree of splendour, interior or exterior, had no moral or social sanction from the Bible. This was of course no discouragement for wealthy builders from fortifying themselves with the belief in their wealth as the will of God. Their architectural works were a testimony of his favour.

Alberti deftly summarised a man's needs as 'la casa, la possessione, e la bottega', which shifts the crucial onus of the Christian's life from the macrocosm of society to its microcosm, the family. A short step from this stance takes us to the first principle of numerous medieval theories of charity, that it should begin in the home. Once all provision has been made for dependants any surplus resources shall be put to charitable use outside the home.[2] In *Della famiglia* Alberti asserts that the increase of possessions is a key ingredient in family happiness. He calls wealth the source of friendship and praise, of fame and of authority in the individual, and leaves aside any questions of philanthropy as matters for individual consciences.[3] The definition of the acceptable limits of conspicuous expenditure on non-essentials posed an elemental moral, social and political problem for the open or closed elites in most western European post-feudal kingdoms or city-states. Abuse of wealth by others is always an issue to absorb thinkers and legislators in boom times or famine alike. In the late Middle Ages and the Renaissance Venice stands out as the great centre where laws proliferated to contain expenditure on funerals, feasts, weddings, dowries, and every imaginable detail of attire from clogs to jewels and uncovered breasts.[4]

Venetian sumptuary laws

The airing of social tensions amongst the top ranks of Venetian society drew attention to the economic and moral consequences of luxury, which naturally included interior decoration and furnishings. In 1512 Venice was in dire military peril. The sumptuary decrees of 1512 were issued 'to placate the anger of Our Lord'. They summarised many earlier, moribund laws concerned with dress, housing and festivities.[5] For us one of the major puzzles of the 1512 laws, and of many other such pieces of futile legislation, Venetian and non-Venetian, is that the main aim is to discourage and curtail ostentatious waste of money. Yet never is there any mention of house or palace facades and their decorations. To set an upper limit, as was done in the 1512 decrees, of 150 ducats for the decoration of any room, and to scorn excessive gilding of panelling and stucco was thought sensible by the Doge Leonardo Loredan himself.[6] Jewels, precious metals and rare clothes are ruled out as unsuitable and undesirable materials for a wide range of household effects and furnishings including mirrors, cutlery, coffers and cradles. The trains of women's dresses and their hair fashions came in for particular attention, especially given the imagery conjured up by influential Franciscan preachers, who saw in dress trains 'a place where the devil always has a bed'. Fancy hair styles were a clear metaphor for the Tower of Babel.[7] An explanation of why grandiose palace facades with all their pagan imagery were left out of the defined categories of vain or wasteful expenditures must be that, when it came to architecture, Albertian rather than Franciscan principles prevailed in the minds of patrician law-makers. The Grand Canal palace built for Andrea Loredan between 1502 and 1509, the most conspicuous private pile from this period, certainly makes one wonder why proud architecture was exempted from the strictures of sumptuary law (figure 105).

Francesco Sansovino

Any answer has to be dug out of the slowly shifting sands of politics, patronage and dynastic precedence within the upper echelons of Venetian society. There seems to exist no trace of contemporary complaint or satire concerning this astonishing private monument. Francesco Sansovino's *Venezia città nobilissimà et singolare* of 1581 lists Andrea Loredan's spectacular house as one of the four finest in the city. This is a considered compliment from a writer well versed in architectural theory. He was perfectly in tune with taste and opinion on art and architecture of the

161

105   Venice. Palazzo Loredan, now Vendramin-Calergi. Begun *c.*1502, completed *c.*1509.
Architect Mario Codussi.

generations since Loredan's day. The size and nobility of the palace were the
criteria by which Sansovino judged this exceptional building to be amongst the most
noteworthy and creditable secular structures in a city more fully stocked with grand
palaces than any other. In such a setting where remarkable buildings jostle for
attention it is far from surprising that the particular circumstances of building and
the meanings attached to the form and style of this great columnar facade have been
forgotten. The name of the palace's architect, Mauro Coducci (1440?–1504), was
passed over by or was genuinely unknown to Francesco Sansovino, whilst little to
nothing is known of the personality and culture of Andrea Loredan. Neither in
official records of public service nor in the copious writings of diarists is there a
single line which gives any impression of them. Any admirer of the Palazzo from
the mid-sixteenth-century onwards ought to have queried Alberti's proposal that
wealth invested in building is a durable investment in fame.

In his chapter on the *Palazzi di Venezia* Sansovino emphasises that lofty building
by private citizens was a recent development. Traditionally all houses had been of
approximately the same height, which showed the unity and equality of the city's
inhabitants. Only at a late stage had an *appetito* amongst owners led to buildings
which rose conspicuously above the general roof-line. The palaces he names in this

162

context are those of Loredan, Calergi, Corner, Dolfin and Grimani, all of the six-teenth century. Confirmation of this change in social values and conventions in building, reported and defended by Sansovino, can be found in Domenico Morosoni's *De bene instituta Re publica*, begun in 1497. Morosoni came from a family of patrician philanthropists, who built rent-free apartments for impoverished aristocrats. He demanded uniformity of houses in deference to Venetian traditions of social cohesion.[8] He would have deplored the changing face of the Grand Canal, commended by Sansovino to all Venetians and foreigners.

The builder Andrea Loredan was of the same *casa* as the reigning doge, which does not help us to understand the thinking behind this prestigious building, since Doge Leonardo Loredan was an outspoken critic, in his public utterances, of grand expenditure. In a speech to the Great Council in October 1513 he ranged over many reasons for the moral *malaise* corrupting Venice from within, of which the chief symptom was self-indulgent luxury. In reviewing all manner of public and private abuses, he singled out the large hall on the ground floors of palaces, which in earlier times had served for the transaction of business, and which were plainly decorated with weapons hanging on the walls. Now, he complained, such places have been transformed into festival dining-rooms. He himself, he admitted, had been guilty of departing from the traditional custom.[9] What he thought of his kinsman Andrea's Grand Canal palace is not recorded, but the well-known disclaimer of earthly pride from Psalm 115, 'Non Nobis Domine, Non Nobis, Sed Nomini Tuo Da Gloriam' inscribed on the ground floor, reveals the patron's sensitivity. It is impossible to take seriously such a pious disclaimer on a private house of enormous proportions. A near-contemporary inscription on the Palazzo Trevisan-Cappello behind Doge's palace on the Rio Canonica once read 'Soli Deo, Honor Et Gloria', which is from the First Epistle to Timothy, I,17.[10] Such inscriptions might reveal unease on the part of the builders about immodesty and extravagance, but none then or now could mistake grand architectural palace facades for monuments of piety. The Ca' Dario of 1487 on the Grand Canal is much smaller than Loredan or Trevisan-Cappello; nevertheless the proud builder in inscribing his name on the front of his house showed himself to be more in tune with Aristotelian thought on *magnificentia*. Those floating past read 'Urbis Genio Iohannes Darius' (figure 106), which is to say, he has built well and the city is the beneficiary.

Ferrara and Bologna

Without becoming too sidetracked by inscriptions on houses, two others deserve consideration as evidence of a widespread consciousness of wealth being wasted on lavish building by private individuals. The house built by the poet Ludovico Ariosto for himself and his large family in Ferrara in the first or second decade of the

106　Venice. Ca' Dario. Begun *c.*1487. Architect unknown.

sixteenth century bore the following declaration upon the cornice for the passer-by 'Parva Sed Apta Mihi. Sed Nulli Obnoxia Sed Non Sordida; Parta Meo Sed Tamen Aere Domus.' (figure 107) It would very interesting to know from what quarter, equals, superiors or inferiors, Ariosto was anticipating criticism to have his disclaimer so spelt out on his home. Roughly translated, the inscription announces: 'It is small, but suitable to my needs and built with my own money.' In the early 1540s the Bolognese patrician and educationalist Achille Bocchi (1488–1562) had a palace built for himself and for his academy, which offers interesting texts all around the frieze above the rusticated base (figure 108).[11] His scholarship and piety are impressed on any who can read Hebrew and Latin. There are quotations from Psalm 119 in Hebrew to the left of the main door, and a long quotation from Horace's Letters in Latin, starting at the right of the main door and continuing round into the side-street. The quotation from Horace can be translated 'Yet boys at play cry "You'll be King if you do right". Be this our wall of bronze, to have no guilt at heart, no wrongdoing to turn us pale.' The application of this text out of context is unique and intriguing. Bocchi has had a lengthy disclaimer written on his palace, to state plainly that he has been a good man, and that all in the present and future should know this. Some might have assumed that so splendid a house could only have been the fruit of some sort of corruption. Such sensitivity about his reputation, and the notion that a great display of wealth in architecture was prone to be interpreted unfavourably are essential elements for a constructive understanding of 'anti-Renaissance feeling' concerning the arts in general and architecture in particular. Eugenio Battisti set an agenda for a debate which did not materialise on just this tack, with his *L'antirinascimento*, published in 1962.

Venice and Caravia again

The controversies which punctuated the building activity of the mightily well-endowed lay confraternity of the Scuola Grande di San Rocco of Venice have already taken pride of place in our first chapter (figure 13).[12] Caravia the man and his criticisms of extravagant use of an institution's wealth on architecture and decoration are of further value here. He was no ordinary middle-class merchant. In the conduct of his business as a dealer in precious stones Alessandro Caravia (1503–68) had a reputation for both shrewdness and absolute honesty. He was the trusted representative of Duke Cosimo de' Medici (1519–74) at the all-important jewellery market of the Rialto. Judging from correspondence of the 1560s in the Medici archives, he served his client's interests with some spectacular purchases at the best possible prices.[13] The Duke's compulsion to buy rough and cut stones of outstanding quality was not only driven by a conventional passion of princes to outshine each other with their personal treasure. There was also the

107 Ferrara. House of Ludovico Ariosto. Early sixteenth-century structure remodelled rather than built for the poet.

166

108 Bologna. Palazzo Bocchi. Begun 1545. Architect Vignola.

belief that such objects were talismans of extraordinary power.[14] The Medici
Dukedom of Florence was barely thirty years old, and Cosimo inclined to justify
to himself and to others the necessity of such trappings, both for the temporal
honour of his house and as a defence against ill-fortune. Large-scale expenditure,
which is political and symbolic, rather than an investment for future profit, was
always a potential for political embarrassment to rulers in the changing and
varied climates of ethical and economic opinion during the fifteenth and sixteenth
centuries.

The case of Caravia, the astute valuer-jeweller, is of unexpected importance in
a discussion of the uses of wealth. As the agent of an exceptionally wealthy or
'splendid' prince, sympathiser with the Reform, critic of the building and builders
of the grandest Venetian scuole and hack moralist in *venetiana lingua in bulesco*,
his loyalties at first sight seem contradictory.[15] Ultimately Caravia was just a keen
critic of the artistic and architectural ambition of the disenfranchised yet affluent
Venetian middle-class, of which he was a member. He exaggerated in his printed
'dream' of 1541, pretending that the cost of building and decorating the Scuola
di San Rocco had been 80,000 ducats. In his view 6,000 would have sufficed.
Despite being at odds with the truth of the matter up to that date, this is entirely
in keeping with his profession as a valuer and negotiator in the most exclusive
and fickle of all markets. His understanding of value in his professional capacity
was reserved for a very small aristocratic caste, who were his clients. Between
1516 and 1564, 47,000 ducats were spent on the Scuola di San Rocco, of which
2,500 were for interior decoration. The disparity between the facts and Caravia's
denunciation matters less than his motive. Waste is unforgivable in an urban
merchant class, whose business sense and ethics had failed them in this instance.
Although Caravia is not explicit, there is a strong underlying feeling that when
spending other people's money, men singly or collectively will not apply even
common sense. The complicated and congested facade of the Scuola di San Rocco
is the strange and hardly beautiful result of spending to the limit.

Caravia was not alone in deploring lavish building in Venice. About 1539 the
twenty-five year old Niccolò Zen was writing down some thoughts on the reasons
for the weakness of Italy in general and Venice in particular. One symptom of this
weakness he saw in the work of architects. *Mediocritas*, or modesty in appearance,
argued Zen, was virtuous in individuals, peoples and their buildings, which, as
Francesco Sansovino was to note in 1581, was a thing of the past.[16] Reaction against
luxury architecture within the patriciate is exemplified in the palace built by
Leonardo Loredan's successor as doge, Andrea Gritti. The large house he remodelled and enlarged opposite the church of San Francesco della Vigna, far from the
truly aristocratic quarters of the city, was fashioned externally *in lingua severa*.
(figure 109). His biographer thought it unsuitable for a great man in the highest
office, calling it 'troppo angusto'.[17] The significance of the *mediocritas* of Gritti's

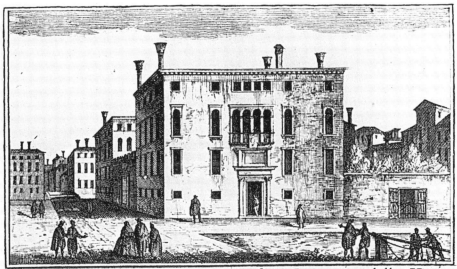

Palazzo del Nunzio Ponteficio a San Francesco della Vigna

109   Venice. Palazzo Gritti at San Francesco della Vigna.

private residence becomes the greater, when his role as patron of Jacopo Sansovino and prime mover in major public building works is remembered. There is a clear distinction between Gritti's patronage of architecture in the name of the State and his provision for himself. The contrast is an eloquent testimony to a powerful man's views on the proper use of public and private money. Fortunately for Jacopo Sansovino it was inevitable that Gritti's personal example was not followed by all of the wealthiest of Venice's patricians, who wanted and paid handsomely for 'Roman' style palace facades on the Grand Canal.

The Florentine or Venetian view of men's affairs and appetites is always of outstanding interest at any point in the Renaissance period. The indulgent attitude of Florentine 'civic humanists' towards the creation of wealth for expenditure on personal gratification is far from being a complete expression of public opinion at the time. Equally, if only Venice's sumptuary laws had survived, we would imagine a people very different from the image presented in paintings by Gentile Bellini or Vittore Carpaccio. Florentines and Venetians were equally proud of the wealth of their cities, but the example and influence of government in those centres was very different. Possibly a common factor would have been approval of the parable of the talents as told by the retired tax-gatherer Matthew (XXV, 14–30, omitted by Mark, Luke and John). Lords and commoners of commerce could draw special comfort and reassurance from this passage, if disturbed by Christ's unequivocal denunciations of usury.

169

During a long absence a master entrusts three of his servants with sums of five, two and one talents, a talent being a very substantial unit of currency. Those with five and two talents have doubled the money for their master's return by investing with bankers. The servant left with the single talent buried it in the ground for safety. The master's reprimand for the servant left with the single talent, who did not put the money into the market, is astonishing and anachronistic. It does not fit with any other of Jesus' pronouncements, and is not followed by any denunciation of the mentality exemplified in the manner in which the master sacks his timorous servant.

You wicked and slothful servant! You knew that I reap where I have not sowed, and gather where I have not winnowed. You ought to have invested my money with the bankers, and at my coming I should have received what was my own with interest. So take the talent from him, and give it to him who has the ten talents. For to everyone who has will more be given, and he will have abundance; but from he who has not even what he has will be taken away. Cast the worthless servant into the outer darkness; there men weep and gnash their teeth.

Then there follows a brisk coverage of a miscellany of sayings by Jesus, before Matthew gives his account of the Last Supper. The master in the parable of the talents is neither reprimanded nor praised. He is called 'a hard man', but this might apply equally to an autocratic prince or a stern father, whose power was based on traditions of obedience and devotion.[18]

Parables were told by Christ so that wider and deeper meanings might be drawn from simple tales, but in this case the story is told with so many details as to make its meaning and purpose clear. Whether the power of the privileged master is just or unjust is not the issue. The assets left behind by the master were to be put to use for his benefit; the servant who buried the single talent neither understood nor respected its use. The crime from the point of view of the master is waste. He has not benefited from his trust and charge to the servant, and so he has been wronged.

To the good man money does not matter, it is an expedient. Christ's pronouncements on tax as a mere temporal problem, not a spiritual matter, are consistent. The history of taxation by royalty or the Church in western Europe abounds in references and allusions to the story of the Tribute Money, and in visual art there is an abundance of medieval or Renaissance images showing what to do with money. The initial to Psalm XV (illustrating verse 5) from the late thirteenth-century English Cuerden Psalter is a crude and effective expression of '*Dominus pars haereditatis meae*' or 'The Lord is the portion of my inheritance' (figure 110).[19] Here God descends to take delivery of his pile of coins. Masaccio's *Tribute Money* of 1426–27 in the Brancacci chapel in Santa Maria del Carmine in Florence is famous as a revolution in composition and style, which has distracted attention from the patron's venality and corruption in his exploitation of public offices (figure 111). If paying for the decorating of the chapel was an elaborate act of penance for Felice Brancacci's abuses, the choice of the subject of the Tribute Money is his confession in a sacred allegory.[20]

Uses of wealth in painting

In fifteenth-or sixteenth-century European painting the most dignified images of wealth as personified by merchants are German; the rawest satires of obsession with money are almost all Flemish (figure 112). Prosperity is a consequence of managing resources to the best effect, and whether by Dürer or Holbein or Mabuse such portraits of merchants are calculated to interest, rather than impress with any expensive trappings of conspicuous expenditure. The portraits give a minimal number of clues, towards knowing what such men bought for personal gratification. Good-quality clothes appropriate to their rank certainly in all cases, but close-up studies only exceptionally show luxuries, such as a small part of an expensive carpet, as in Holbein's famous portrait of the London-based Cologne merchant Georg Gisze. The apparatus of the office are the attributes to be shown, if anything at all. Not one 'private' individual or family portrait of the fifteenth and sixteenth centuries from the middle to the top ranks of society shows the subject or subjects set amongst large quantities of very expensive possessions. Some prestige objects do appear, but no one, king or pope or merchant, wished to be portrayed with their treasure. Furthermore, with the singular exception of donor portraits, where there may be an architectural model of a church or chapel being offered, the rich or powerful were uniformly not interested in being recorded in front of their buildings. The first combined image of patron with villa, palace or town house seems to be Veronese's lavish *Virgin and Child with Saints John the Baptist, Jerome and the Coccina family* of 1571 (figure 113). In the background is the recently completed family palace on the Grand Canal (figure 114). Many contemporaries must have found such a combination of sacred and profane distasteful. The Coccina from Bergamo were in terms of the Venetian oligarchy *nouveau riche* outsiders, who would never attain any titles or prestigous offices. This is perhaps the earliest sixteenth-century image of a family with their palace. Even without any devotional excuse, the display of actual worldly wealth in such a fashion would have looked vulgar.[21] In their defence it should be remembered that this picture was not painted for public view in a church, but for the family oratory inside the palace, and it would have given an intimate sense of divine presence to the room.

This is not to gloss over the considerable number of painted and engraved views of Renaissance private houses, gardens and estates, Italian, French or English,

110   Initial to Psalm XV from the Cuernden Psalter. Thirteenth-century English.

111   Tommaso Cassai, called Masaccio. *The Tribute Money.*

112 Van Rymerswaele. *A Merchant, Banker or Tax-collector and his wife*, portrayed in an unusually sympathetic manner.

113 Veronese. *The Coccina Family before the Virgin and Saints*.

114 Venice. Palazzo Coccina, now Tiepolo, at Sant'Apollinare. Completed *c.*1560.

but it is not the ownership of splendid buildings that is commemorated, as became the fashion from early in the seventeenth century and then continuously onwards. Renaissance men are not recorded for posterity in front of their architectural facades. Perhaps because there was no pictorial tradition of integrating buildings into portraits, architecture has always tended to be treated by historians as a subject apart. The study of rank, elites and the 'gorgeous apparatus of rule' needs to embrace architecture.[22]

Towers, coaches, and funerary monuments

Towers

It is when and where wealth is used in competitive, strange or novel ways, that critics and Aristotelians were moved to polemic. The commonest subjects for economic or ethical complaint over waste of wealth amongst the peerage, at least as far as France and England are concerned, were building, food, clothes, transport, funerals and tombs, in that order.[23] Subjects from these categories such as towers, coaches and funerary monuments have a direct bearing on the social and stylistic history of architecture in most countries. Within the general subject of luxury and architecture towers for private houses are particularly rewarding subjects for study. Whatever practical defensive value the tower-house in town or country had in the early Middle Ages, by the late fourteenth century many Italian towns and cities had become afforested with skyscraping towers (figures 115–7). Nobles and family clans of central and northern Italy became caught up in a competitive mania to build higher and higher. The decrees of civic authorities to regulate and ultimately to demolish them provide firm evidence of concern not just about order but also about waste. As far back as 1257 Rome was *capitozzata*, with no fewer than 140 towers belonging to the nobility being lowered or demolished.[24] By 1400 Bologna boasted at least 194 towers known by family names. Only two survived the demolitions of the seventeenth century, because they were publicly owned (figure 117). At Florence, with as many as 400 private towers, the highest of which reached to 250 feet, the Commune methodically condemned them during the late thirteenth and early fourteenth centuries as a challenge to its authority over private interests.[25]

The consolidation of communal government in the course of the fourteenth and fifteenth centuries in central and northern Italy was the death-knell for private towers. Psalm LXI uses the metaphor of a tower as a symbol of hope and strength. The association of towers with wisdom and learning is a commonplace in ancient and medieval literature. As claustrophobic faction evolved into collective self-interest, towers lost their purpose and meaning. Perhaps the last grandiose tower to be built in a city on the peninsula was for the Bentivoglio in Bologna. Shortly

115   Lucca. Family towers.

116   San Gimignano (Tuscany).

117 Bologna. The Asinelli and Garisendi towers (97.6 and 47.5 m high respectively).

after the Malvezzi conspiracy against their rule, Giovanni Bentivoglio and his sons laid the foundation stone early in 1490 in circumstances of great pomp, reminiscent of the behaviour of Filippo Strozzi. The Bentivoglio's tower was completed in 1495. It was designed with living-apartments and was second only to the Asinelli in height. God and the mob guaranteed its early demise. A minor earthquake in 1505 destabilised it, and the hostile citizens rased it to the ground three years later. The political and architectural language of the Bentivoglio was far out of date.

Architectural dinosaurs they may have been, but unlike dinosaurs the reasons for their extinction are understood. Their workings and functions and precise role as status symbols are often hard to fathom. San Gimignano delights, bemuses and puzzles its visitors, and the sight of the giant Garisenda and Asinelli towers at Bologna has moved travellers to wonder about human folly in general, and to ask what were the long-forgotten reasons for such rivalry and competitiveness.[26] Book VIII, chapter 5 of Alberti's *De Re Aedificatoria* is devoted to watchtowers and their ornaments. In this unique insight he starts with a discussion of how impressive lofty towers can be in choice positions 'on appropriate lines' across the countryside. They can make agreeable landmarks and afford splendid views. He adds 'if grouped closely together, they make an imposing sight from afar'. With that said he cautions immediately against the follies of about two hundred years before, that is to say the mid-thirteenth century, when men succumbed to 'a mania . . . for building towers even in the smallest towns. It seemed that no head of a family could be without a tower; as a result forests of towers sprouted up everywhere'.[27] A vaguely suggested amenity value of towers in town and country is all Alberti sees in towers built by his compatriots, and much the greater part of his text is devoted to describing some principles, forms and components for monumental tower building, as well as praise for the greater achievements of the ancients in this type of endeavour. The ancients built useful things such as light-houses and strategic watch-towers, which served to protect more than mere factions.

The uselessness of such gigantic structures for later generations is shown by their systematic destruction in the major centres of the peninsula in the course of the sixteenth and seventeenth centuries. The most amusing of the many bemused accounts of later travellers is Goethe's, in the *Journal of his Italian Journey of 1786* (18 October) writing of the towers at Bologna (figure 117):

The leaning tower is frightful to look at, but it was probably built that way on purpose. My theory is that, during the time of the civic feuds, every great building became a fortress and every powerful family built its own tower. After a period of time, this became both a hobby and a point of honour; everybody wished to boast of having a tower. In due time perpendicular towers became too commonplace, so someone built a leaning one. If so, one must admit that the architect and owner achieved their aim, for people are no longer interested in all the straight towers but only in the crooked one.

I went up it later. The layers of bricks run horizontally. Given a good mortar and iron bars, it is possible to build the craziest things.

Secular towers of any height were certainly thought of as both anachronistic and archaic by all architects and patrons of building in the new style of fifteenth- and sixteenth-century Italy. No Florentine, Venetian or Roman palace incorporated a tower, and it would be absurd to conceive such bombast as being compatible with the visual language of classicism. If secular towers are perceived as the quintessential architectural emblem of prestige in a medieval Italian town or city, the human condition of collective folly so finely and ironically satirised by Goethe would seem to be confined to one region in one period. But this is not the case. Toulouse is one well-known example of a city which prospered during the sixteenth century, and is well stocked with town houses boasting splendid staircase towers with belvedere cabinets on top.[28] Such towers are always functional and integrated into the house plan, and never was a free-standing structure contemplated *à l'italienne*. The emblem of the tower as representing greatness was a commonplace across Europe, but the motives of tower-builders in towns risked being seen as arcane pretension.

There is in all the intriguing history of tower-building a salacious interpretation. Luxury, by the late sixteenth century, was a metaphor for an exaggerated sexual appetite. In Italian *uno maschio* meant and means a male; boy; man; tenon; shaft; keep of a castle; fortress; main tower. Equally a tower was a masculine metaphor *par exellence* of strength, *fortezza*, or competitive success. Were Italian cities and towns emblems of phallocratic competition out of control?

The spread of town house towers seems to have reached London via Antwerp as late as the 1530s. Twice in his *Survey of London* of 1598 John Stow (1525?–1605) records high towers, one of brick and the other of timber, which in both instances had been built 'to overlooke his neighbours in this Citie'. Angell Dune, grocer and alderman of London, who built a brick tower, was punished with blindness. The builder of the tall tower of timber was Richarde Wethell, a merchant tailor, then a young man, whose fate was to be 'so tormented with goutes in his joyntes, of the hands and legges, that he could neither feede him selfe, nor goe further than he was led, muche lesse was he able to climbe, and take pleasure in the height of his Tower'. Stow was himself a merchant tailor, and the seemingly divine retribution on the tower-builders is recorded with a relish in tune with his obvious distaste for such basely motivated fellow-citizens. London's secular towers all disappeared in the great fire of 1666, but in Hollar's panorama of London from Bankside, published in 1647, there are five or six towers discernible, which do not appear to belong to churches. Their form roughly echoes the stately tower of the Hôtel Busleyden at Mechelen (figure 36), which was the grandest and possibly the last great tower built to enhance a patrician town house in the Low Countries.[29]

Sixteenth-century architectural pattern books of domestic design all leave towers out of the repertory of components and set pieces suitable for middle-or upper-class houses in town or country. The sole exception is a plate in the *Architectura* of Hans Vriedeman de Vries, published at Antwerp in 1577, where there is a design with variant of a town hall or public building rather than a private house. The reason for adding the pagodas, classically styled in the Antwerp fashion, is explained in the vaguest terms in the caption to the plate (figure 77). In part it reads 'constructions avec tours à l'usage des princes et des seigneurs. L'accès aux étages supérieures des tours se fait par un éscalier de bois car il y a des personnes qui apprécient de pouvoir y monter'.[30] Such towers have no more significance or purpose than for lords and princes to enjoy the view, a patrician Eiffel or Blackpool tower. It is a most interesting insight into the social assumptions and mentality of a populariser like de Vries that he should instinctively make fancy towers one of the features and pleasures of buildings not of the greatest imaginable scale but of the greatest status. Just such a building was the Loggetta at the foot of the giant campanile in the Piazza San Marco designed by Sansovino and begun in 1537 (figure 118). It was no more than a meeting-place for nobles, a key spot where they could see and be seen.[31] With its polychromatic architecture and rich sculptural iconography celebrating the 'Myth of Venice' for citizen and foreigner alike, the Loggetta is a pure luxury building, rich in its materials and allegories, and with no formal or practical function. There were several reasons for the siting of the Loggetta, the most obvious of which is that it faces the main ceremonial entrance to the Doge's palace. The Loggetta might easily have been built as a free-standing structure, but by attaching it to the tallest belfry in the city with unrivalled views, the patriciate symbolically awarded themselves precedence on the stairway to heaven.[32] If this was generally understood to be part of the meaning of the Loggetta, those who were favoured with an established high rank must have found it reassuring, and its cost wholly justified.

Coaches

The architectural consequences of the spread of the fashion for coaches on the design and organisation of the town or country houses of the wealthy have never been explored. There is plenty of written material from across sixteenth-century Europe of the considerable social impact made by the new invention. Covered carts and waggons for the transport of goods and people in peace or war were nothing new. However, when the structure incorporated a device of straps, chains or springs between the carriage body and the axles, the sole purpose was for the comfort of those on board. A good horse, well-ridden, was the method used by well-to-do men or women to travel short distances, hunt or go on pilgrimage. The metamorphosis of the working cart into the luxury coach took major strides in late fifteenth-century Hungary during the reign of the Italophile King Matthias Corvinus.[33] In the first or second decades of the sixteenth century, according to

118 Venice. The Loggetta. Begun 1537. Architect Jacopo Sansovino.

the antiquarian and architect Pirro Ligorio, the first coach was imported into Italy by the nephew of the Queen of Hungary, Ippolito d'Este, Cardinal of Ferrara. Within fifty years the development of the coach was rapid. It became the public status symbol *par excellence* of wealth and luxury, and inevitably became in the eyes of many a pure expression of sloth, immorality and vanity. As early as 1508 in his prose comedy *La Cassaria* Ariosto mocks the public pretensions of great ladies who '. . . are loth to leave their homes on foot, nor will they even cross the street unless they have a rocking gig beneath them, and their gigs they must have fully gilded and draped with precious stuffs, and want them drawn by sturdy chargers'.[34] If the great and haughty were collected at their front door, then the coach and horses might be kept adjacent or close by, and be summoned when required. If not, the house would have to have a courtyard, and provision within the gates for horses and coaches in sixteenth-century Italy as elsewhere was of considerable importance in the organisation and planning of new or remodelled aristocratic to *haut-bourgeois* town houses. For the owner or the guest to be driven into a house and deposited at the main door he needed a courtyard big enough for the horses and apparatus to turn. In Roman palazzi and Parisian hôtels from the mid-sixteenth century onwards the size of forecourts and courts grew perceptibly.[35]

181

The proliferation of coaches in the sixteenth century is a recurrent and popular topic in satirical literature across Europe. One of the most incisive is a satire on family life by Juan Costa, published at Saragossa in 1584. In it there is the complaint that even the wives of merchants are no longer content to be taken pillion behind a groom, as had been the custom some forty years before. Now they demand a coach drawn by four horses to glorify their 'facticious ennoblement'.[36] The evidence of topographical paintings and engravings of the late sixteenth and seventeenth centuries shows that a coach pulled by four or more horses was rare and impractical in older towns and major cities. Costa seems to have been exaggerating for effect. The norm for a coach for show and routine use was certainly just two horses. Paul V, pope from 1605 to 1621, thought that a cardinal's obligation to appear magnificent in public required six horses.[37] Courtesans and cardinals were as one in their vanities, in the eyes of poets and writers who viewed ancient Rome as a melancholy symbol and modern Rome as a hive of abuses.[38] A coach was by definition a luxury, and it is known that a total of 883 coaches existed in Rome in 1594. Eleven households boasted four or more coaches, and no fewer than eight of these households belonged to cardinals. No other city is known to have been so invaded by coaches as Rome in the late sixteenth century.

Paris in 1550 probably had not many more than the three recorded by within her walls a contemporary. One belonged to Catherine de Medici, one to Diane de France and the third to Jean de Laval, seigneur de Boisdauphin, who needed such a sprung carriage because he was exceptionally overweight. The author who noted these facts did so in order to underscore his personal contempt for these people and their artificiality. The most striking sixteenth-century French image of a luxury coach is the engraving by Jacques Androuet du Cerceau of one made or to be made for King Charles IX, published in 1569 (figure 119).[39] Pagan figures of satyrs and winged female herms adorn the suspended body of the massive carriage for the Most Christian King. It is drawn by at least two pairs of horses. This state-of-the-art prestige vehicle would have needed almost all roads in town and country redesigned and enlarged for it to pass. Its use could only have been very occasional. When the urge to spend on coaches filtered down to the lesser aristocracy and the upper bourgeoisie the organisation and scale of houses, their courtyards and approaches had to accommodate the new fad. Henry IV was assassinated in 1610, when exposed in an open coach in a congested part of Paris. He had forbidden any to keep a private coach in the city without royal consent, but it is certain that many were hidden. By 1619 a text reports '... it is now one of the principal conditions of marriage contracts to stipulate the provision of a house with carriage gateway and a carriage for madamoiselle'. The plans of *haut-bourgeois* houses in Jacques Androuet du Cerceau's *Livres d'Architecture* of 1559 and 1582 show no specific provision for costly coaches, whilst the plates of the grander houses in Pierre Le Muet's *Manière de Bien Bastir,* first published in 1623, clearly show this added consideration.[40]

NOVVM VEHICVLI REGALIS GENVS, QVOD QVIDEM VVLGATIS PAVLO VASTIVS EST, SED MVITO
COMMODIVS VT QVOD VI I LOCO INÆQVALI, PONDERE SVO LIBRATVM TAM LEVITER FERATVR
QVAM CYMBA, AQVA TRANQVILLA, NEC EIVS LECTICA SVBVERTI VLLO MODO, VEL CVIQVAM
QVI VEHATVR INCOMODARE POSSIT-

119 Jacques Androuet du Cerceau. Coach for King Charles IX.

The grand coach-house as a distinct element of country or town house belongs to the architectural history of the following centuries. As building types western European coach-houses, riding-schools and a host of other specially designed structures for man and horse in urban and rural contexts cry out for collective and thematic study. The carriage and horse for work or the coach for show or play changed the face of towns, cities and the countryside. The yeoman, bourgeois and aristocratic building and architecture which mirrored these changes is a social, economic and artistic barometer of immense interest. Polemics about ever-grander and more ostentatious coaches abound with the keynote accusations being that coach owners were immoral, vain and wasteful of money.[41]

Tomb monuments

Immorality, vanity and waste of money might be taken as salient features of any discussion of the worth, interest or uselessness of tomb monuments. Many a rich family within the Renaissance period, who did not spend notably on fine houses to perpetuate their name, invested in indoor monuments of architecture and sculpture. Whether tabernacles attached to walls or free-standing baldachins, the stylistic history of 'Renaissance architectures' across Europe is not complete without an account of tomb monuments. Here we can do no more than mention a few suggestive and revealing cases, where the form of a commemorative structure raised wider issues of decorum, ethics and taste.[42] Expenditure on funerals left no physical trace, whilst future generations at prayer had to live with monumental expressions of personal pre-eminence by the departed. In England throughout the Middle Ages there was a constant stream of complaints and laments, that it was inappropriate for decomposing bodies to be covered with fine marble. One of the most vigorous of these sallies is Robert of Bourne's cautionary tale in his *Handlyng Synne* of 1303, in which a sinner is pulled from his grave within a church by demons. He writes, 'His soul has greater pain for his pomp in lying there.' De Bourne even suggests that those lords 'busy about acquiring proud stones, lying on high on their graves, may be damned for that pride, even though they had no sin before'.[43] If we turn to sixteenth-century Verona, the impact of the intervening Reformation and Counter-Reformation on thought about ethics and the decorum of a tomb monument in a church are finely illustrated in the story surrounding the Fregoso monument (figure 120).

From early in the second decade of the sixteenth century there grew up an articulate lobby amongst senior clergy against those who would erect tombs in 'eminent places' that 'exceeded' altars.[44] Gian Matteo Giberti, Bishop of Verona (1495–1543), was a dedicated reformer, whose educational and disciplinary pro- grammes put him in the vanguard of Catholic Reform. His diocesan legislation for Verona, published in 1542, covers a wide range of concerns, amongst which is a reasoned denunciation of large and vainglorious wall-monuments. His influence was widespread in northern and central Italy, and within his own see his opinions guided the form of important new monuments.

The monument to Giano Fregoso in Sant' Anastasia, Verona, which is signed by the Tuscan sculptor-poet Danese Cattaneo and dated 1565, is by no stretch of the imagination inconspicuous. It was expensive, and takes the form of a large triumphal arch prominently located near the west entrance of the church. It is against a background of extravagances in secular tomb-building, with the example of Venice particularly in mind (figures 121–2), that the piety if not the modesty of the Fregoso monument can be read. The figure of Christ showing his wounds in the centre, flanked or attended by statues of Giano Fregoso on the left and of Military Virtue on the right is a novel arrangement. It has turned a tomb monument, whose aim is to commemorate a mortal and to display the remains in a sarcophagus, into a shrine for the laity to venerate. The Fregoso monument is an altar, with a repertoire of motifs in architecture and sculpture befitting the soldier-donor. Conspicuously omitted is a sarcophagus, against which there had been barrages of protest from leading ecclesiastics by 1565. The placing of 'stinking corpses as though they were relics of holy bodies, exalted in a high and ornate position in churches, with arms, standards, trophies and other signs of victory and remembrances around them', as Carlo Borromeo, Bishop of Milan, put it in the mid-1560s, caused a reaction: a widespread policy of reburial below ground.[45] Borromeo is only the most famous to have attacked secular clutter, which impeded worship, in word and deed. The *vani*

120   Verona. Sant'Anastasia. Monument to Gian Fregoso. Completed 1565. Architect
and sculptor Danese Cattaneo.

121 Venice. SS. Giovanni e Paolo. Monument to Doge Pietro Mocenigo. Commissioned 1476. Architect and sculptor Pietro Lombardo.

122 Venice. Frari. Monument to Doge Nicolo Tron. Completed 1479. Architect and sculptor Antonio Rizzo.

trofei of Milan Cathedral were targets for scorn, irrespective of artistic quality or of the greatness of those commemorated. In such an atmosphere the executors of Giano Fregoso had to try to spend a lot of money on a monument which at one and the same time would be spectacular and modest. In this they seem to have succeeded. By changing the central element of the composition from the departed to Christ, and by discreetly placing the remains under a simple oval gravestone in the floor in front of the monument, the Reform's principles were respected. 'Non nobis Domine' they might have, but did not inscribe on the structure.

'The Reform mode' as it has come to be known, of church commemorative (not tomb) monuments had a new iconography. The message of the Fregoso monument was well understood, and its influence considerable. Paradoxically, it was in countries where the Reformation held sway, specifically and especially in the southern half of England, that tomb monuments proliferated in the chancels and aisles of parish churches small and large. The tradition of the monarch being entombed above ground did not alter with the Reformation, and Westminster Abbey is the supreme example of a consecrated warehouse bulging with royal and aristocratic monuments.[46] The wall tabernacle or free-standing canopied monuments churned out in mixed marbles, gaudily painted, by the Southwark workshops, are an amazing social and economic phenomenon. Italian patrician notables moved aside for Christ or more commonly contented themselves with a portrait bust.[47] Meanwhile the English Protestant aristocracy and an increasing number of the gentry spent large sums to ensure that their kneeling or recumbent effigies would be prominent. The tombs of beneficiaries of 'the age of plunder', as the reign of Henry VIII has been called,[48] followed by the men of the new order of Elizabethan England, equalled anything erected for the memory of one of ancient lineage. The well-charted history of social mobility in Tudor England reveals a trickle becoming a stream of first-time-tomb-monument-building families. There was nothing comparable, or on such a scale, in other territories or states which adopted Protestantism. The architecture of 'Romish' marble columns, friezes and pediments of the most fancy tomb monuments, such as that for the greatest of the new men of Elizabeth's reign, William Burghley, speaks a language, which must have been incomprehensible to any ordinary parishioner (figure 123). Burial monuments of the great and the grand surely awed parishioners, but as an investment of money in fame, too many had the same idea for them to become fascinating for posterity.

The symbolism of antique architectural members must have been more tantalising for contemporaries in the case of of monuments where the deceased is not depicted. The wonderful commemorative monument in Hillesden church in Buckinghamshire to Alexander Denton, erected by his mother, the daughter of Lord Mordaunt, in 1576, is an outstanding example of a bookish sophistication which could have been meaningful only to very few (figure 124). The panel within the Flemish strapwork cartouche explains his lineage in English for all to understand. So does the

123 Stamford, Lincolnshire. St Martin's. Monument to William Cecil, Lord Burghley (d.1598). Southward Workshops.

124 Hillesden, Buckinghamshire. Monument to Alexander Denton (d.1577). Commissioned by his mother. Lady Mordaunt. Sculptor Thomas Kirby?

prominent coat of arms, in the language of heraldry, for those who could decipher it. The significance of the base with its three exotic Aztec Indian heads might be no more than a reference to the actual and legendary wealth of the outermost regions of a growing world.[49] The meaning of the finely-carved Doric tabernacle with its superstructure of stone coffin and further frieze with pediment is elusive. Classical architecture is conventional by this date for the tomb of members of the ruling classes who, if raised on a diet of Latin grammar and Roman history, would instinctively equate themselves with the Senatorial class of ancient Rome. The meaning behind the choice of Doric rather than the richer and opulent Corinthian is suggestive to any who had read or had been told of Plato or Vitruvius. The Corinthian acanthus can be associated with death, immortality and healing, according to Plato, but the allure of Vitruvius' characterisation of the Doric with *virtus* and manliness proved the stronger in this case.[50] The clear preference for Corinthian for wall and free-standing monuments inside churches throughout the second half of the sixteenth and the first quarter of the seventeenth centuries is a certain indicator that it was a status symbol for the landed and wealthy of England. It was chosen by convention, which makes the Denton monument the more expressive. Another of three known commissions associated with Thomas Kirby, that for the monument of the first Lord Mordaunt (d.1562), not far away at Turvey in Bedfordshire, has twin fluted Doric columns as well as a recumbent effigy. Here is visual proof, without need of further testimonials, of virtue meaning status and great rank.

As a display of affluence the Denton tomb might be read as a 'Reform mode' monument in a Protestant context. The omission of statuary must have been a deliberate choice, based on a notion of propriety. The very elaborateness of the ensemble precludes any notion that cost was the reason why Denton was not commemorated in a direct and personal way by a portrait. His rank and position are set out with care. Such a monument demonstrates the culture of the obscure man. Compared to the riot of colour and the visual congestion of statues, columns, inscriptions and heraldry which characterise large numbers of late sixteenth-century English tomb monuments, the Denton monument at Hillesden is an exercise in restraint. It is not parochial in its range of reference, and it is imposing. It might be imagined that it greatly impressed the literate as both a learned and a modest display, whether they knew the family, or came across the church on their travels, in its lush out-of-the-way setting.

The appearance in this life of the man celebrated was passed over with the preference for a composite of finely observed, crisply cut foreign architectural motifs, erudite and eloquent of the man's status and exclusiveness. If the memorial at Hillesden might be said to represent his mind, Alexander Denton's (marble) body is elsewhere. At far-away Hereford Cathedral, prestigiously located in the south transept, is a more conventional monument to him, his wife Anne and their stillborn baby child (figure 126).[51] In post-Reformation England elaborate debates

125   Turvey, Bedfordshine, Monument to the lst Lord Mordaunt (d.1562). Sculptor Thomas
Kirby?

126 Hereford Cathedral. Monument to Alexander Denton and his wife Anne Willison (d. in childbirth 1566). Commissioned by the father of Anne Willison. Sculptor Richard Parker (d.1571).

formulated a theory of permissible images in churches, which legitimised the representation of the dead.[52] Representations of virtuous people were not regarded as idolatrous or corrupting. The Fregosos and the Dentons both lived in political and cultural milieux in which the purpose, form and value of commemorative art was being scrutinised. The antagonisms of the Reform and the Counter-Reformation stimulated self-analysis of remarkably similar character directed against vanity and waste on monuments. The results in terms of sculpture are diametrically opposed. Christ could not preside over Denton, but Fregoso needed a statue of the Redeemer to justify the scale of his grandiose cluttering of a church.

Social objectives and reactions

The social objectives of tower-builders, carriage-owners and tomb monument builders might be summarised as follows. Tower-builders were motivated by rivalry to excel. Carriage-owners sought comfort and prestige with a novel and costly vehicle which was a status symbol for pure display. The most complex of these categories is that of tomb monuments as an ethically justifiable use of wealth. A waspish quip by a character in a play by Thomas Middleton (1570–1627) must represent the reaction of large numbers of ordinary Londoners of the time. He complains of those who 'left their carcasses as much in monument as would erect a college' and so 'lie rotting under a million spent in gold and marble'. If this reaction was common, the social objectives of magnificent tombs as admirable legacies of admirable people had failed with the bourgeoisie. We have to imagine what might have been the more robust but less articulate reaction amongst the proletariat. In my first chapter, I quoted Thomas Lever, who told the Court why 'the commens do not love, trust, nor obey the gentlemen and the officers'. Research on other categories of luxury expenditure such as furniture, goldsmith's work and jewellery is highly rewarding, but unfortunately even a cursory survey of texts would be difficult to justify as being relevant to architecture. Nevertheless, if we restrict ourselves to a small sample of anecdotes from just one famous book, Benvenuto Cellini's *Vita*, written between 1558 and 1566, the passion for permanence in buildings can be contrasted vividly with the impermanence of the goldsmith's luxurious products.

Money into art into money into oblivion

Rubble and scrap have much in common for the historian. The sole survivor of Cellini's oeuvre as a goldsmith is the marvellous salt-cellar, completed in 1543, made for Francis I. All the rest of his considerable output, of which we read in his bustling autobiography, disappeared so early that not even drawings or engravings of them are extant. Even a goldsmith of Cellini's reputation and status must have known that the precious materials in which he was working condemned his works to destruction as soon as they became unfashionable or the owner needed ready money. The brief life of such ultimate luxury objects, which has been estimated by one scholar at 'some thirty years or so at best',[53] would have been doubly clear to the artist, because his materials very rarely came to him in the form of bullion and unmounted stones. He used the highest possible class of scrap in the form of old, damaged or unfashionable pieces. This impermanence is the more saddening and alarming when we contemplate the Cellini saltcellar, and read of its falling out of favour after the death of Francis I. In 1566 Charles IX included it in a list of treasure to be melted down, but it was spared to be given away in 1570 to Archduke Ferdinand of Tirol, as one of three precious tokens of gratitude for his standing as Charles' proxy in his wedding to Elizabeth of Austria. The object only survives because the Habsburgs were inclined to hoard possessions, and were the first to make provision for their protection as heirlooms.[54] Another factor which influenced the survival of objects in precious materials was utility. Cellini relates how, while he was working in Rome, he was commissioned by the Bishop of Salamanca to make a great water-vessel some three feet high, to stand on a sideboard. Such an article was of use, which the great majority of plate set out for display on sideboards at feasts and great receptions was not. In 1550 the Milanese medallist and rock-crystal carver Jacopo da Trezzo wrote from Spain to Duke Cosimo de' Medici to enquire whether the vessel he had commissioned was 'a cup to drink from or only to look well'.[55] So the owner of such an object might enjoy being surrounded by his capital assets made up in entertaining ways, but capital assets they always remained, to be liquidated, literally, when needs dictated. The artist's achievements in this domain, at this period, had no book value other than the fee paid to him, which for the owner was a debit.

Heirlooms and tombs also have a lot in common. Benvenuto Cellini and Thomas Kirby have never been written of in the same paragraph, far less shared the same sentence in any writings on sculpture. However capricious it is to link their names, there is something of significance to be garnered in the way in which fate and posterity have treated them and their work. Much of the wealth which Cellini's patrons concentrated in pieces made by him was retrievable at a loss. The moment the meaning and prestige attached to the object fades or is forgotten, the furnace is stoked. The artistic and social value of the finest of such work did not last from one generation to the next. In another land, and way down the social scale, Thomas Kirby's monument for Alexander Denton might not at first sight look flamboyant in any way analogous to Cellini's work. Cellini's workmanship was highly perishable in the social, political and economic contexts of later times. The taste for it had gone. The Denton monument was designed to be longer-lasting, made of deeply carved stone that would have been of little value for any reuse. None would covet the memorial, and so its message and artistic quality might survive to be understood or at least admired far into the future. Treasure, like memory, is vulnerable and finite. If treasure is hidden for long enough, it may survive to be recovered, preserved and appreciated. The meaning of objects made of non-precious materials perishes for different reasons. Quite simply there was and is no guarantee, that any major or minor work of art will survive and be understood without good luck, good will and the efforts of historians.

The social orders of Renaissance Europe were hierarchies in which wealth found a natural and conducive expression in the classical language of architecture. As one modern writer has put it succinctly, it was a language in which 'the rich were eloquent and the poor dumb'.[56] This oversimplification is hardly surprising, for effective material and monumental expressions of distinction are by nature confounding to those who are intended to be awed. Articulate criticisms from economists, churchmen or playwrights of wealth devoted to non-practical architectural glory are scattered and unco-ordinated. Where and when we have insights into private expenditure on luxuries, from fripperies to monuments, the common factor usually is that such things are indulgences which have a detrimental effect on others.

The impressionable young, the impecunious nobility and women were the components of society most prone and vulnerable to ruination because of luxuries. This holds true if we are to take seriously the caveats of sumptuary laws which sought to define the borderlines between propriety and excess. Venice is the richest western European source for legislative tinkering with all manner of private expenditure on luxuries, which was held to affect and influence public morals for the worse. By the fall of the Republic, over thirty-five general categories of sumptuary laws had been drawn up, whose scope ranged from minor details of attire, to the interior decoration of gondolas and palaces, and feasting. Morality and public order were amongst the highly subjective criteria which were the express concerns of the *magistrato alle pompe*. The interests of families and individuals could easily be at odds with the political order and the social traditions of the state, especially in the economic sphere, in which private wealth was employed in a strategy of private advancement. Private economic advantage once gained and consolidated could not remain static or unexpressed in a competitive society, however civilised or ordered. Intervention by the state was rarely effective except in the very short-term in such matters.

Political and philosophical debate about wealth and its uses and abuses during the Renaissance was profoundly influenced by the concept of 'the effective truth of things'.[57] Man 'as he really is' becomes a theme in many literatures, which at its best is ethical pragmatism, not to be confused with cynicism. Leonardo da Vinci believed in 'sound envy', and Florentine 'civic humanists' of the fifteenth and sixteenth centuries excavated and adulterated more and more ancient writing to strengthen the case of merchants and princes who expressed their wealth in different ways in order to outdo others. Such behaviour is a passion and an interest born in men.[58] The most blatant expression of such feeling must have been that of the burgomaster of Gdansk who had 'Pro Invidia' inscribed on the facade of his house.[59] Once the passion or vice of luxury has been transformed into a natural expression of advantage, great expenditure can be justified as being in the interest of some and to the harm of none. The social and intellectual framework has been erected in which all are expected to admire secular architectural splendour. This is a little-recognised legacy of the Renaissance which is still alive today.

'Quo vadis?'

The reader will have noticed that no one particular great Renaissance building comes in for direct attack amongst all the material assembled here. The optimists or the 'magnificence school' sing the praises of great men and commend their works. The pessimists or the enemies of luxury usually expressed their concerns in generic terms, in which extravagant building was an important component. Several themes from all the preceding chapters can be drawn together, by visiting

127 Chenonceau (Indre-et-Loirt). Begun *c.*1515, bridge and gallery 1556 onwards.

in our mind's eye the very famous Chenonceaux (figure 127). The exquisite 'châtelet' (not the gallery on the bridge, which was added in the 1560s) was built for Thomas Bohier and his noble wife Catherine Briçonnet between 1515 and 1522. Beginning in 1496, Bohier, a royal financier and tax-gatherer, accumulated his estate by extending to the previous owners, the Marques family, a series of ever-growing loans at impossible rates of interest, which they could not repay.[60] He stalked his prey ruthlessly. Bohier was a skilled and successful asset-stripper. The 'magnificence school' of the sixteenth century lives on in modern art history. Bohier's wealth produced a biographical fiction in architecture. The romantic appeal and the historic symbolism of this masterpiece, wholly deflects any meaningful reaction in the onlooker to the truth of the man. Would a guide or a visitor express heartfelt sentiments about social inequality or venality in such a setting? To most, such behaviour would seem small-minded. Poggio Bracciolini's followers have won the argument, it is the 'have-nots' who are envious and avaricious.

Whether Chenonceaux is magnificent or luxurious is a question for the individual, on which there can never be agreement. It is not a matter of historical dispute that Chenonceaux is a product of a society in which the 'rich were eloquent and the poor dumb'. I conclude with a short essay on social attitudes to the poor and their architectural imagery.

5

POVERTY, LUXURY AND
ARCHITECTURE

The Renaissance period, however defined in terms of dates, was not an age of peace or liberality in any European state. Eminence and success amongst the wealthy and powerful, where expressed in material ways such as buildings, were statements of social and cultural distinction. As a state of grace, poverty amongst the laity is never celebrated. Poverty in literature is almost universally associated with sloth. The intensity of the contempt for the poor and the common stock of society can be one of the most chilling features of Renaissance history for the modern mind.[1] From the second quarter of the sixteenth century a more sympathetic treatment of peasants in literature and visual art emerges in the Venetian territories.[2]

A choice example of the disaffection of the 'haves' for the 'have-nots' is found in the crude population censuses taken at Vicenza in 1558 and 1570. The Vicentine nobility, in their palaces and villas designed by Palladio, have left a stock of buildings which are eloquent testimony to their affluence and pride. The basis of their prosperity was based on such assets as good and plentiful labour. So it is the more surprising to read that in 1558, from a total population of 19,899, a total of 6,867 were classified as *anime de fattione*, that is to say useful or busy people, whilst 13,032 were marked down as *anime inutile*. By 1570 the proportion of useful and useless had changed significantly with a slight drop in useful people, to 6,272 and a considerable rise of the useless to 20,074.[3]

It would be preposterous to imagine that the great majority of the population of such a prosperous small city was made up of beggars. The distinction between useful and useless must have been between those with significant interests and holdings, so that they were liable to make a contribution to the state in taxes, and those (including women and children?), who could be called on for little or nothing. The great majority of the useless were the minor artisans, casual labourers and the service staff of all sorts, whose livelihood derived directly or indirectly from the nobility. Until social and economic statistics were developed, in the late seventeenth and early eighteenth centuries, into a far more refined procedure with numerous special categories, the general headcount, with its stark and misleading distinction, persisted. For us, the pejorative and apparently natural and acceptable use of a term like 'useless' is echoed with force and clarity in paintings of peasant subjects and in 'comic mode' literature. To offset what seems to be an overwhelming consensus in art and literature that the poor were viewed by the middle and upper classes as a burden on society, there is the emergence in the manuscript literature of architecture of a visual account of housing for all classes, from the poorest to the richest.

Sebastiano Serlio designed houses for a 'poor peasant of three degrees of poverty', for a 'middling peasant of two degrees of mediocrity', for a 'rich peasant of two degrees of wealth', for a 'poor artisan of three degrees of poverty outside the city' and so on up and across the classes to designs for palaces for a king. His 'true' sixth book on domestic architecture pioneered ideals of building for the lower orders (figures 64–71), but his social categories measured in *gradi* are far from easy to understand. The social and intellectual milieu which produced and inspired Serlio's social nomenclature must have been Venetian, but his source remains mysterious.[4] The heart of the matter is a view that very humble free men can be lodged decently, thus fitting their station. This is the antithesis of that of the census-makers or playwrights, amongst whom, there is barely any trace of such a developed sense of fine distinctions amongst the lower orders, with vested interests in property.

The appearance of buildings in real or imagined scenes of rustic life is usually at odds with the disorder or self-indulgence associated in satirical plays with peasant festivities.[5] Indeed, Serlio shared with Bruegel an innate sense of the honourable status of the manual labourer. If the houses and barns of wood and thatch in Bruegel's landscapes and peasant moralities were intended to read as part of an indictment of country folk, they would presumably have been shown as decrepit or decayed. Neglect is an obvious outward sign of sloth. The buildings in his paintings are always picturesque, even quaint, and would have been so read by contemporaries. They are always neat and well-maintained with all roofs and wall-renderings sound. Here, all, in terms of housing, from the smallest cottage to a substantial farmhouse, is in good condition, amounting to a clear statement not of chaos but of order. Bruegel's villages are not haunted by plague or blighted by the crop failures which were ever-present threats to life in the rural Low Countries, as everywhere. The only circumstances in which disorder invades are where the villages are turned into stages for biblical subjects such as the *Massacre of the Innocents*.[6] Cruelty and poverty are consequences of tyranny, and in their contrasting ways both Serlio and Bruegel depict a universal malaise.

Palaces or fortresses for tyrants figure prominently amongst Serlio's designs for the upper echelons. Serlio's social ladder, which informed his organisation of the several grades of lowest and low hovels to middle-class houses, is analogous to Bruegel's repertoire of cheap but not humble buildings. The symmetry imposed by Serlio on humble buildings was a requirement for presentational order in an architectural pattern book. Serlio, as a painter by training, would easily have grasped the symbolic intentions of Bruegel's use of rural buildings, if he had lived to see engravings after him. In his old age Serlio was undoubtedly poor, but not destitute. Personally and intellectually, he met a challenge to fix the dwellings of the poor into a sequence and order which all knew to exist, but to which none had thought worthy of giving extensive description or analysis.

To artists in northern or southern Europe the ultimate hovel which had to be represented was Christ's birthplace. Curiously the setting for the great event did not concern the writers of the Gospels. Matthew merely refers to a house to which the shepherds were guided by the star. Luke alone makes the key statement, that the baby was wrapped and laid in a manger, which defines the place as a stable. A fantasy architecture of crumbling walls, rafters and holed roofs was vividly portrayed in popular prints or great altarpieces to impress the message of the decay of the world, which Christ had come to redeem. The greatest of care had to be taken to make the buildings look forlorn, but to avoid any appearance of squalor. That Christ was born in a shambles of timbers and crumbling brick is an embroidering of the story of his nativity, essential for a potent impact on the faithful. As conjured in Dürer's prints or the avant-garde stage set invented by Tintoretto in the opulent setting of the Scuola Grande di San Rocco, the architecture of poverty is a humiliation transcended by the serenity of the Holy Family (figure 128). The blame for their condition rests not just with some anonymous innkeeper, but with all mankind, then and now. From this it is a short step to the well-worked thesis that poverty is the natural condition of the useless.

Any appropriate emotion of remorse aroused by the setting of the nativity should have extended amongst Christians to influence their view of their own society. There is no shortage of evidence celebrating works of charity by individuals and institutions in every part of Catholic or Protestant Europe. To make provision of food or clothing to the poor in times of particular need or crisis was always a highly selective and subjective process. The most common criterion for help is one where those in need are deemed 'worthy'. An individual English lord or the collective of a Venetian Scuola would incline to select their beneficiaries on the basis of a limited range of qualifications, such as tradition of service, social association or trade.[7] The needs of destitute strangers or 'useless' citizens were for the conscience of the Church. Only very rarely were vagrants seen as a call on the purse of the useful. Shelter of the most elementary kind was excluded by all writers on architecture during the Renaissance, with the sole exception of Sebastiano Serlio. We are indebted to him alone for showing us that such concerns at least

128   Jacopo Robusti, called Tintoretto. *Adoration of the Shepherds*. 1570–80.

129 Jacopo Bassano. *Adoration of the Kings. c.1540–c.1550.*

existed on the periphery of thinking, writing and planning of luxury architecture. The French Serlio, Jacques Androuet du Cerceau published in his first *Livre d'Architecture* of 1559 a sequence of fifty designs on an ascending scale, whose point of departure is well up Serlio's social ladder.[8] To build well is the right of rank and the reward of the useful, and it is the most precise affirmation of the actual state of social and economic differentiation. Serlio tried to break the mould made by Alberti, but in the pattern book genre du Cerceau re-established it.

If there was a dilemma for the urban or rural rich, whose Christian faith gave them no authority for fine building, it was one which they circumvented. There is a perfect Venetian example of the censoring of the ideals of poverty in Jacopo Bassano's magnificent *Adoration of the Kings*, of the 1540s, in the National Gallery of Scotland (figure 129). The stable, which was good enough for the shepherds to approach to adore the child, is relegated to the middle distance, isolated in a lush landscape. Played in this painting by an unknown patrician family and retinue, all in gorgeous festival attire, the secular kings would have looked far less grand if shown kneeling in the debris of a farm building. One of the revelations of the picture is that a key New Testament episode has been revised in terms of sixteenth-century social and architectural decorum. In the finer surroundings of a classical patio, the blessing of Christ is administered by gentlemen. Although set in the open air, the Holy Family have moved to a site appropriate for the reception of dignitaries. The adjustment may seem small, but it is profoundly significant. The rich are accorded an audience in a setting commensurate with their high rank in the world of Venice and the Veneto of the 1540s. The only sour note might be the broken column-shaft. This had become a recurrent feature in devotional and non-devotional portraits of great churchmen and laity from the late fifteenth century. The broken column had the ideal connotation of representing *vanitas* as past vainglory and mortality, but not present decadence.[9] Here, as in the real world, there is a sumptuary code of architectural forms, where with divine approbation fine architecture is one of the luxuries of appearance essential not for a celebration of abundance, but for an overt expression of the visible distinctions. Thus the useful are separated from the useless. In such terms most 'Renaissance cultures' devoted deep thought and enormous resources to display the magnificence which God could bestow. At one and the same time this abandoned the definition of luxury in Genesis as 'anything unneeded', and adopted that found in Samuel and Kings 'anything to which one has no right or title'. Do we admire both the buildings and works of art which express this? If we do, the legacy of any past age can be assimilated to the times in which we live, and the ways in which we conform, question or rebel. If 'not needed' is the study of wealth and didactic architecture luxurious?

NOTES

Notes to chapter 1

The inspiration for the present book came from reading John Sekora, *Luxury, the concept in Western Thought from Eden to Smollett*, Baltimore 1977, especially chapter 1, 'Necessity and Hierarchy. The Classical Attack upon Luxury', pp. 23–62. Sekora's admirable work made the initial research for this book far more efficient and fruitful than would have been possible without his thorough and perceptive scholarship. He writes (pp. 297–8, note 5) 'Since 1800 approximately four hundred books and articles have appeared, that discuss luxury in one connection or another. The usual context is of course the History of Rome.' Since the publication of Sekora's book in 1977 a thesis on the subject has appeared. See Edwoud Slob, *Luxuria. Regelgeving en maatregelen van censoren ten tijde Romeinse Republick*, Utrecht 1986. The principal economic studies of luxury as meaning exorbitant spending are not modern. They are E.J. Urwick, *Luxury and the Waste of Life*, London 1908; R.I. MacBride, *Luxury as a Social Standard*, New York 1915; Werner Sombart, *Luxury and Capitalism*, English translation, Ann Arbor 1967; Emile De Laveleye, *Luxury*, London 1891. See also Richard A. Goldthwaite, 'The Renaissance Economy. The Preconditions for Luxury Consumption', in *Aspetti Della Vita Economica Medievale. Atti del Convegno di Studi nel X Anniversario della morte di Federigo Melis*, Florence-Pisa-Prato, 10–14 March 1984, pp. 659–75, and his 'The Empire of Things. Consumer Demand in Renaissance Italy', in *Patronage, Art and Society in Renaissance Italy*, F.W. Kent and Patricia Simons (eds), Oxford & Canberra 1987.

1 See Richard G. Schlatter, *Private Property. The History of an Idea*. London 1951.

2 For references to relevant Roman texts see Andrew Wallace-Hadrill, 'The Social Structure of the Roman House', in *Papers of the British School at Rome*, 1988, pp. 43–97, especially p. 44, note 5. See also René Martin, *Recherches sur les agronomes latins et leurs conceptions économiques et sociales*, Paris 1971, and Moses Finley, *The Ancient Economy*, Berkeley 1973.

3 See James S. Ackerman, *The Villa. Form and Ideology of Country Houses*, Princeton 1990, chapter 2, 'The Ancient Roman Villa', pp. 35–61.

4 See Andrew Wallace-Hadrill, *op. cit.* (note 2), p. 47, note 18. The most thorough account of ancient Greek urban domestic architecture and planning is Wolfram Hoepfer & Ernst Ludwig Schwander, *Haus und Stadt im Klassischen Griechenland*, Munich 1986.

5 See Yvon Thebert, 'Private Life and Domestic Architecture in Roman Africa', in *A History of Private Life*, I, *From Pagan Rome to Byzantium*, Paul Veyne (ed.), Cambridge (Mass.) 1987, pp. 313–409.

6 See Umberto Eco, *Art and Beauty in the Middle Ages*, New Haven 1986, pp. 6–8.

7 The quotations come from St Bernard's *Apologia ad Guillelmum*. See Conrad Rudolf, *The 'things of greater importance'. Bernard of Clairvaux's Apologia and the medieval attitude towards Art*, Philadelpia 1990.

8 For the fullest discussion of these writers of the Paris Schools on matters of architecture see Victor Mortet , 'Hugue De Fouilloi, Pierre Le Chantre, Alexandre Neckham et les critiques dirigées au douzième siècle contre le luxe des constructions', in *Mélanges d'Histoire à M. Charles Bemont*, Paris 1913, pp. 105–37. See also J.W. Baldwin, *Masters, Princes and Merchants. The Social Values of Peter the Chanter and his Circle*, 2 vols, Princeton 1970.

9 Petrarch, *Familiares*, VI, 2. See Angelo Mozzacco, 'The Antiquarianism of Francesco Petrarca', in *Journal of Medieval and Renaissance Studies*, 7, 1977, pp. 203–24.

10 This text is studied by both L.F. Salzman, *Building in England down to 1540*, London 1969, pp. 513–14, and John Harvey, *The Medieval Architect*, London 1972, pp. 252–3. Harvey calls the text evidence of 'aesthetic puritanism', which is not a wholly satisfactory concept for the fifteenth century.

11 See Bertram Wolffe, *Henry VI*, London 1981, p. 142.

12 See Wolffe, *op. cit.* (note 11), p. 145.

13 See Francis Woodman, *The Architectural History of King's College Chapel and its Place in the Development of Late Gothic Architecture in England and France*, London 1986, pp. 178–81.

14 See A.D. Fraser Jenkins, 'Cosimo de Medici's Patronage of Architecture and the Theory of Magnificence', in *Journal of the Warburg and Courtauld Institutes*, 1970, pp. 162–70. See also Odd Langholm: *The Aristotelian Analysis of Usury*, Bergen 1984.

15 *Giovanni Rucellai ed il suo zibaldone. Vol. II. A Florentine Patrician and his Palace.* Studies by F.W. Kent, Alessandro Perosa, Brenda Preyer *et al.* London 1981, especially part of the contribution by Brenda Preyer, V, 'The patron, his palace and his loggia', pp. 202–7.

16 See F.W. Kent, '"Più superba de quella de Lorenzo." Courtly and family interest in the building of Filippo Strozzi's palace', in *Renaissance Quarterly*, 30, 1977, pp. 311–23, and Richard A. Goldthwaite, *The Building of Renaissance Florence. An Economic and Social History*, Baltimore 1980. The economic climate at this period was unsteady see R.S. Lopez, M.A. Miskimin & C.M. Cipolla, 'The Economic Depression of the Renaissance', in *The Economic History Review*, second series, vols. XIV & XV, 1961–62, pp. 408–28, & 1963–64, pp. 519–27. The authors observe 'When the excitement and profitability of business waned . . . one finds the combination of price recession, financial extravagance and cultural brilliance'.

17 See Werner L. Gundersheimer, *Ferrara , the style of a Renaissance Despotism*, Princeton 1973, especially pp. 248–71.

18 Richard Krautheimer, *Three Christian Capitals. Topography and Politics. Rome, Constantinople, Milan.* Berkeley 1983, p. 56.

19 See André Chastel, *The Sack of Rome 1527*, Princeton 1983, especially part II, 'Rome-Babylon', pp. 49–90.

20 See Christoph Luitpold Frommel, *Die Farnesina und Peruzzis Architektonisches Frühwerk*, Berlin 1961, and Wilde Tosi (editor), *Il Magnifico Agostino Chigi*, Rome 1970.

21 Quoted and translated by Ingrid D. Rowland, 'Some panegyrics to Agostino Chigi', in *Journal of the Warburg and Courtauld Institutes*, 1984, pp. 194–9. The painted decorations inside Chigi's villa showed a very different range of cultural and ethical values. See David R. Coffin, *The Villa in the Life of Renaissance Rome*, Princeton 1979, pp. 87–109. See also Michel Jeanneret, *A Feast of Words. Banquets and Table-Talk in the Renaissance*, Cambridge 1991, for an excellent account of the protocols and rituals of entertainment in polite society, which were often abused.

22. Blosio Palladio, *Suburbanum Augustini Chisii per Blosium Palladium*, Rome 1512.

23 See Richard G. Schlatter, *op. cit.* (note 1), pp. 77–123.

24 See James S. Ackerman, *op. cit.* (note 3), pp. 62–87. See also Brian Vickers: 'Leisure and Idleness in the Renaissance, the ambivalence of "otium"', in *Renaissance Studies*, IV, 1990, pp. 1–37 & 107–54.

25 See David R. Coffin, *op. cit.* (note 21). See also John F. D'Amico, *Renaissance Humanism in Papal Rome. Humanists and Churchmen on the Eve of the Reformation*, Baltimore 1983.

26 On houses painted by Holbein see Hans Alfred Schmid, *Hans Holbein der Jüngere*, Basle 1948, pp. 106–27. On the very different character of painted facades in Italy see Maria Errico, Stella Sandra Finozzi & Irena Giglio, 'Ricognizione e schedatura delle facciate affrescate e graffite a Roma nei secoli XV e XVI', in *Bollettino d'Arte*, 1985, pp. 53–134.

27 On the *Hasenhaus*, whose site was on the former Seilergasse 5/7, now the Kartnerstrasse 8/10, see *Historisches Museum der Stadt Wien. Schausammlung*. Bearbeitet von Robert Waissenberger, Vienna 1984, pp. 74–5.

28 See Christiane Andersson 'Polemical Prints in Reformation Nuremberg', in *New Perspectives on the Art of Renaissance Nuremberg, Five Essays*, Austin 1985, pp. 41–62. On the subject of allegorical inversion see Barbara A. Babcock (ed.), *The Reversible World. Symbolic Inversion in Art and Society*, Ithaca and London 1978, especially David Kunzle : 'World Upside Down, The Iconography of a European Broadsheet Type', pp. 39–94.

29 See Paul F. Grendler, *Critics of the Italian World 1530–1560*, Madison 1969 and his *The Roman Inquisition and the Venetian Press 1540–1605*, Princeton 1977, and Edward Muir, *Civic Ritual in Renaissance Venice*, Princeton 1981, especially chapter 1, 'The Myth of Venice', pp. 14–61.

30 See Antonio Foscari and Manfredo Tafuri, *L'Armonia e i Conflitti. La Chiesa di San Francesco della Vigna nella Venezia del '500*, Turin 1983.

31 See Brian Pullan, *Rich and Poor in Renaissance Venice*, Oxford 1971, pp. 117–21, and Enrica Benini, 'Alessandro Caravia, gioielliere dei Medici a Venezia', in *Quaderni di Teatro. Rivista trimestriale del Teatro Toscano*, Anno II, 1980, pp. 177–94.

32 See Manfredo Tafuri, *Venezia e il Rinascimento*, Turin 1985, pp. 125–54.

33 Robert Dallington (1561–1637), *A Method for Travell, showing by taking the view of France as it stoode in the Yeare of our Lord 1598*, London n.d., p. 17. See Pauline M. Smith, *The Anti-Courtier Trend in Sixteenth Century French Literature*, Geneva 1966, and Sydney Anglo, 'The Courtier and changing ideals', in *The Courts of Europe, Politics, Patronage and Royalty*, edited by A.G. Dickens, London 1977, pp. 33–53. On theories of regal magnificence of the fifteenth and sixteenth centuries in Northern Europe, see Gordon Kipling, *The Triumph of Honour. Burgundian Origins of the Elizabethan Renaissance*, Leiden 1977, and W.O. Harris, *Skelton's 'Magnyfycence' and the Cardinal Virtue Tradition*, Chapel Hill 1965, pp. 71–126. See also George Weise, *L'Ideale Eroico Del*

Rinascimento, 2 vols., Naples 1961–5, especially vol. 1, chapter 3, 'Il Nuovo Senso di Maestà', di Dignità' e di Distanza', pp. 121–36.

34 On Seyssel see Alberto Caviglia, *Claudio Seyssel, 1450–1520*, Turin 1928, and *The Monarchy of France by Claude Seyssel* translated by J.H. Hexter. Edited, annotated and introduced by Donald R. Kelley, New Haven 1981.

35 On Bodin the fullest biography is still M.H. Baudrillart, *Jean Bodin et son temps*, Paris 1853. The expenditures and economic problems of the nobility in France during this period are the subjects of two important articles. See J. Russell Major, 'Noble Income, Inflation, and the Wars of Religion in France', in *American Historical Review*, 1981, pp. 21–48, and Denis Crouzet, 'Recherches sur la Crise de l'Aristocratie en France au XVIe siècle. Les Dettes de la Maison de Nevers', in Histoire, Economies, Sociétés, 1982, pp. 7–50.

36 For an earlier discussion of the interest of this text see my *Renaissance Paris. Architecture and Growth 1475–1600*, London 1984, pp. 98–104.

37 On the building documents of the Hôtel des Ligneris see Jean-Pierre Babelon, 'Du Grand Ferrare à Carnavalet. Naissance de l'hôtel classique', in *Revue de l'Art*, 1978, pp. 83–108, & 'Bonnes et Mauvaises Lectures', *ibid.*, 1981, pp. 56–60. See also the summary of the architecture in this sectc· of Paris in *Le Marais, mythe et réalité*, (Exhibition catalogue, Hôtel de Sully, Caisse Nationale des Monuments Historiques et des Sites/Ministère de la Culture), 1987, pp. 74–85.

38 See Helen C. White, *Social Criticism in Popular Religious Literature of the Sixteenth Century* [in England], New York 1944, p. 123.

39 See Mark Girouard, *Robert Smythson and the Elizabethan Country House*, New Haven 1983, pp. 39–76, and Paul Drury, 'A Fayre house, Buylt by Sir Thomas Smith', the Development of Hill Hall, Essex, 1557–1581', in *Journal of the British Archaeological Association*, Vol. CXXXVI, 1983, pp. 98–123.

40 Girouard, *op. cit.* (note 39), pp. 18–28.

41 Helen C. White, *op. cit.* (note 32), pp. 235–236.

42 All these issues are brilliantly covered by Felicity Heal, 'The Idea of Hospitality in Early Modern England', in *Past and Present*, 1984, pp. 66–93. Dr. Heal has published a full-length study, *Hospitality in Early Modern England*, Oxford 1991, which appeared after this essay was revised for printing. An invaluable background study for the sixteenth century in England is Bridget Ann Henisch, *Feast and Fast. Food in Medieval Society*, University Park, Pennsylvania 1976.

43 William Harrison was born in London in April 1534, and educated at both Oxford and Cambridge. He was rector of Radwinter from 1558 to 1593. He was a close associate of Sir Thomas Smith, the builder of Hill Hall, and they drew on each other's work. He was appointed a canon of Windsor in April 1586, where he died. All the quotations from Harrison are taken from Book II, chapter 12, 'Of the Manner of Building and Furniture of our houses'. I have used the edition edited by Georges Edelen, Ithaca 1968, pp. 195–204.

On the real troubles with foreign 'artificers' at Longleat and at Somerset House see Mark Girouard, 'Some Alien Craftsmen in Sixteenth and Seventeenth Century England', in *Proceedings of the Huguenot Society of London*, 1956, pp. 26–35, especially p. 28.

44 See Anthony Quiney, *House and Home, A History of the Small English House*, London 1986, pp. 37–55, and R. Machin, 'The Great Rebuilding, a Reassessment', in *Past and Present*, 1977, pp. 35–58.

45 Much modern historical research has transformed architectural history from descriptive accounts of style to an analytical branch of social history. An important contribution for the Renaissance period will be the forthcoming volume *'Architecture et vie sociale'* in the series 'De Architectura' edited by Jean Guillaume from the conference held at the Centre d'Etudes supérieures de la Renaissance at Tours in 1990. Notable recent studies of case histories in France and England include Bertrand Jestaz, 'Etiquette et Distribution Intérieure dans les Maisons Royales de la Renaissance', in *Bulletin Monumental*, 1988, pp. 109–20; Kristen B. Neuschel, 'Noble Households in the Sixteenth Century, Material Settings and Human Communities', in *French Historical Studies*, XV, 1988, pp. 595–622; Alice T. Friedman, *House and Household in Elizabethan England, Wollaton Hall and the Willoughby Family*, Chicago 1989.

46 Erasmus, quoted by W.G. Hoskins, *The Age of Plunder*, London 1976, p. 2.

47 The 'delight in great light' in England was mentioned by Sebastiano Serlio in the earlier manuscript of *c.*1545–*c.*1550 for his sixth book, written in France. See Myra Nan Rosenfeld, *Sebastiano Serlio On Domestic Architecture*, Cambridge (Mass.) 1978, project XLIX, the bottom line. It would be fascinating to find out who told him about English building fashions. I am very grateful to Professor Jean Guillaume for pointing this passage out to me.

Notes to chapter 2

1 William A. McClung, *The Architecture of Paradise. Survivals of Eden and Jerusalem*, Berkeley 1983, p. 83, quoting from Aldous Huxley, *Heaven and Hell*. For medieval accounts of fabled or legendary architecture beyond Europe, see Patrick Connor, *Oriental Architecture in the West*, London 1979, pp. 9–11 and footnotes for references.

2 The term 'Court Society' is coined from Norbert Elias' classic study of that title. On the subject of the reworking of the Trojan Legend during the late Middle Ages and the Renaissance see Fritz Saxl, 'The Legends of Troy in French and Italian Art', in *Lectures*, London 1957, pp. 125–38; M.R. Sherer, *The Legends of Troy in Art and Literature*, New York and London 1964 and Hugo Buchtal, *Historia Troiana. Studies in the History of Medieval Secular Literature*, London 1971.

3 See John Onians, *Art and Thought in the Hellenistic Age. The Greek World View 350–50 BC*, London 1979, pp. 7–16.

4 Frank E. & Fritzie P. Manuel, *Utopian Thought in the Western World*, Cambridge (Mass.) 1979, p. 64, and McClung, *op. cit.* (note 1), p. 62. See also J.C. Davis, *Utopia and the Ideal Society. A Study of English Utopian Writing 1516–1700*, Cambridge 1981. There seems to be little comparable in modern French or Italian scholarship.

5 For example, see the quotation from Horace inscribed on the plinth of a column in a *Portrait of a Gentleman* by Moroni of 1554, now in the Ambrosiana in Milan. The quotation is 'Impavidum ferient ruinae' meaning roughly 'fearless amongst the ruins'. See *Giovanni Battista Moroni*. 400th Anniversary Exhibition, National Gallery, London 1978, pp. 12–13. For Cicero's comments on architecture see A. Desmouliez, *Ciceron et son goût*, Brussels 1976, p. 245, where *De Oratione* III, 180 is discussed.

6 Revelation of John, XXI, 16–21.

7 Ezekiel, XL–XLIII. For the resonances of this text in art see Carol Herselle Krinsky, 'Representations of the Temple of Jerusalem before 1500', in *Journal of the Warburg and Courtauld Institutes*, 1970, pp. 1–19.

8 See James A. Freeman, 'The Roof was Fretted Gold', in *Comparative Literature*, 1975, pp. 254–66, especially pp. 260–261.

9   See William A. McClung, 'The Matter of Metaphor. Literary Myths of Construction', in *Journal of the Society of Architectural Historians*, 1981, pp. 279–88, especially p. 279.

10   McClung, *op. cit.* (note 1), pp. 119–23.

11   See Joseph Rykwert, *On Adam's House in Paradise*, New York 1972.

12   Quoted by Tilmann Buddensieg, 'Criticism of Ancient Architecture in the 16th and 17th Centuries', in *Classical Influence on European Culture*, AD 1500–1700, edited by R.R. Bolgar, Cambridge 1976, pp. 335–48. For Petrarch see Angelo Mazzocco, 'The Antiquarianism of Francesco Petrarca', in *Journal of Medieval and Renaissance Studies*, 7, 1977, pp. 203–24.

13   See Filarete (Antonio di Piero Averlino), *Treatise on Architecture*, translated and edited by John R. Spenser, 2 vols., New Haven 1965, and Manuel, *op. cit.* (note 4), pp. 153–61.

14   See John Onians, 'Alberti and ΦΙΛΑΡΕΤΗ. A Study in their sources', in *Journal of the Warburg and Courtauld Institutes*, 1971, pp. 96–114, especially pp. 107–9.

15   Antonio Francesco Doni. The dialogue 'Mondo Savio', in his *I Mondi Celesti, terrestri, e infernali, de gli accademici pellegrini*, Venice 1552.

16   See Lawrence Stone, 'Social Mobility in England, 1500–1700', in *Past and Present*, 1966, pp. 16–55.

17   I. Insolera, *Storia d'Italia*, Vol. 6, Milan 1976, p. 320.

18   Richard Goldthwaite, *The Building of Renaissance Florence*, Baltimore 1980, p. 14.

19   For a good, contextual introduction see Charles Mitchell, 'Archaeology and Romance', in *Italian Renaissance Studies*, edited by E.P. Jacob, London 1961, pp. 455–83. The fundamental study is M.T. Casella & G. Pozzi, *Francesco Colonna. Biographia e opere*, 2 vols., Padua 1959.

20   In France Rabelais assumed his readers would be familiar with the *Hypnerotomachia* as shown in several amusing plagiarisms in both *Gargantua* and *Pantagruel*. A French translation by Jean Martin appeared in 1546, and a shortened English translation in 1597. See also Anthony Blunt, 'The Hypnerotomachia Polifilii in Seventeenth Century France', in *Journal of the Warburg Institute*, I, 1937, pp. 117–37.

21   Jacob Burckhardt, *The Civilisation of the Renaissance in Italy*, part III, chapter 1.

22   Mitchell, *op. cit.* (note 19), p. 470.

23   Quoted by Mitchell, p. 470.

24   '*Rome poudreuse*' as a term to describe the emotional impact of the decaying monuments comes from the French poet Joachim Du Bellay's *Antiquitez de Rome contenant une générale description de sa grandeur et comme une deploration de sa ruine* &c. of 1558. See G. Dickinson, *Du Bellay in Rome*, Leyden 1960. See also David Lowenthal, *The Past is a Foreign Country*, Cambridge 1985, especially pp. 138–59.

25   See *The King's Good Servant. Sir Thomas More 1477/78–1535*, (Exhibition Catalogue), National Portrait Gallery 1977, p. 38.

26   On Busleyden see H. de Vocht, *Jérôme de Busleyden, Founder of the Louvain Collegium Trelinghie. His Life and Writings*, Turnhout 1950. On the style of contemporary bourgeois town architecture see the bewildering study by Henry Russell Hitchcock, *Netherlandish Scrolled Gables of the Sixteenth and Early Seventeenth Centuries*, New York 1978.

27   Alberti, IV, 5.

28   Amongst many contemporary panegyrics on More's character see especially Juan Luis Vivès' introduction to St Augustine's *City of God*, Basle 1522, p. 41.

29   The names are from the Greek and mean Northern, Airy, Eastern, Southern, Western and Glacial.

30 On Bonnivet, Chambord and Chantilly see Wolfram Prinz & Robert Kecks, *Das französisches Schloss der Renaissance*, Berlin 1985, pp. 553–9, 399–415 & 512–19. See also Jean-Pierre Babelon, *Châteaux de France au Siècle de la Renaissance*, Paris 1989.

31 See Charles Lenormant, *Rabelais et l'Architecture de la Renaissance. Restitution de l'Abbaye de Thélème*, Paris 1840.

32 See Carlos G. Norena, *Juan Luis Vivès*, The Hague 1970 and Alain Guy, *Vivès, ou l'Humanisme engagé*, Paris 1972.

33 See exhibition catalogue, *op. cit.* (note 29), p. 95.

34 See article by Freeman, *op. cit.* (note 8).

35 For a discussion of this tradition in planning for town houses in the case of one city see David Thomson, *Renaissance Paris*, London 1984. See also *La Maison de Ville à la Renaissance. Recherches sur l'habitat urbain en Europe au XVe et XVIe siècles*, (De Architectura, collection dirigée par André Chastel et Jean Guillaume), Paris 1983, for essays on plan types in various European towns and cities, see especially the contribution of Sylvia Pressouyre, 'L'image de la maison dans la littérature au XVIe siècle', pp. 117–34.

36 See Pressouyre, *op. cit.* (note 35), p. 126.

37 Spanish humanists such as Juan Luis Vivès, Diego Gracian and Antonio Guevara attacked the Amadis cycle and others in the genre, which they considered to be inferior, unclassical and unprofitable for the mind or soul. Churchmen often concurred about the effect the secular morality of Amadis would have on credulous readers, especially women. See John O'Connor, *Amadis de Gaule and its influence on Elizabethan Literature*, New Brunswick 1970, pp. 9–10.

38 See Henry Thomas, 'Amadis de Gaula, and its continuations', in *Transactions of the Bibliographical Society of London*, XI, 1912, pp. 251–84, and his *Spanish and Portuguese Romances of Chivalry*, Cambridge 1920.

39 On Francis I's literary tastes and policies of patronage and collecting see E. Quentin Bauchart, *La Bibliothèque de Fontainebleau 1515–1589*, Paris 1891. On the Palace of Apolidon see Gerhard Goebel, *Poeta faber. Erdichtete Architektur in der italienischen, spanischen und französischen Literatur der Renaissance und Barok*, (Beitrage zur neueren Literaturgeschichte, XIV) Heidelberg 1971, and André Chastel, *The Palace of Apolidon*, (The Zaharoff Lecture 1984–5) Oxford 1986, reprinted in his *Culture et Demeures en France au XVIe siècle*, Paris 1989, pp. 81–116. For a consummate thesis of real brilliance see Anne-Marie Lecoq, *François Ier Imaginaire. Symbolique et politique de la Renaissance française*, Paris 1987.

40 Joachim Du Bellay, *Ode au Seigneur des Essarts sur le discours de son Amadis*, written about 1548. François De La Noue, *Discours politiques et militaires*, Basle 1587, pp. 164–6.

41 On some affinities between Chambord and Thélème see W. Metternich, *Schloss Chambord an der Loire*, Darmstadt 1985, pp. 1–6.

42 See the magisterial study by Anne-Marie Lecoq, *op. cit.* (note 39).

43 See O'Connor, *op. cit.* (note 37), pp. 13–14 and chapters IX, for the influence of Amadis on Spenser and X, for the use made of it by Sydney.

44 See Ruth Putnam, *California, the name*, (University of California Publications in History, IV, no. 4) 1917, pp. 293–365.

45 Quoted by Chastel, *op. cit.* (note 39), p. 9.

46 See Jean Guillaume & Rafael Moreira, 'Le premier description de Chambord', in *Revue de l'Art*, 79, 1988, pp. 83–5.

47 See Mary Patchell, *The Palmerin Romances in Elizabethan Prose Fiction*, New York 1947, reprinted 1966, and E. Asensio, 'El Palmerin de Inglaterra, conjecturas y certezas', in *Estudios Portuguêses*, 1974, pp. 445–53.

48 Francis I probably spent fewer than fourteen nights at Chambord in his whole reign. His itinerary can be plotted from *Catalogue des actes de François 1er*, 10 vols, Paris 1887–1910.

49 On the dilapidation of Chambord during the second half of the sixteenth century and the early seventeenth century see Jean Martin-Demezil, 'Chambord', in *Congrès Archéologique de France, Blésois et Vendomois*, Société française d'archéologie, 189e Session, 1981, Paris 1986, pp. 1–115.

50 See J.W. Jolliffe & D.E. Rhodes, 'Some Sixteenth Century Books with Turin Imprints', in *Gutenberg Jahrbuch*, 1962, pp. 251–93, and E. Droz, 'Fausses adresses typographiques', in *Bibliothèque d'Humanisme et Renaissance*, T. XXIII, 1961, especially p. 292.

51 E. Droz, *La Veuve Berton et Jean Portau 1573–1589, L'Imprimerie à La Rochelle*, 3, (Travaux d'Humanisme et Renaissance XXXIV), Geneva 1960, pp. 23–30.

52 On Marguerite de France see the biographies by R. Peyre, Paris 1902, and W. Stephens, London 1912.

53 See Etienne Jodelle. *Oeuvres complètes*, edited by Enea Balmas, 2 vols., Paris 1965 & 1968, especially vol. 1, pp. 99–102, 163–85. Ronsard published his lengthy *Tombeau de Marguerite de France* in 1575.

54 On the techniques of embalming practised during the Middle Ages see Alain Erlande-Brandenburg, *Le Roi est mort*, Paris 1975, pp. 27–31.

55 See Michael Greenhalgh, 'A Paduan Medal of Queen Artemesia of Caria', in *Numismatic Chronicle*, Vol. XII, 1972, pp. 295–303.

56 Libanius of Antioch, *liban* according to 'Er', AD 314–93. His numerous surviving writings include a life of Demosthenes and synopses of his orations. He is credited as founder of a school of rhetoric at Constantinople. See also Howard Colvin, *Architecture and the After-Life*, New Haven & London 1991, p. 323, note, where the *maison de liban* is identified as Diocletian's palace at Antioch.

57 See Vittore Branca, 'Ermolao Barbaro and late Quattrocento Humanism', in *Renaissance Venice*, edited by John R. Hale, London 1973, pp. 218–43.

58 W.G. Hoskins, *The Age of Plunder. The England of Henry VIII 1500–1547*, London 1976.

59 See T.C. Izard, *George Whetstone, mid-Elizabethan gentleman of letters*, (Columbia University Studies in English and Comparative Literature), New York 1942.

60 'Segnior Phyloxenus' apparently means Giraldi Cinthio, whose *Hecatommithi* was the basis for many of the stories in Whetstone's *Heptameron*. The real Philoxenus (436–380 BC) was a dithyrambic poet of whose works only a fragment survives. Giambattista Giraldi called *il Cinthio* (1504–73) was a dramatist, chiefly remembered for his *Ecatommiti* (the hundred stories), which Shakespeare made use of for the plots of *Othello* and *Measure for Measure*.

61 Quoted by Chastel, *op. cit.* (note 39), p. 9, note 8.

Notes to chapter 3

After this text was finalised, *The Renaissance in National Context*, edited by Roy Porter and Mikulas Teich, Cambridge 1992 was published. The eleven essays in this book are little concerned with luxury or architecture, but all have a considerable bearing on the issues raised in this chapter. It is to be highly recommended to any reader of these pages.

1 Vitruvius, VII, 5.

2   See Nicole Dacos, *La Découverte de la Domus Aurea et la formation des grotesques de la Renaissance*, Leyden 1969, and on a parallel theme for northern Europe of the sixteenth century the dull but useful work of Sune Scele, *Cornelis Bos. A Study of the Origins of the Netherland Grotesque*, Stockholm 1965.

3   George Hersey, *The Lost Meaning of Classical Architecture*, Cambridge (Mass.) 1988, p. 3.

4   See Carol Herselle Krinsky, 'Seventy-Eight Vitruvius Manuscripts', in *Journal of the Warburg and Courtauld Institutes*, 1967, pp. 36–70, Joseph Rykwert, 'On the Oral Transmission of Architectural Theory', in *Les Traités d'Architecture de la Renaissance*, (Collection De Architectura) ed. Jean Guillaume, Paris 1988, pp. 31–48, especially p. 34 note 17.

5   See Rykwert, *op. cit.* (note 4), p. 44.

6   On the discovery of Vitruvius see *Architectural Theory and Practice from Alberti to Ledoux*, ed. Dora Wiebenson, Chicago 1982, unpaginated section I.

7   For Portuguese examples see Robert Smith, *The Art of Portugal, 1500–1800*, New York 1968 p. 82, George Kubler, *Portuguese Plain Architecture. Between Spices and Diamonds 1521–1706*, Middletown (Connecticut) 1972. For Spain see 'The Image of Roman Architecture in Renaissance Spain', in *Gazette des Beaux Arts*, Vol. 52, 1958, pp. 329–46, especially p. 343 note 1. For France see Catherine Grodecki, *Documents du Minutier Central des Notaires de Paris. Histoire de l'Art (1540–1600)*, 2 t, Paris 1985–86. For the Low Countries see I. Vandevivere, *Renaissance Art in Belgium*, Brussels 1973, pp. 18, 22 & 31. For England see Maurice Howard, *The Early Tudor Country House. Architecture and Politics 1490–1550*, London 1987, especially chapter 6.

8   For example Ambrosio de Morales, *Las Antiguedas de las ciudades de Espana*, 1575, p. 2.

9   See Johan Huizinga, *Men and Ideas*, London 1960, especially the chapter 'Patriotism and Nationalism in European History', pp. 97–155. Unfortunately he gives no reference for the earliest appearance of the words. See also Anthony D. Smith, *National Identity*, London 1991. 'Nationalism' as portrayed by E.D. Marcu in her *Sixteenth Century Nationalism*, New York 1976, has been queried by John Breuilly, *Nationalism and the State*, Manchester 1982, pp. 6–7. For an incisive discussion of nationalism shorn of ideologies see David Lowenthal, *The Past is a Foreign Country*, Cambridge 1985, pp. 332–7 & 393–4.

10   See Cecil Grayson, *A Renaissance Controversy, Latin or Italian?* Oxford 1960 and Françoise Choay, *Le Règle et le modèle*, Paris 1980.

11   See Paul Oskar Kristeller, *Renaissance Thought and the Arts*, Princeton 1980, pp. 70–1.

12   On the these debates see Robert A. Hall, *The Italian Questione della Lingua. An interpretative essay.* (Studies in the Romance languages and literatures, no. 4.) Chapel Hill 1942, and Maurizio Vitale, *La Questione della Lingua*, Milan 1960.

13   See E.D. Marcu, *Sixteenth Century Nationalism*, New York 1976, p. 25, and J.H. Parry, *The Spanish Theory of Empire in the Sixteenth Century*, Cambridge 1940.

14   See Lionello Puppi, *Scrittori Vicentini d'Architettura del Secolo XVI*, Vicenza 1973, pp. 79–86.

15   See Wallace K. Ferguson, *The Renaissance in Historical Thought. Five Centuries of Interpretation*, New York 1940, p. 14. More recently for the situation in France see Donald R. Kelley, *Foundations of Modern Historical Scholarship. Language, Law and History in the French Renaissance*, New York 1970.

16   Pierre Villey, *Les Sources italiennes de la Deffence et Illustration de la Langue Francoyse de Joachim Du Bellay*, Paris 1908.

17 *Deffence et Illustration* &c., I, 11. See also Margaret Ferguson, 'The exile's defence. Du Bellay's La Deffence et illustration de la langue francoyse', in *Publications of the Modern Language Association*, 93, 1978, pp. 275–89.

18 See G.P. Norton, 'Translation theory in Renaissance France. Etienne Dolet and the rhetorical tradition', in *Renaissance and Reformation*, X, 1974, pp. 1–93, and *idem*, 'Translation theory in Renaissance France. The poetic controversy', in ibid, XI, 1975, pp. 30–44.

19 Translated by Terence Cave, *The Cornucopian Text. Problems of Writing in the French Renaissance*, Oxford 1979, p. 336. See also Thomas M. Greene, *The Light in Troy. Imitation and Discovery in Renaissance Poetry*, New Haven 1987, and G.C. Fiske, *Luclius and Horace. A Study in the Classical Theory of Imitation*, Madison 1920. For literary sources for painters see Ernst Gombrich, 'The Style "all'antica", Imitation and Assimilation', in *Norm and Form. Studies in the Art of the Renaissance*, London 1966, pp. 122–8.

20 On late sixteenth-century nationalism and xenophobia in England see E.D. Marcu, *op. cit.* (note 13), pp. 73–85. Also W.S. Maltby, *The Black Legend in England*, Durham, NC, 1971 and P.W. Powell, *The Tree of Hate*, New York 1971.

21 This is not strictly true. See Hugh Plommer, *Vitruvius and later Roman building Manuals*, Cambridge 1973.

22 The most important of the annotators was Guillaume Philander. See Dora Wiebenson, 'Guillaume Philander's Annotations to Vitruvius', in *Les Traités* &c. *op. cit.* (note 4), pp. 67–74.

23 See Carol Herselle Krinsky, 'Cesariano and the Renaissance without Rome', in *Arte lombarda*, 1971, pp. 211–18.

24 On the social, political and cultural milieu of Milan of the 1500s and 1510s see *Storia di Milano*, Milan, Fondazione Treccani Degli Alfieri, Vol. VIII.

25 See James S. Ackermann, 'The Certosa of Pavia and the Renaissance in Milan', in *Marsyas*, V, 1947/49, pp. 23–34.

26 See E.S. de Beer, 'Gothic. Origin and Diffusion of the term; The Idea of Style in Architecture', in *Journal of the Warburg and Courtauld Institutes*, 1948, pp. 143–62. Also Paul Frankl, *The Gothic*, Princeton 1960 and Erwin Panofsky, 'The First Page of Giorgio Vasari's "Libro". A Study on the Gothic Style in the Judgement of the Italian Renaissance &c.' in his *Meaning in the Visual Arts*, London 1970, pp. 206–65.

27 I am grateful to Professor John Onians for this translation.

28 See John White, *Art and Architecture in Italy 1250–1400*, Harmondsworth 1966, pp. 336–50.

29 Eulogistic descriptions of Milan abound. See especially the earliest, written about 1288 by Bonvesin della Riva, discussed by J.K. Hyde, 'Medieval Descriptions of Cities', in *Bulletin of the John Rylands Library*, 1965/66, pp. 308–40.

30 Quoted by E.S. de Beer, *op. cit.* (note 26), p. 147, and by Erwin Panofsky, *op. cit.* (note 26), p. 214. See also T.S.R. Boase, *Vasari the Man and his Book*, Princeton 1979, especially chapter IV, 'The Maniera Tedesca', pp. 93–118.

31 See Jan Bialostocki, *Dürer and his Critics, 1500–1971. Chapters in the History of Ideas.* Baden-Baden 1986, pp. 37–52.

32 Quoted by Paul Frankl, *op. cit.* (note 26), p. 249.

33 Etienne Dolet, *Commentarii linguae latinae*, Vol. 2, Lyon 1538, cols. 1156–7; J. Peletier du Mans, *L'Arithmetique*, 3rd edn, Geneva 1607, p. 7; Henri Estienne, *Henricus Stephanus II Francofordiense Emporium . . . Anno 1574*, Amsterdam 1574.

34 See Heinrich Rottinger, *Die Holzschnitte zur Architektur und zum Vitruvius Teutsch des Walther Rivius*, Strassburg 1914.

35   See George Hersey, *op. cit.* (note 3), p. 119.

36   His book was finally translated by Miguel de Urrea, Alcala 1582.

37   See Earl Rosenthal, *op. cit.* (note 7), p. 334.

38   See Nigel Llewellyn, 'Diego de Sagredo and the Renaissance in Italy', in *Les Traités* &c., *op. cit.* (note 4), pp. 295–306.

39   In the British Library. Republished by the Sociedad de Bibliofilos Espanoles, Madrid 1898.

40   Villalon, *op. cit.*, p. 163.

41   The Latin reads : Hic Te Admonendum Lector Putavimus, Quod Ante Hanc Nostram Impressionem, Quidam Sebastianus Serlius Bononsiensis Inter Multorum Locorum Antiquitates, Quarum Volumen Ab Se Compositum Dedit. Veronensium Etiam Monumentorum Aliquot Se Antiquarium Professus Est, Quae, Quia Ipse Non Vidit, Imprudenter Fortasse Ab Alterius Incuria Sumpta, Aut Non Recte Designavit, Aut Non Cognita Subticuit. Atquae Ideo, Si Quid Erit Hoc Nostro In Libro Compertum Ab Eo Discrepans. Scias In hisce Nostris Expressa Esse, Quae vera sunt, & Germana, Quemadmodum Vel Incola Veronae Certior Fieri Potes, Vel Peregrinus, Si Tibi Quandoque Visuro Veronenses Antiquitates Adire Contigerit. Bene Vale.

42   See John Bury, 'Renaissance Architectural Treatises and Architectural Books, a Bibliography', in *Les Traités* &c.*op. cit.* (note 4), pp. 485–503, especially pp. 499–500.

43   See M.N. Rosenfeld, *Sebastiano Serlio On Domestic Architecture*, Cambridge (Mass.) 1978 for the earlier version of the manuscript, now in the Avery Library, Columbia University, New York. For the later version in the Bayerische Staatsbibliothek, Munich, see Marco Rosci, *Il Trattato di Architettura di Sebastiano Serlio*, 2 vols, Milan 1967.

44   This writer believes some French translations of Serlio's inscriptions in the Avery Library manuscript to be in du Cerceau's hand. This view is not accepted by others. See Myra Nan Rosenfeld, 'From Drawn to Printed Model Book. Jacques Androuet du Cerceau and the Transmission of Ideas from Designer to Patron, Master Mason and Architect in the Renaissance', in *Revue d'art canadienne/ Canadian Art Review* (RACAR), XVI, 2, 1989, pp. 131–45, especially p. 143 note 89. Time will tell. I am very grateful to Dr. Rosenfeld for a copy of her essay.

45   Du Cerceau's pastiche is based on Serlio's designs for the chateau of Ancy-le-Franc in Burgundy. See Jean Guillaume, 'Serlio, est-il l'architecte d'Ancy-le-Franc', in *Revue de l'Art*, 1969, no. 5, pp. 9–18. See also David Thomson, *Jacques Androuet du Cerceau. Les Plus Excellents Bâtiments de France*, Paris 1988, pp. 142–7, and Jean-Pierre Babelon, *Châteaux de France au siècle de la Renaissance*, Paris 1989, pp. 384–93.

46   It was his eldest son Baptiste who is documented as the first practising architect of the dynasty. See David Thomson, 'Baptiste Androuet du Cerceau, architecte d'Henri III', in *Bulletin Monumental* 1990, pp. 47–81.

47   See Madeleine van de Winkel, 'Hans Vriedeman de Vries', in *Les Traités* &c., *op. cit.* (note 4), pp. 453–8.

48   On Coecke van Aelst see Johannes Offerhaus, 'Pieter Coecke van Aelst et l'introduction des traités d'architecture dans les pays-bas', in *Les Traités* &c., *op. cit.* (note 4), pp. 443–52.

49   Philippe de Béthune, *Le Conseiller d'Estat*, Paris 1633, quoted by Jean-Pierre Babelon, *Demeures parisiennes sous Henri IV et Louis XIII*, Paris 1965, p. 23.

50   See Jean Guillaume, 'Philibert de l'Orme, un traité different', in *Les Traités* &c., *op. cit.* (note 4), pp. 347–54.

51   Guillaume *op. cit.* (note 50), p. 348.

52   Jean-Marie Pérouse de Monclos, *L'Architecture à la française. XVIe, XVIIe et XVIIIe siècles*, Paris 1982.

53 See Howard Burns, in *Andrea Palladio 1508–1580. The Portico to the Farmyard.* (Exhibition catalogue), Hayward Gallery, London 1975, p. 219.

54 See Earl Rosenthal, 'The Diffusion of the Italian Renaissance Style in Western European Art', in *Sixteenth Century Journal*, 1978, pp. 33–45. On Andrea Sansovino in Portugal see Janez Höfler, 'New Light on Andrea Sansovino's Journey to Portugal', in *Burlington Magazine*, April 1992, pp. 234–7.

55 On Chambord see the magisterial study by Jean Martin-Demezil, 'Chambord', in *Congrès Archéologique de France, Blésois et Vendomois*, (Société française d'archéologie), 189e session 1981, Paris 1986, pp. 1–115. On the Emperor Charles V's Alhambra palace see Earl Rosenthal, *The Palace of Charles V in Granada*, Princeton 1985. For Nonsuch see Martin Biddle, 'The stuccoes of Nonsuch', in *Burlington Magazine*, 1984, pp. 411–16. On the Louvre see *Jacques Androuet du Cerceau : Les plus excellents Bastiments de France*, facsimile of Destailleur edition, introduction and historical notices by David Thomson, Paris 1988. On the Escorial see George Kubler, *Building the Escorial*, Princeton 1982, as well as Catherine Wilkinson, 'Planning a style for the Escorial. An architectural treatise for Philip of Spain', in *Journal of the Society of Architectural Historians*, 1985, pp. 37–47.

56 See Kubler, *op. cit.* (note 55), p. 16 & p. 44. for Philip II's interest in Chambord.

57 See Rosenthal, *op. cit.* (note 55), p. 52. Charles V is known to have commissioned or encouraged Jacques du Broeucq's designs for a pentagonal villa or palace in or near to Brussels in 1553 or 1554. See Robert Wellens, *Jacques du Broeucq. Sculpteur et Architecte de la Renaissance (1505-1584)* Brussels 1962, p. 134 (with no references) and the du Broeucq 'Receuil d'Etudes' published by Europalia, Mons 1985, p. 27, again with no references to the sources.

58 See Martin Biddle, *op. cit.* (note 55).

59 See David Thomson on Pierre Lescot *op. cit.* (note 55), pp. 27–31.

60 Quoted in full by Catherine Wilkinson, *op. cit.* (note 55), p. 43, note 31.

61 Quoted by John Onians, 'Brunelleschi, Humanist or Nationalist?', in *Art History*, 1982, pp. 259–73, especially p. 262 & p. 268.

62 Rudolf Wittkower's *Architectural Principles of the Age of Humanism*, London 1962 remains the touchstone for most later arguments about architecture's relations with humanism in its many guises. See also Augusto Campana, 'The Origin of the Word Humanist', in *Journal of the Warburg and Courtauld Institutes*, 1946, pp. 60–73, and most recently John Stephens, *The Italian Renaissance. The Origins of Intellectual and Artistic Change before the Reformation*, London 1990, pp. 15–36.

63 Central and eastern Europe, despite strenuous efforts there and here, has proved impossible to integrate into this study. The first foyer of Italian Renaissance art and design undiluted was the Hungarian court of Matthias Corvinus. The best general survey is Jan Bialostocki, *The Art of the Renaissance in Eastern Europe*, Oxford 1976. See also *Matthias Corvinus und die Renaissance in Ungarn*, (Exhibition Catalogue), Schallaburg, Austria 1982. For Poland see *Polen im Zeitalter der Jagiellonen 1386–1572*, (Exhibition Catalogue) Schallaburg, Austria 1986. For Bohemia and Moravia see Jirina Horejsi *et al, Renaissance Art in Bohemia*, London & New York 1979, and *Dejiny Ceskeho Vytvarneho Umeni*, II/i, (edited by Jiri Dvorsky and others), Academia Editions, Prague 1989. Magisterial studies of relevance are R.J.W. Evans, *Rudolf II and His World. A Study in Intellectual History, 1576-1612*, Oxford 1984, and Thomas da Costa Kaufmann, *The School of Prague, Painting at the Court of Rudolf II*, Chicago & London 1988. For bibliographical references to all Rudolphine artists and architects, the reader should consult the same author's *Art and Architecture in Central Europe 1550-1620, an annotated bibliography*, Boston

1988. See also *The Stylish Image, Printmakers to the Court of Rudolf II*, (Exhibition Catalogue, National Gallery of Scotland), Edinburgh 1991. The issue of Tuscan architectural imports in eastern Europe is addressed by Adam Milobedski, 'Architecture under the Last Jagiellons in its Political and Social Context', in *The Polish Renaissance in its European Context*, Bloomington and Indianapolis 1988, pp. 291–300. This article is invaluable for its bibliography. Professor Milobedski's first sentence is crucial. 'Pure Renaissance architecture in its Tuscan version was adopted by only two European countries: Hungary and then Poland. 'Of further significance is his observation on page 292 that '... buildings of stone and brick were extremely few as compared to those of wood: around the year 1500, only about 0.4 per cent of city and village construction was in masonry'.

64   See Pedro Dias, *A arquitectura de Coimbra na transição do gótico para a renascença*, Coimbra 1982, and Robert C. Smith, *The Art of Portugal, 1500–1800*, New York 1968, pp. 157–9.

65   For England and the colonies of Italians, French and Flemings see Mark Girouard, 'Some Alien Craftsmen in Sixteenth and Seventeenth Century England', in *Proceedings* of the Huguenot Society of London, 1966, pp. 26–35.

66   See J.W. Burgon, *The Life and Times of Sir Thomas Gresham*, 2 vols, London 1839, I, p. 115.

67   A precedent had been set at Somerset House on the Strand, for which £41 5s was spent on 'marble pyllers bought in Fflaunders'. See Maurice Howard, *The Early Tudor Country House, Architecture and Politics 1490–1550*, London 1987, p. 194.

68   See Robert Wilkinson, *Londina Illustrata*, Vol. II, London 1825, p. 13.

69   See also J.G. White, *History of the Three Exchanges, The Gresham Lectures and Gresham Almshouses*, London 1896. Gresham's Exchange cannot have been too dilapidated, for it survived fully operational up to the Great Fire in 1666.

Notes to chapter 4

1   Bracciolini quoted in Quentin Skinner, *The Foundations of Modern Political Thought*, 2 vols, Cambridge 1978, vol. 1, p. 174. On Poggio Bracciolini see E. Walser, *Poggio Bracciolini's Leben und Werke*, (Beitrage zur Kunstgeschichte des Mittelalters und Renaissance, *Bd.* 14), Berlin 1914. See also Lauro Martines, *The Social World of Florentine Humanists 1390–1460*, London 1963. For a contemporary socio-economic analysis of wealth outside the period considered here see George Golder, *Wealth and Poverty*, London 1982, especially chapter 5, 'The Nature of Wealth', pp. 54–69.

2   See Brian Tierney, *Medieval Poor Law. A sketch of canonical theory and its application in England*, Berkeley 1959.

3   *Della Famiglia*, edited by F.C. Pellegrini & P. Spognano, Florence 1946, pp. 153–4, 210 & 330–2.

4   Giulio Bistort, *Il Lusso nelle vita e nelle legge. Il magistrato alle pompe nella Republica di Venezia*, Venice 1912, reprinted Bologna 1969. A very useful bibliography of literature on sumptuary law is provided by N.B. Harte, 'State Control of Dress and Social Change in Pre-Industrial England', in *Trade, Government and Economy in Pre-Industrial England*, edited by D.C. Coleman & A.H. John, London 1976, p. 157 notes 5–8. See also Rosita Levi Pisetzky, *Storia del Costume in Italia*, Milan 1964, vol. III, p. 280, for bibliography. A magisterial account of the subject for the whole of the Italian peninsula is Diane Owen Hughes,

'Sumptuary Law and Social Relations in Renaissance Italy', in *Dispute and Settlements*, edited by John Bossy, Cambridge 1983, pp. 69–99.

5   Bistort, *op. cit.* (note 4), pp. 240–1 and Sanuto, *Diarii*, XIV, pp. 114–17.

6   See Felix Gilbert, 'Venice in the Crisis of the League of Cambrai', in *Renaissance Venice*, edited by John Hale, London 1973, pp. 274–92, especially p. 279.

7   See Diana Owen Hughes, 'Ear Rings, Jews and Franciscan Rhetoric', in *Past and Present*, 1986, pp. 3–59, especially p. 25. On the Tower of Babel as a symbol of luxury and folly in painting, see the poor but well-illustrated book by Giovanna Massobrio & Paolo Portoghesi, *L'immaginario architettonico nella pittura*, Rome-Bari 1988, pp. 53–81.

8   *De bene instituta Re publica*, reprinted Milan 1969, p. 98. See also Gaetano Cozzi, 'Domenico Morosoni e il De bene instituta Re publica', in *Studi Veneziani*, 12, 1970, pp. 405–58.

9   See Gilbert, *op. cit.* (note 6), p. 277. See also Peter Thornton, *The Italian Renaissance Interior 1400–1600*, London 1991.

10   See Loredana Olivato & Lionello Puppi, *Mauro Codussi*, Milan 1977, p. 241, and John Onians, *Bearers of Meaning*, Princeton 1988, p. 128.

11   See Giancarlo Roversi, *Palazzi e Case Nobili del '500 a Bologna*, Bologna 1986, pp. 47–57.

12   See Enrica Benini, 'Alessandro Caravia, gioielliere dei Medici a Venezia', in *Quaderni di Teatro. Rivista trimestrale del Teatro Toscano*, Anno II, 1980, no. 7, pp. 177–94.

13   Benini, *op. cit.* (note 12), p. 178.

14   Benini, *op. cit.* (note 12), pp. 179–180. Amongst philosophers who consider the supernatural powers of jewels Benini mentions Marsilio Ficino, Pietro d'Abano and Thomas Aquinas. See Yvonne Hackenbroch, *Renaissance Jewellery*, London-Munich 1979.

15   Benini, *op. cit.* (note 12), pp. 192–4, and Manfredo Tafuri, *Venezia e il Rinascimento*, Turin 1985, pp. 125–49.

16   Tafuri, *op. cit.* (note 13), pp. 3–5.

17   See Antonio Foscari & Manfredo Tafuri, *L'Armonia e i Conflitti. La Chiesa di San Francesco della Vigna nella Venezia del '500*, Turin 1983, pp. 24–9.

18   See Steven Ozment, *When Fathers Ruled. Family Life in Reformation Europe*, Cambridge (Mass.) 1983, and David Herlihy, *Medieval Households*, Cambridge (Mass.) 1985.

19   See *Age of Chivalry, Art in Plantagenet England 1200–1400*. Exhibition catalogue edited by Jonathon Alexander and Paul Binski, Royal Academy of Arts, London 1987, p. 36 & 354.

20   On Felice Brancacci's career see Anthony Molho, 'The Brancacci Chapel, Studies in its Iconography and History', in *Journal of the Warburg and Courtauld Institutes*, Vol. 40, 1977, pp. 50–99.

21   See Elena Bassi, *Palazzi di Venezia*, Venice 1976, pp. 140–5 for the Palazzo Coccina. Approximately twenty years later Niccolò Balbi had his portrait painted with his new palace on the Grand Canal in the background. See Elena Bassi, *Tre palazzi veneziani della Ragione Veneto : Balbi, Flangini-Morosini, Molin*, Venice 1982, p. 61.

22   This is a quotation from Edward Gibbon, the reference for which I have mislaid.

23   For England see Lawrence Stone, *The Crisis of the Aristocracy 1558–1641*, Oxford 1965, Chapter X on 'Conspicuous Expenditure'. For France with an up to date bibliography see Kristen B. Neuschel, 'Noble Households in the Sixteenth Century. Material Settings and Human Communities', in *French Historical Studies*, Vol. XV, 1988, pp. 595–622.

24   See the review of Peter Partner, *Renaissance Rome. A Portrait of a Society 1500–1559*, Berkeley 1977, by André Chastel, in *Journal of the Society of Architectural Historians*, 1978, pp. 202–4.

25   See Richard Goldthwaite, *The Building of Renaissance Florence. An Economic and Social History*, Baltimore 1980, p. 4, and Giovanni Fanelli, *Firenze, architettura e città*, Florence 1973, p. 29.

26   On Bologna's towers see G. Rivani, *Le Torri di Bologna*, Bologna 1966. Writing in the last quarter of the fifteenth century the humanist and man of action Giovano Pontano (1422–1503) commented that private towers '. . . seem to show that it was thought praiseworthy for the most prominent citizens to raise square towers by which they could compete with each other in loftiness'. Pontanus, 'De Magnificentia', in *Opera*, vol. 1, Venice 1518, fol. 128 verso. See also Naomi Miller, *Renaissance Bologna, A Study in Architectural Form and Content*, (University of Kansas Humanistic Studies, Vol. 56), New York &c. 1989, pp. 26–33. At least 170 towers were packed closely together when Dante was a student in Bologna between 1304 and 1306, but it was the leaning Garisenda, which riveted his attention.

27   Alberti, VIII, 5, from the translation by Joseph Rykwert, Neil Leach & Robert Tavernor, Cambridge (Mass.) 1988, p. 257.

28   See Bruno Tollon, 'Toulouse', in *La Maison de Ville à la Renaissance*, (Collection De Architectura, edited by André Chastel and Jean Guillaume) Paris 1983, pp. 51–8, especially p. 54.

29   See *Bouwen door de eeuwen heen. Inventaris van het cultuurbezit in Belgie. Architectuur.* Deel 9n. *Stad Mechelen.* (Ministerie van de Vlaamse Gemeenschap), Ghent 1984, pp. 101–4. The authors date the building of the major components of the house to 1503–8. My claim that London's secular towers were inspired by Antwerp is based on careful scrutiny of a woodcut bird's-eye view of Antwerp of 1565. The only surviving copy is in the Plantin-Moretus Museum, Antwerp. It is reproduced in facsimile as a pull-out for Leon Voet, *Antwerp, The Golden Age. The Rise and Glory of the Metropolis in the Sixteenth Century*, Antwerp 1973. On the close economic relations of Antwerp with London see R.D. Ramsey, *The City of London in International Politics at the Accession of Elizabeth Tudor*, Manchester 1975, especially chapter 1, 'Antwerp : the metropolis at its zenith', pp. 1–32. See also Ralph Davis, 'The Rise of Antwerp and its English Connection 1406–1510', in *Trade, Government and Economy in Pre-Industrial England*, D.C. Coleman & A.H. John (eds), London 1976, pp. 2–20.

30   See M. Van De Winckel, 'Hans Vriedeman de Vries', in *Les Traités d'Architecture de la Renaissance*, (Collection De Architectura, edited by Jean Guillaume), Paris 1988, pp. 453–8.

31   See Deborah Howard, *Jacopo Sansovino. Architecture and Patronage in Renaissance Venice*, New Haven-London 1975, pp. 28–35.

32   There are an infinity of literary imaginings of the stairway to heaven throughout the Middle Ages and the Renaissance. See Howard Hibbard, *Poussin, The Holy Family on the Steps*, London 1974, pp. 89–90.

33   See Lazlo Tarr, *The History of the Carriage*, London 1969, pp. 191–215.

34   '. . . uscir si adegnano Di casa a piedi, ne passar pur vogliono La strada, se non hanno al cullo il dondolo Della carretta, e le carrette vogliono Tutte dorate e che di drappi sieno Coperte e gran corsieri che le tirino.'

35   For Rome see Wolfgang Lotz, 'Gli 883 cochi di Roma del 1594', in *Miscellanea della Società Romana di Storia Patria*, (Studi offerti a Giovanni Incisa della Rochetta), Rome 1973, pp. 247–66. See also Patricia Waddy, *Seventeenth Century Roman Palaces, Use and Art of the Plan*, New York 1991, chapter 7, on coaches, pp. 61–6. For Paris see my *Renaissance Paris. Architecture and Growth 1475–1600*, London 1984, pp. 163–4.

36   Juan Costa (1550–97) in his *Govierno del cuidadano, trata de como se ha de regir*

a si, su casa, y republica, Saragossa 1584. Quoted by Claude Chauchadis, *Honneur, Morale et Société dans l'Espagne de Philippe II*, Paris 1984, p. 133 and note 116 for further references to Spanish texts on coaches.

37   See J.F. Orbaan, *Sistine Rome*, Rome 1910, p. 14.

38   See André Chastel, *The Sack of Rome*, Princeton 1983, pp. 49–90.

39   Plate 17 in Jacques Besson, *Livre premier des Instruments Mathématiques et Méchaniques* &c. Orléans 1569, reprinted at Lyon 1578.

40   See the introduction and notes by Claude Mignot in a reprint of Le Muet, Paris 1981. Surprisingly there is no discussion of integrated stabling and housing for coaches in Michael Dennis, *Court and Garden. From the French Hôtel to the City of Modern Architecture*, Cambridge (Mass.) 1986.

41   Although it dates from slightly later than the period on which this book focuses, my favourite example of this type of tract is by the eccentric 'Water Poet' John Taylor. His *The Worlde Runnes on Wheeles or Oddes betwixt Carts and Coaches* was printed in London in 1623. His lurid imagination saw the only motive for curtains in coaches as screens for fornication. He may have been right.

42   Alberti VIII, 2, 3 on sepulchres.

43   Robert de Bourne of Lincolnshire. Quoted by T.A. Heslop in *Age of Chivalry, op. cit.* (note 18). For the full text see Early English Texts, Vol. 119, Old Series, London 1901. De Bourne says that he has translated his essay into the vernacular for the common man.

44   See Kathryn B. Hiesinger, 'The Fregoso Monument. A Study in Sixteenth Century Tomb Monuments and Catholic Reform', in *Burlington Magazine*, 1976, pp. 283–93. An early and influential treatise on episcopal reform was Gasparo Contarini, *De officio episcopi* &c. of 1516. The role of images, monuments and the subject of the furnishing of churches in post-Tridentine Italy is studied in some depth by Marcia B. Hall, *Renovation and Counter-Reformation. Vasari and Duke Cosimo in Sta. Maria Novella and Sta. Croce, 1565–1577*, Oxford 1979. See also Howard Colvin, *Architecture and the After-Life*, New Haven & London 1991, chapter XI, 'Triumphal Tombs and the Counter-Reformation', pp. 217–30. On the subject of Carlo Borromeo and architectural reform see Sandro Benedetti, *Fuori dal Classicismo. Sintetismo, Tipologia, Ragione nell'architettura del Cinquecento*, Rome 1984, especially 'Praticità e Normativà razionale nel Trattato di Carlo Borromeo', pp. 105–31.

45   Hiesinger, *op. cit.* (note 44), pp. 284–7.

46   See Nigel Llewellyn, 'The Royal Body. Monuments to the Dead, for the Living', in *Renaissance Bodies*, edited by Lucy Gent and Nigel Llewellyn, London 1990, pp. 218–40.

47   This is especially true of Venice as attested by the large number of busts commissioned by Procurators of Saint Mark's for personal commemoration in the destroyed church of San Gemignano at the far end of the Piazza San Marco from the basilica, many of which are now in the Cà d'Oro. They were placed discreetly above head height. Regrettably, the only engraving from Coronelli (1708–9) of the interior of San Gimignano before its destruction shows the location of just one bust. See John McAndrew, *Venetian Architecture of the Early Renaissance*, Cambridge (Mass.) 1980, p. 540.

48   The term was coined by W.G. Hoskins in his book on *The England of Henry VIII 1500–1547*, London 1976. See especially the preface.

49   Aztec heads first appeared in the capitals of the arcades of the Bishop's palace at Liège *c.*1510–15. See *Le Patrimoine Monumentale de la Belgique. Province de Liège. Arrond. de Liège, Ville de Liège*, Vol. 3. (Ministère de la Culture française.) Liège 1974, pp. 326–31, and S. Collon-Gevaert, 'Le palais des princes-évêques à Liège et la Renaissance française', in *Bulletin de la Société de l'Art et d'Histoire*, 39, 1955, pp. 53–83. By the

middle of the century the import of Central American pillage can be traced as decorative exotica across western Europe. See F. Anders & D. Heikamp, 'Mexikanische Altertümer aus suddeutschen Kunstkammern', in *Pantheon*, XXVIII, 1970, pp. 205–20, and Jean-Jacques Gloton, 'Les cheminées du château de Lourmarin', in *Archives de l'Art français*, t XXV, 1978, pp. 136–45.

50   See John Onians, *op. cit.* (note 10), p. 22 & 38.

51   Alexander Denton seems to have had an uneventful life. He held no known office of state, and his name is not associated with any social, political or military event of the times. For his will see PCC 29, Langley, 1577 = Prob. II /60/ 227r–228v. I am very grateful to Dr Nigel Llewellyn for this reference.

52   See Nigel Llewellyn, *The Art of Death. Visual Culture in the English Death Ritual c.1500–c.1800*, London 1991, p. 123.

53   Quotation from J.F. Hayward, *Virtuoso Goldsmiths and the Triumph of Mannerism*, London 1979, p. 32.

54   J.F. Hayward, *op. cit.* (note 53), pp. 34–5.

55   J.F. Hayward, *op. cit.* (note 53), p. 45. See also Peter Thornton, *The Italian Renaissance Interior 1400–1600*, London 1991.

56   Andrew Wallace-Hadrill, 'The Social Structure of the Roman House', in *Papers of the British School at Rome*, 1988, pp. 43–97, especially p. 58.

57   See Albert O. Hirschman, *The Passions and the Interests. Political Arguments for Capitalism before its Triumph*, Princeton 1977, pp. 12–14.

58   Hirschman, *op. cit.* (note 57), p. 33.

59   See M. Bogucka, 'Les bourgeois et les investissements culturels. L'example de Gdansk', in *Revue historique*, vol. 259, 1978, pp. 429–40.

60   See George Huppert, *Les Bourgeois Gentilhommes. An Essay in the Definition of Elites in Renaissance France*, Chicago 1977, pp. 34–6. See also Jean-Pierre Babelon, *Les Châteaux en France au siècle de la Renaissance*, Paris 1989, pp. 119–23.

Notes to chapter 5

1   For Italy see Domenico Merlini, *Saggio di ricerche sulla satira contro il villano*, Turin 1894. This book may be old, but it is still the most useful.

2   See James S. Ackerman *The Villa*, Princeton 1990, p. 120.

3   Lionello Puppi, *Scrittori vicentini d'Architettura del secolo XVI*, Vicenza 1973, pp. 23–4. See also James Cushman, *The Decline of the Venetian Nobility as a Ruling Class*, (The Johns Hopkins University Studies in Historical and Political Science, ser. 80, no. 2), Baltimore 1962, and Brian Pullan (ed.), *Crisis and Change in the Venetian Economy*, London 1968, for social categories of 'useful' and 'useless'.

4   Serlio's Venetian milieu is impressively documented by Hubertus Günther, 'Studien zum venezianischen Aufenthalt des Sebastiano Serlio', in Münchener Jahrbuch der bildenden Kunst, XXXII, 1981, pp. 42–94, and *Sebastiano Serlio, Sesto Seminario Internazionale di Storia dell'Architettura*, Vicenza, agosta–settembre 1987, (Centro Internazionale di Studi di Architettura 'Andrea Palladio' di Vicenza, Christof Thoenes (ed.). The mystery of the source and inspiration for Serlio's social nomenclature is discussed by Myra Nan Rosenfeld, *Sebastiano Serlio, On Domestic Architecture* &c., Cambridge (Mass.) & London 1978, pp. 41–3. Dr Rosenfeld well summarises the social grades as follows:

Country dwellings. 1: Farmhouses of the poor and middle-class citizen for three levels of poverty &c.; 2: Farmhouse of the rich citizen of two levels of wealth; 3: House of the artisan of three levels of poverty; 4: Houses for the citizen or merchant; 5: Houses for the richer citizen or merchant; 6: Houses for the rich citizen or merchant; 7: Houses for noble gentlemen; 8: Houses for Princes; 9: Houses for the King (i.e. Francis I, for there was no other).

City dwellings. 1: Houses for the poor artisan; 2: Houses for the better-off artisan; 3: Houses for the rich artisan; 4: Houses for the citizen or merchant; 5: Houses for the rich citizen or merchant; 6: Houses for noble gentlemen; 7: Palace for the *Capitano*; 8: Palace for the *Podesta*; 9: Palace for the Governor; 10: House of the Prince; 11: House of the King.

Almost all of these 'social labels' can be found dispersed through the chapters of Alberti's ten books. The origin of most are given as ancient authors. The top strata such as *Capitano*, *Podestà* or Governor were obviously modern. Between Alberti in the 1450s and Serlio in the 1540s someone must have tabulated or ordered them. If it was not Serlio, who should take the credit for collating scatterings in Alberti? It remains regrettable that Serlio offered no precise information on social and economic distinctions amongst the lower and middle ranks. What did he mean by 'three levels (or degrees) of poverty' or 'two levels (or degrees) of wealth'?

5   The subject of satires and polemics about peasants in the Low Countries has become a fashionable subject in recent years. See Margaret D. Carroll, 'Peasant Festivity and Political Identity in the Sixteenth Century', in *Art History*, 1987, pp. 289–314, and Jonathan Alexander, 'Labeur et Paresse. Ideological Representations of Medieval Peasant Labor', in *Art Bulletin*, 1990, pp. 436–52. Both articles have valuable bibliographies of recent literature in their notes.

6   As far as I know, there is no study of the buildings in Bruegel's paintings in relation to the real social conditions and economic structures of his times. Might they be graded in Serlian terms?

7   For Venice see Brian Pullan, *Rich and Poor in Renaissance Venice*, Oxford 1971. For England see W.K. Jordan, *Philanthropy in England*, London 1959, and A.L. Beier, *The Problem of the Poor in Tudor and Early Stuart England*, London 1982.

8   See Françoise Boudon, 'Les Livres d'Architecture de Jacques Androuet du Cerceau', in *Les Traités d'Architecture de la Renaissance*, (Collection De Architectura), edited by Jean Guillaume, Paris 1988, pp. 367–96.

9   In mid-sixteenth-century north Italian portraiture, broken columns and architectural debris served as foils to contrast with the courage and endurance of subject of the portrait. See Allan Braham, *Giovanni Battista Moroni*, (Exhibition catalogue, National Gallery), London 1978, p. 13.

Appendix 1

Amadis de Gaule
vol. 4, feuillet V, Paris 1543

Le plant de ce palais tant magnifique, parc et jardin ensemble estoit quadrangle, & contentoit en longeur six ces vingtcing toyses, & en largeur trois cês soixante & quinze, à prendre la toyse pour six pieds, le pied de douze poulces, & le poulce de dix grains d'orge, cloz de haulte muraille de marbre noir, auec colonnes doriques de marbre blanc. Au frôc d'iceluy plant, estoit assis le palais qui auoit en son carré cêt quarâte & un toyses, au quatre coigns duquel estoient esleuées quatre grosses tours. L'une de pierre d'Azur, l'aultre de pierre d'Iris, la tierce de Grisolite, & la quarte de Iaspe: lesquelles auoient en leur dymettre de la circonference du dedans huyt toyses deux piedz trois poulces. En chascune y suoit deux chambres, quatre garde robbes, & autant de cabinetz, en ce comprins la chambre deffendue: laquelle estoit dedans la tour de pierre d'Azur. Et pource que cestoit la plus excellente de toutes, ie vous descripray par le menu les singularitez d'icelle. Elle auoit le lambris le licorne à culz de lampe renforcé dallouez, Basme & cedre le tout fait en manequinaige de fin or, & fleurons diuersisiez par plusieurs sortes desmaulx. Le paué estoit de Grisolite en las d'amour, enrichy de coural & cypres taillé en escaille, retenue par filletz d'or. Les luys & fenestraigles de beyne enchassees de moulures d'argent, auec des vitres de cristal. Et vouoit on les cloysons de garderobes & cabinetz estoffées d'agathes, taillés en lozenges dedans lesquelles se representoient naturellement infinies figures de tous animaulx. Au plancher de cette chambre pendoient deux lampes d'or, au cul desquelles estoient enchassées deux escarboucles qui donnoient telle clarté au circuit de lieu, qu'il ny estoit besoign d'aultre lumière. Mais telles richesses estoient de peu de valeur au respec d'ung miroir saphir blanc, les plus oriental que l'on veit oncques, qui auoit trois piedz en carré, assis sur une lame d'or, tant bordée & garnie de gros Dyamês, Esmeraudes, Rubis & Perles, que cestoit chose plus que admirable. Entre ces quatre tours desquelles ie vous parle, estoient assis quatre grands corps d'hostelz d'ung seul estaige, faitz en plate forme de six toyses en largeur dedâs oeuure tous de pierre de porphire, en haulteur, assises sur basses de bronze, coeffées de chappeaulx d'ox, dessoubz architraues de porseline, sur lesqukelz estoient frizes d'yoire, marquetées de plusieurs richies de Turquoyses. Et vis à vis de portail de ce palais auoit Apolidô aultresfois assis les perrôs, desquelz il vous a esté parlé au premier & second liure, & tout ioignant l'arc des loyaulx amans. Puis passans oultre entroit ou en vne bien belle court, contentant cinquante trois toyses en son carré, sur lignes ortogonelles, laguelle estoit pauée de Iaspe, en carreaulx brisez à la mosaique. Et vng donion ayant aussi en son carré cinquâte vne toyses & demye. Au milieu duquel estoit assis vne viz double, contenant neuf toyses en son dymettre. Et à l'entour quatre aultres sumptueulx corps d'hostelz de vingt toyses en profondeur, separez de tours nô moins belles & excellentes que les premieres. Et estoit ceste viz de cuyure doré, faite en forme de lâterne, retenue d'arcs boutans, & soustenue de colonnes attiques de pierre de crateritte fort dure, taillée à l'antique: & ne se rêcontroient aulcunement les deux montées d'icelle viz, en ligne ortogonne ny ambligonne. Ce donion auoist quatre estagaiges subz vne platte forme, ou estoient seize grandes salles. Et un meilleu la viz esleuée, & quatre pauillons oultre les quatre tours, dont nous auons parlé cy dessus, lesquelles auex lesditz

223

pauillons surmontoient ladite plate forme de deux estaiges soubz leur couuerture. Et pour vous declarer la premier estaige estoit de Calcydoyne, enrichy de colonnes Yonicques de fine topaze, moulures, chapiteaulx bases & assietes telles que les premieres. La tiers estaige estoit de marbe rouge griuollé à colonnes de corinte d'Yuoire: & le quart de Iacinte auec colonnes tuscanes de proesme d'Esmeraulde. Et voyoit on aiséement les plates formes dont cy dessus nous auons parlé, au dessoubz desquelles estoiêt ces quatre estaiges pauées de Porselaine & celles des quatre pauillons & tours qui surmontoiêt icelles plattes formes, faites de boys de Cypres, Cedre & Cethin non corruptible, couuertes de Naque de perle, & la reste d'icelles de myrouers de fin acier retenues par filletz d'or. Tous les porteaulx de ce palais estoient d'Albastre desmasquin auec moulures, Tympannes & Frôtissonnes de pierre d'Ambre, Agathe & vermeilles, le tout taillé auec ouuraige antique, auquel l'on pouoit veoir maintes batailles & haulx faitz, tant des Grecz, Romains, que Gaulloys. Et au dessus les ymaiges de Priapus, Bacchus, Mars & Apollo, auec celles de Venus, Ceres & Minuerve, de plus polly marbre blanc qu'on veit onques. Et auoit Apolidon expressement fait faire les moulures diceulx portaulx d'aymant, & les portes d'acier, à ce que ainsi que l'on les ouuriroit olles se refermassent d'elles mesmes par la vertu de ceste pierre. Or estoiêt les pauillons & tours garnies chascun de cinquante six chambres, quatre vingt garderobbes, & autant de cabinetz doubles, le mieulx dorez & estoffés qu'il seroit possible de penser: puis sortant hors de ceste second court, entroit on dedans vng jardin ou parterre de mesme mesure de son carrée que tout l'edifice cy dessus descript, plâté par nature de toutes sortes de fleurs & bônes herbes que l'on sçauroit soubhaiter, au millieu dequel sortoit la grosse fontaine, qui tumboit (par les tetins d'une Venus dagathe, esleuée sur vng hault pillier de proesme d'Esmeraulde) dedans vng grand bassin de pierre d'Azur, & estoit ceste ymaige si bien taillé qu'il ny restoit que la parolle, parce que l'Agathe auoit en soy tant de naturel, que Venus visue ne fut oncques plus belle: laquells tenoit en sa main dextre (vng peu plus auancée que l'aultre) la mesme pomme que Paris luy adiugea, lors, qu'il fut esleu arbitre par les trois déesses en la forest de Yda, dont depuis sortit la malheureuse guerre entre les Grecz & les Troyens, & l'auoit aultresfois Iuno desrobbée à Venus par le moyen de Vulcanus ialoux, & par despit donnée à Agamenon, & depuis tumbée de main en main iusques a Apolidon, qui la trouua entre les grands thresors du Roy son père, auec la perle aultrement dite Lunion, que cleopartra eut si long temps en sa possession depuis qu'elle eut humée l'autre en la présence de Marc Anthoine: laguelle aussi il auoit fair pédre à l'aureille gauche de ceste déesse, par telle art qu'elle ne luy pouoit estre ostée, tât que la belle qui entroit en la chambre deffendue eut beu de l'eaue de ceste claire fontaine. Et lors cest ymaige luy deuoit presenter, & la perle & la pomme, côme digne du premier lieu de parfaite beaulté. En l'aultre aureille luy pendoit l'anneau de Pirrus, auquel estoit enchassé l'Agathe, en laquelle par vne tresgrande admiration & varieté de nature, estoient representees au vif neuf muses auec Apollo tenant sa Harpe, duquel anneau Vaspasian faisoit si grand cas, qu'il n'estimoit brague tact que caste la, ainsi que Pline la tesmoigné. Ce iardin la duquel ie vous parle estoit clos de galleries doubles de dix toyses & demie de large, soustenue par asseaulx soubz grosses colonnes doriques, & tuscanes de Cassidoine & amatiste de trente piedz de hault, aux deux angles desquelles (regardâs directement le parc) on auoit gaigné vne châbre, garderobbe en double estaige. Et estoit la plus basse de ses galleries au modelle du parterre, paintes d'excellêtes paintures de toutes sortes de venerie, chasse & faulcônerie car on y veoit pourtrait' au vif, le plaisir que preignent gentilz hommes, dames, & damoyselles estans à l'assemblée, couchez sur l'heerbe fresche & deuisans ensemble, attendês le rapport du veneur, lequel peu apres on veoit retourner sur sa brisée auec son limier, que rant ses voyes à route, tât qu'il faisoit lancer le cerf. Et à veoir la contenance de cest homme, it sembloit preprement qu'il sonnait vng long mot, pour aduertir qu'il auoit trouué le repos de la beste. Puis estoient paintz en mainequinaige

les aultres chiês qui luy bailloient le meutte & route, & les picqueurs lesquels couroient
apres à bride auallé, tenans leurs trompes contre leure bouches (à ioues enflées) de si bonne
grace, que l'on se persuadoit quasi d'entrentre l'air rentir, comme si la chose eust esté
vraye. Mais ou est celuy qui ne prendroit vng plaisir extresme à descouurir ce cerf sommé
de seize cors sortât du fort, brossant les hayes & buissons; puis trauerser la lâde tenant
la teste haulsée, & la langue tirée gaignant a didlgence l'eaue prochaine, tâdis que les chiês
sont en default par les ruses & faultz qu'il a faitz. Et meantmois cela n'est riens au pris
que de la veoir sortir d'estang, & à force estre mis aus abboys, lors gue les chiês courans
luy pendent aux fesses, en sorte qu'ilz abatent & rendent mort, par le moyen dequoy a
instant mesmes leur en est fait curée. Et vng peu à costé voyoit on le sanglier ou laye que
le vaultroy auoit contraint habondonner le buisson, trausersant vng cours ou estoient
atiltrez leuriez, parquoy ceste beste trop fiere, entêdant le son des trompes passe entre
chiens et veneurs, ronflant, grognant, & iectant par terre tout ce q'elle recontre. Et que pis
est auec ses deffenses rompt, decouppe, & trenche les plus hardis leuriers qui s'approchent
pour l'arrester. Et non obstat la force de leurs iaquées en deffait les aulcuns sans partir de
sa place: mais le veneur prompt & adroit d'une grande asseurâce luy presente l'espieu &
l'enferre en le tumbant sur l'herbe. Lors na il plus pouoir de resister à l'effort des chiens
qui sont au tour de luy, dont les vgns le pinssent aux suites, les aultres aux aureilles &
cuisses, tant qu'ilz le font mourir. Certes ce seroit chose trop longue à descripre par le
menju tant de sortes de venerie, & de chasse que l'on voit pour traites de long de ceste
gallerie si plaisante, & est le paintre digne de tresgrande louenge gui fit oeuure de telle
excellance, & auec si grande perpectiue, mesmes en ce qu'il figuroit le deduict de la
faullconnerie; car il representoit tant au naturel (entre sultres) le vol du Heron buffeté par
trois sacres tyrans à mont, lors qu'il veult faire sa montée si halt que l'on les voyoit dedans
les nues: puis tout a coup l'apperceurent on fondre, & eulx quand & quand, qui le qui
le forcêt se rendre entre les dens du leurier qui attêdoit de pied quoy. Et neantmoins se
telles painctures apportoient plaisir aux regardans, trop plus leur en dônoiêt celles de la
gallerie plus haulte, en laquelle estoient figurez la plus part des batailles de Semiramie &
de Ninus, la deffaite d'Astiages par les Perses, la mort de Marchesie Royne des Amozones
au pays d'Asie. La desconfiture de Cyrus par la Royne Thomoris. Les affaulx d'Hercules
contre Antroge & Otrera. La fuyte de Vexores Roy d'Aegipte assaillât les Scythes, &
infiniz aultres combatz dignes dememoire perpetuelle. Ainsi estoirent ces galleries decorées
par la singularité du paué d'icelles, qui estoit de Ieracotte plus noire que meure, & de
l'embrissement en forme Ouale de Zedrosusos de poisson, que les Roys d'Arabie ont en
tres grâde estime. La couuerture estoi9t de Gestz, & la reste de dessus de jpur argent à
figures de petis mensequins & Animaulx esmaillez, auec goustieres & eschinaulx d'Albastre,
qui sortoient le long de la muraille entre les croisées, enrichies de feuillages & ouuraiges
taillez à la damasquine. La veoit on les huys & fenestraiges de boys du deluge, & vitres
de strin. Sortant de ce parterre entroit on au parc: auquel estoit en crouppe de montaigne
vng buisson des trois cens arpens de bois ou environ, planté de Pins, Cypres, L'auriers,
Houx francs, Palmiers & Trebentins. Et le bas estoit partie approprié pour vng verget tât
plaaiksant & delectable qu'il sembloit nature auoir mis toute son industrie a le faire
singulier: car l'on y veoit vne infinité d'Orengers, Grenadiers, Cytronniers, & Myrtres tous
plantez a la ligne, aues les plus doulx fruitaiges qu'il est possible de souhaiter. Et l'aultre
partie estoit prairie arrousée par vne infinité de petis ruysseaulx. Au moyê dequoy la terre
fresche & deliée produisoit la petite herbe verde auec violettes, Margueritttes, Pêsées, &
aultres fleurs odoriferantes. La venoit iardinerpar chascû an au moys de May le Phenix,
lequel pour l'amenité du lieu y prenoit tel plaisir, qu'il y mua aussi tost que Apolidon eut
parfait les enchantemês de son palais: parquoy faisant songueusement receuilly son pennaige
l'appropria a vng Euentail enricht d'ung Dyament si large qu'il seruoit aisément de mirouer,

accompaigné de la plus belle Esmeraulde & gros Ruby que l'on veit onques. Et ordonna iceluy Apolidon quand il partit pour aller en Constinople, que ce pênaige si precieulx fust gradé auec les singularitez de l'isle, comme la chose plus excellent d'icelle: Parquoy Amadis le presenta à Oriane le iour mesmes qu'elle se desembarqua. Et affin que le lieu tât plaisant demeurast embelly de tout ce qu'il estoit possible, iceluy Apolidon y auoit laissé deux licornes que le poince de Quisay luy enuoya, lesquelles y vesquirent tant, que le Roy lisuart les y trouua encore apres le mariage solemmisé de la princesse Oriane & Amadis. Et y auoit dauâtaige maingtes cyuettes & musqs, qui rendoient l'air si odoriferât que rien plus: Au moyen dequoy le Pelican y faisoit quelque fois son ayre. Assez d'aultres bestes viuoient au lieu si delectable, comme cerfz, Daings, Cheureulx, Lieures & Connins & tant de diuersité d'oyseaulx s'y brancherent que cestoit chose diurne de les ouyr desgoyser: specialemêt le Rossignol & le passe solitaire. D'ung hault rocher ioignant descêdoit vng ruysseau, qui enfloit le lac, duquel il vous a esté parlé au second liure, ou se perdoit le cerf poursuiuy par les chiens comme il vous a esté recité & la se tenoit ordinairement le Castor baignant sa queue, & vne infinité de Cignes, Crues, Signoignes, Corbeaulx de medr & Aigrettes, auec toute sultre espece de telz oyseaulx. Mais cela ne le rendoit tant singulier comme le grequentation d'une seraine, laquelle on oyoit quasi continuellemêt chanter, si doulcement que oncques plus grande melodie fut ouye. De ce lac sortoit vne infinité de ruysseaulx qui faisoient diuerses petites Isles en ceste prairie: En l'une desquelles y auoit ung Dedalus contenant seulement quatre arpens en carré, planté de plus précieulx baulme que creut oncques en Angady, lequel estoit ordinairemenrt gardé par deux serpens de l'espece de celuy qui veilloit les pommes d'or au iardin des Esperides. Et droit au meilleu de ce Dedalus estoir vng colloce de brouze doré de la haulteur de six vingt couldées, tenant en la main gauche (esleuée sur sa teste) vne lanterne de Cristal: & au dedans la verge bruslante encores (auec laquelle Prometheus garde le feu qu'il auoit desrobbé au ciel) rendant tant de clairté iour & nuict sans diminuer, que de cent lieus à la ronde les Mariniers y prenoient leur adresse, comme ilz faisoient au Pharos pres Alexandrie & auoit Apolidon recouuert icelle verge par grande industrie des prebstres & magiciens de Caldée. Et quiconue pouoit veoir ce feu inextingible au naturel, & sans aultre couuerte, il acqueroit vne tresgrande prouidence. Mais les serpens garderoient trop bien le lieu, sans toutes fois faire aultre nuysance à ceulx qui prenoient plaisir au parc, poureau qu'ilz n'entreprinssent entrer au Dedalus, lors, iectoiêt feu & flamme si aspre quk'ilz espouentoient les plus hardis. Et tout ce auoit esté ainsi ordonné par Apolidon, qui estoit (comme vous auez entendu) l'ung des plus grands enchanteurs du monde: Mais quand la belle qui entroit en la chambre deffendue en approcheroit, les enchantements deuoient finir, & pourroit veoir a son ayse ce few tant requis. Or iugez donques en voz espritz gentilz lecteurs, si facilement l'on pourroit au iourdhuy trouuer vng palays semlable, ny accompaigné de tant de singularitez que y veit Oriane, laquelle apres estre descêdue de cheual fut conduite auec ses dames & demoyselles en l'ûg de plus sumptueulx corps de leâs cheualiers de l'Isle ferme la laisseerent, luy donnant tous le bon soir: car il estoit ia tard, & heure de reposer.

Appendix 2

L'OMBRE ET TOMBEAV DE TRESHAVTE ET TRESPVISSANTE Dame Marguarite de Frāce en son viuant Duchesse de Sauoie & de Berri. Fait et composé premierement en lā gue latine par R.dER. Et puis traduit en Francés par ENDI. Imprimé a Thurin le 17 Octobre 1574 Par Baptiste d'Almeida.

DESCRIPTION tant de L'ichniographie que de l'orthgraphie, Plan & montée de la sepulture & Mausolée de MARGUARITE DE FRANCE, Duchesse de Savoie & de Berri, traduitte de latin en vulgaire Francés pour gratifier les studieux de l'Architecture.

Parce qu'il est approuué par toutes les écritures tant saintes que profanes, & grandement louable, d'hononer ceux qui ont bien & saintement vaicu, principalement les grans Rois, & Princes, par sepultures & monumens, sur tout non remplis ne deffamez d'idolatries, sculptures, écris ne peintures indignes: afin que par l'hystoire muëtte, non seulement les sours, mais aussi les ignorans, à qui la veüe est demeurée, puissent apprendre & connoitre la bonne memoire & grandeur des gestes des grans personages & des dames qui ont cet' honneur merité: Noz peres (cōme assez il appert par le sepulchre de IESVS CHRIT, de Dauit & d'infinis autres) erigent & bastirent deuerses façons de monumens aux grans & illustres seigneurs, & pareillement aux chastes & vertuëuses Princesses & dames: qui fut cause qu'Artemisie iadis opulente & memorable Roine de Carie, pour perpetuer la valleur & amitie de Mausolée son cher mari, beuuant ces cendres, (reliques & temoignage étenel d'vne si viue amitié) dans le crane & testz de la teste d'iceluy Mausoliée qu'ell auoit expressement gardé pour cet'vsage, luy fit eriger vn sepulchre tel qu'auiourdhui la renommée encores viuante par son excellence à tan gangée sur la posterité que lon nomme toutes sepultures qui ont quelque dignité & ornement d'architecture, Mausolées. Et pource que tant de la structure, symmetrie, innentions & enrichissemens d'icelles, & tout ce que les estrangiers de la foy y obseruerent le passe, que de ce que lon y doit continuer, nous en auons traité bien amplement & vn discours qui quelque iour (si iamais l'europe & la chretienté lasses de tant & tant de maux sont si heureuses que de trouuer franchise, seurité, & quelque azyle pour la conscience oppressé par tant de blaphemes idolatries, & heresies, desquelles l'vlcere & la peste pires que la camarine, ne les etables d'Augée, attendent la sacrée main d'vn Péon, & la puissance d'vn Hercule galois) prédra la hardiesse de sortir en publique, au nom & pout le reuerance d'vn tresguand, égal à tout ce qui fut iamias de preux ne vaillent parmi les fis des hommes: ie n'en diray pour le present autre chose: sinon qu'il est certein que les viues ruines des antiques pyramides conditoires colomnes tombeaux, obelisques, tombes, cochleares, trophées monumens, monts-ioyes sepultures, & sepulchres de l'orient, de l'Egypte, & de Romme lo'rguilleuse, sont encores asses parler les pierres muettes & les marbres, de la grandeur & bonne vie des braues & signalez personages: voire qu'ē arrachāt & en efātāt des pinceaux des peintres, & des marteaux des sculpteurs, & des plumes des hystoriographes & poetes la souuenance & imortalité, ils ont graué & eternizé dans la memoire de noz neueuz & à iamais, la reputation, les triomphes, les palmes les lauriers & la gloire des vertueux: tellement que sans cela Alexandre, Cesar, Annibal, Scipion, & Achile, enterrans aueques eux leurs prouësses & vaillenties, fussent

227

pieca oubliez & effacez, voire deux fois mors en ce monde, raclez & aneantis en la memoire de la posterité, seule arbitre & iuste iuge des bōnes ouures: si les burins des Lysippes & Praxiteles les coleure d'Appele, les plumes de Liue d'Herodien, de Curse, d'Homere & de Virgile ne les eussent maugre la mort renduz viuās. Voila pourquoi cet'Alme, tresgrande, & vertueuse Princesse doibt conuier pas ses gestes & vertus, tous les prophyres de l'Egypte & de Paros: tous les Phidies, Ianets, Titians & Michel-Anges, tous noz historiographes, peintres, sculpteurs & poëtes, dirai-ie toute l'Academie des sauās l'olympe & le parnasse de la grece & de la frāce à vanter & decrire son diuin iugement, sa sainte conscience, son esprit tout celeste, sa main liberale sa bouche faconde, ses moeurs irreprochables & sa conuersation & creances toutes bonnes & toute douces, affin de la faire viure hors de la tome, & maugré Proserpine en siecles inombrables & infinis. Attendant doncques que la liberalité des grans-grans, le docte inuentiō des plussages & auises: l'art & la plus docte main des meilleurs ouuriers construize à son eternelle memoire, diuers trophées, sepulchres, arcs monumans, & poémes: n'aiant apresent aucun graueur pour vous dresser & faire voir, par planches bien faites selon l'optique, les plans, erections & scenographie de son sepulchre, pour aucunement contenter l'esprit & le desir des curieux de l'architecture, & montrer à lhuilleuse, gothique, & beste ignorance de ces egrattigneurs & sanglans meurtriers de marbre, que ont tousiours beu de vin en Parnasse, combien ils offensent la maiesté de noz tresillustres, tresaugustes, & tressacrez Rois Ducs & Princes, pau leurs babouines & badines inuentions desquelles à grandes & insupportables despes, ils leurs dressent des sepultures n'y apportans que les plus, vains, & barbares ornemens que Cherile eust peu songer: sans art, sans forme, sans mesure, beaulré de iugemēt: tous confus, & fainans plustost des estuues, & Apodyteres (que les sacristes appellent Reuetoirs) que des sepulchres, auseroi ie dire des Thalames & lits nuptiaux: anatomies & Mascarades, plenes de drouilleries (comme londit) que des monumens? Iay pensé qu'il estoit raisonnable (voire & en attendant meilleure chose) que Archimede fit quelque chose en Syracuse: & que comme les troisfois diuins poites de ce tems (non seulement des latins ia de longtemps en possesiō de cet'honneur, ains aussi ceux de la France, égaux si plus nesont, sans contredit aux oracles des grecz ie veux dire aux Illiades Anacreontides, & Olympies) déploians leurs poëms sacres, & inimitables: ont etonnans & chassans ces nouuelles grenoilles couassantes, & corbeaux malplaisans & enrouëz de la cour des Rois, & des plusgrans: voire de la bouche, des yeux, & des oriilles tendres & lestes des dames, & des sauantes Academies, des sages senats, graues compagnies, & peuples, enseuely ces petits barbouilleurs & dysenteriques decrire, ces petis rimeurs & fatistes du tēs de n'augueres, dond la memoire auecques la naissāce auorta & peritsi tost que cette guerriere troupe Mineruale leur apparut, armée de sauoir exquis, de discours, inuentions, & eloquences admirables leur imposant silence comme l'aigle fait geay & Apollon à Marsyas. Que parallement ouurant le pas à diuinité de la Tectonique & Structoire, trop & trop bigarrée & meconneuë lon cōmence en voiant pluseler à apprendre que cest que de loger vn Roy & vn Prince viuant & mort. Bondieu qui ne void ces petis maçons, que (ô sacrilege trop effronté, ausent d'vne plusque pariure impudence swe nommer architectes) parce qu'ils sauent trois ou quatre sections de quelque elangourée Trompe, rachetée auecques sept ou huit trais égarez: vne arête de voute, & quelques vis suspenduë, mélans les cieux auecques les enfers, munis de compas impareils, & de regles lésbiennes, Ageometres, & Anaphabetes, ne sachās qu'vne chanson (qui est vn cours de logis, & vn bel escalier entre deux pauillons) prophaner l'orgueil des Roiales, des Theatres, Thermes, Cirques & autres pareils ennemis de leur ignorāce & soit par le desordre Corynthiē, ou Ionique donner de si grans soūflets à la sacresainte Architecture, que pour vn batiment de Roy, ils font souuent celuy, d'vn banquier, & pour le temple de Ianus celuy d'Hercules? sans sauoir qu'elles parties, membres, ornemens, ne syminetries sont decentes aux palais roiaux, aux capitoles, basiliques, & senats, aus marchans: aux ieux, à la danse, aux priuez ou auz publiques? ignorans toute l'antiquité, ie puis dire, lassiette seule, & recontre des places: rencontres ie di, qui deuroient bsen souuent, comme ce memorable Septizone de Rome, faire peur aux arriuans: aussi eloignez de ce que les doctes appellent Decét, comme ils sont bestes & truëlliers, Mais cete vague dixieme maient porté plus auant que ie ne pensoi: ie reuien d'ou ie suis parti. Pour dōcques vous faire entendre l'harmonie conuenance & dignité de ce sepulchre, & sa decence, cōme chose adaptée aux moeurs, vie, & gestes, grandeur & nom de defunte MARGVARITE fille de Fance: & la bōne volonte qu'elle portoit aux lettres, & a toutes choses vertueuses: fault que vous sachiez premierement que le sepulchre est assis en vue place plane & libre en toutes ses arriuees & de tous costz: qu'en premiere assiete de ce qui se void par le dehors à fleur de terre il y à vn Plynthe ou degré de marbre noir, quarré, hault d'vn pié portant en chacune face cent septente & noeuf piez de lon: qui est pour tout le tour, & eu tous cens le nombre de sept cens seize piez. Dessus ce plynthe il y à cinq autres marches de marbre noir le premiere faisant retraite de deux piez, & neantmoins pareillement regnantes toutes au tour, aiant chacune d'auancement & saillie pour assiette des piez, douze pouces, & dehault demi pié, de sorte que lon peut arriuer au sepulchre par tans endrois, & de toutes pars, au moien desdites marches: main il fault sauoir que par le meillieu dicelles affin que lon puisse entrer dedans la sepulture, il y à vn passage (car de porte il ny en a point, ienten qui ait aucm prothyre ne closture, ains seulement vn petit escalier à la haultheur des marches mémes pour entrer au dedans par lespace & vuyde des deux colōnes qui le frontyoient, lequel a noeuf piez de largeur, different par ce moien des autres espaces, cōme plusgrand, enuiron de quatre piez:) pour auquel paruenir & arriuer lesdites marches dudit petit escalier font retour, & se continuent à la forme que sensuit. C'est assarruoir que la plus haute & derniere marche qui est la cinqieme, se recoupe en dedans, & retourne en demye ouale: aient ladite ouale huit piez de vuyde en son diametre, & ce afin qu'il puisse demurer six pouces de chacun cousté pour ne heurter les plynthes des colōnes costieres desquelles nous auons parlé: ladite marche comme aussi toute les quate qui le suiuent ha demi pié de haulteur. Au dessous d'elle il s'en continue vne aultre auecques vn pié de saillie en meme retour: audessus de la quelle demeure vn poiler faisant l'ouale toute entiere: lequel poilier (ou repos,) seruant d'vne autre marche, & sauanceant par son oualité en dehors (cōme les precedentes le faisoient en dedans) vous porte & decend dessus vn autre marche, formée & retournée en pareille rondeur ouale, & proportion: faisant lesdites deux dernieres marches leurs demies ouales en dehors, comme les autres le faisoient en dedans. De la se forme ve petit escalier, par lequel vous penetrez dans le sepulchre: & y en à vn pareil en chacune face. En quoi il ne fault oublier que le premier plynthe ou degre qui à deux piex de saillie outre lesdites marches & vn pié de hauteur, retourne (mais quarrement) à lentour des petits escaliers, tellement que faisant seul vne marche, & le pié droit reuenant à pres le second pas a marcher, (limparité estant gardée) vous montez lesdis cinq degrex puis apres. Il faut sauoir aussi que par les marches qui vironent à lentour de peristyle, (don sera tantost parlé,) vous arriuant a la derniers & plushaulte marche, que est à la verité l'are & vestige de tout l'edifice pouuez vous promener autour de la sepulture & peristile, sans pouuoir entrer aucunement dedans (si ce n'est par les petits escaliers:) daultant que la derniere marche à de proiecture & espace auancé, outre les coulōnes du portique, cinq piez: & que de colonne en colonne (cōme il sera dit) il y à vn balustral que sert de closture, & vous en empesche l'entrée: desorte qu'il est aisé neanmoins à ceux qui sont mémes dehors de se contenter, & voir tout ce qui est dedans: voire sans y enter aucunement sur ce plynthe dōques & marche derniere (cinq piez en dedās, & deplus cinqu piez e dedās, & deplus cinq piez laissex en quarre sur chacū angle) sont asisez en chacune face, & en chacun coin deux colonnes: desquelles les plynthes des bases & tailloirs des chapitaux setouchente & ioignent par lun des angles tellement dque leur proximité & mariage les rend plus fortes, pour lesoutien des

fardeaux quelles portent: de ces deux colonnes iusques aux autres il y a seize piez trois
pousses despace ou enuiron: & en chacune quarte partie de faciate quatre assiettes de
doubles colonnes qui sont trois espaces, & dans le meillileu est la porte & les petits
escaliers: desorte qu'en chacune face il y à sept espaces (l'entreé & passage qui est de neuf
piez y compris) & huit assietes de colonnes qui sont size colonnes, & par ce moïē en tout
le tour de l'edifice le nombre de soixante & quatre: cela entendu & compris: laissez vn
espace pour le proumenoir & portique dudedans, & audela de l'alignement desdites colonnes,
& en chacun angle dudit alignement second, eloigné de cinq piez de l'autre, pozes vne
colonne seule en chacun coin laquelle correspondera à la seconde de chacune colonne
angulaire des premieres assises dans le front & par le dehors & puis front à front de toutes
les auttres (ledit espace de cinq piez gardé franc & reserué) posez encores aultant de
colonnne vous aurez conneu & forme vn peristyle & portique qui virōnera toute la sepulture:
aiant à l'endroit de ses colonnes cinq piez de large, & par ses entrecolonnes plus d'onze,
& y en auroit quinze, voire vint, (cōpris les cinq piez d'auancement de la derniere marche
& plushaute) n'estoit que les colonnes de la faciate, sont fermées d'vn ballustral tel qui
sensuit: Qui est que par le mitan de leurs entrecolonnes & à légal de leurs plynthes, sont
posez des cubes de marbre noir, haultz de cinq piez, & larges de trois, épois de quatre:
auxquels cubes de chacun coste est attaché ledit balustral ou accodoir de bronze doré,
regnant & secoduisant tout au tour, & de colonnes à autres, hors mi a lendroit des
portes: Icelluy balustral haut de trois piez trois pouces: composé de petis termes, desquels
les testes & coiffures sont, partie des Diames, partie de Gorgonnes engaînées sur étuis
releuez de rinceaux & feuillages de laurier, mi-parries d'abondances de grenades, & amas
de greins de genieure, & cypres: pour faire expressement entrendre par lesdites gorgonnes
(signifiantes prudence) cōbien ladite dame étoit sage acorte, docte, & bien auisée: Aussi
qu'elle portoit en son embleme & deuise, vne teste de Meduse, béāte, encheuelée de serpens,
& sourscripte de ces mots. RERVM PRVDENTIA CVSTOS. & par les semences de
grenades, genieures & cyprés: qui sont arbres dediez à la terre & à Pluton, conioints aux
tigres de laurier, vne mort vistorieuse & par les testes des Dianes tymbrees de croissans
la chastete, & gentilesse de laquelle ladite dame, à auancé toutes les Lucreces & Porcies
du monde Ce ballustral est enfermé par enhault d'vne petite cornice, & d'vn quarré par
le bas: le tout reuenant à la mesure que dessus qui est de bronze pareillement. Sur lesdits
cubes (qui sont six enchacune face: & parce moien vingt & quatre en tout l'edifice) il y
a partie des statues, partie des lampes & lychóphores de brōze dorez de fin or: lesdits
lychnophores fais les acuns de dauphins, acollez de serpens qui portent leurs bacinetz &
foiers, pout loger les luminōs & meiches, les autres de tortues ouuertes & grosses lymaces
creuzées expres & a cellefin, de representer les feux inextingibles & eternels: par lesquels
la deuotieuse antiquité figuroit l'immortalité de l'ame: encores qu'ils n'en eussent telle
certirude que nous: desorte qu'en chacun desdits cubes (qui sont ceux lesquels des trois qui
se treuuent en chacun quartier, ou quart de chacune face, sont es espaces prochains des
entrees & angles) portans lampe est graué en lettre de cuyure doré et attachées a queüe
d'aronde ce mot grec ΑΣΒΕΣΤΟΝ: qui signifie inextingible: & y'a sur les arestes & coins
desdits cubes, des testes & caifs de beouf, aux cornes desquels pendent iusques enbas, des
festons de fruis hyberaux iettez en fonte & partie dorez, comme les chataignes, melles,
cormes, glan, faine, pommes de mandragore, pommes d'amour, & choses semblables: sus
autres cubes (qui est chacun quartier de faciate, & iceluy posé en l'espace de milleu, &
entre les deux cubes portans lampe) il y a des statues de marbre blanc, telles qu'entendrez
c'y apres. Desorte qu'ē tout le peristile il y a six vings collones, huit Statues, vingt & quatre
cubes, autant d'espaces ou entre colonnes: & quatre entrées. Les huit statues representent
au naturel, lune le grand Roy François son pere: l'autre la Royne Claude sa mere: lesquelles
sont à & à senestre de la face & aux espaces de la partie d'orient: de l'autre costé opposé

a celuy la, sont le Roy Henry son frere, & la Royne Magdalene sa seur, iadis Royne d'Escoce: En la face de midi sont celles des Roys François second & Charles ses neueux: enceluy de septentrion le Roy Henry apresant regnant & celle de François monseigneur son frere ses nepueuz pareillement: toutes lesdiltes Statues armées de leurs cuyrasses, lambellees à l'antique: aiant les testes nuës auecques des litestes de branches de laurier: & à leurs cotez pendans & amoncelez les manteaux, mytres, thiares baudriers, infules, cercles, diademes, sceptres, galons & autres ornemens imperiaux: pour temognage & euidence de leurs maiestez & grandeurs: mais pour mieux les faire connoitre aux regardans, dans le cubes qui les soustiēnent sont engrauez en lettre dor leurs noms & dignitez, auecques leurs ages, emblemes, & deuises: comme les salamandres, les croissans & trousses, les colonnes laçées & tous autres: tellement que par ce moien les cubes montrent vne extreme beaute, & font vn office en cete structure fort à propos: pour signifier vne bonne & grande partie de l'hystoire, & ramener, par les simulacres de si grans Roys & monarques, aux yeux duspectateur, la valeur & les gestes d'vne si memorable & inuincible race: de la qu'elle ladite dame estoit isseue: & auecques lesquels elle flori, & vaicu comme compagne glorieuse, & asociée a tant d'honneurs, triomphes, & merites: enquoi il ne fault oublir que les cubes portant lesdites Statues (affin de se differentier de ceux qui portent les lampes) sont outre lesdits nonsentaillez d'vn relief de bronze (attaché dans le macif de marbre) de Moly & Nepenthe, herbes tant celebrées par Homere, desquelles l'vne faisoit tout sauoior: & l'autre oublier toute douleur sitost qu'on les auoit aualées. Maintenant il faut retourner aux colonnes: elles sont de marbre blanc corynthiennes: canelées, haut de vint & sept pies: & grosses de neuf ou peu s'en fault: aiāt trois piez de diametre: leurs bazes & chapiteaux, taillez de feulages, entrelas, rinceaux ouucs, tortis, & guilochis en perfection, & autant que l'art & la matiere le peuuent permetre. Par dessus ces colonnes & sur leurs chapiteaux tant en dehors qu'en dedans ledit poqtique & peristile, trauersent de gros sommiers & bandes de fer epoisses d'vn pié & ce d'vne colonne à àutre, & en tout cens sur lesquels & aux quels sont attachées & posées vne architraue, la frize & la cornice de brōze telles qui sensuiuēt. L'Architraue à ses trois faces, filets & cimaise taillés de feuilles canaux, & patenotrers: & le fons du dessous de commpartimens, rouleaux, & entrelas attachez à des faisseaux & iarbes de bouq, cyrés & chene eniochez dans les yeux, & oreilles de plusiers testes & larues qui y sont: semées de floccons de feu & de flambes, le tout releué & doré par endrois, comme l'ouurage le requiert & la beaulté de l'oeuvre, si meruelleux. Par dessus cet àrchitraue qui a pres de doux piez de hault, est posée la frize, autrement dit zoophore ou large bande: dans la qu'elle, d'vn excellent relief & haults taille, est decrit le tournnai ou la fatale lance blessa le Roy son frere, auant ses noces, & aussi son depart de la France, & le voiage qu'elle fit par mer à Nice & de la les entcrées & receptions qui luy ont eté faites par les viles de Piémont & de Savoie: le tout selon la proportion requise à l'elongnement de la veuë & de l'oeil de ceux qui les voient du peristyle plane & arc de l'edifice. Dessus cete fryze qui a deux piez est posée la cornice qui salist de trois piez ou enuyron, & haulte d'auttāt composée de ses mouleures filets, doucyne, gorgerins, quarrez & denteleures selon l'ordre & symmetries des colonnes: & adornée & entaillée des plus riches & artistes ouurages, feuilles rameaux, oues, canaux & bozels que lon sauroit voir, memes iceux dorez en certeins endrois: desquels la description en particulier seroit trop longue & possible ennuyeuse, toutesfois ie ne veux oublier que tant la cornice, fryze, que l'architraue font le méme tour & saillie par le dedans que par de dehors: qui est cause que le platfons de l'architraue (qui est comme vn plancher & lacunaire du portique) est fort admirable & excellent: Pareillement aussi le fon de la proiecture de la cornice est releué de bassé taille fort douce & d'infinies beautez & particularitez des choses celestes: comme d'vne Iris, des cheuaux, chariots, rauissemens & chemins de soleil: de celuy de l'aurore: des vens, nuages & eclairs de Boote, orion, Persée, & choses semblables sur la cornice aultant qu'il y à despace de l'vne des colonnes du porail a lautre, c'est à dire sur l'entrée: il y a vn pié destel continué, hault de deux piez & demy, panchant vn peu vers le dehors, sur lequel seruant dacrotere par son meilleu, est vn grād corsellet à lantique entacé parmi vne montioye de diuerses despouilles & armes, & semke en infinis lieux, de rameaux d'Iris, de pin, & d'oliuier, sur lesquels est vng morion pareillement antique, pontanty sus son cymier vne meduse, amortissante par son deffault en vne queuë de cheual teinte de cynabre, & rouge cōme sang quel'etoit celuy de ce preux Hector & Achile en homere: & ha ce trophée ainsi fait, enuyrō cinq piez de haulteur, pour representer la deuise queportoit monsieur le Duc son mair auāt que l'auoir eposée c'est assauoir SPOLIATIS ARMA SVPERSVNT. Aux depouillez il ne reste que lepée. Sur les autres doubles colonnes tant par le dehors, que par le dedans, aultāt que leur cors en emports, îl y à vn pynthe ou latastre, depareille forme & haulteur sur le quel sont de tetis enfans & popolo tous nus trauersez d'vne epaule à la hanche d'vne guhirlande de cedre argenté cercléz par le teste dr rinceaux de Melaise dit larix. & acoudez les vns cōtre les autres, par l'vn des bras lacé, ensemble: en signe d'innocence & de concorde, portans aucuns diceaux des cornets pleins d'abondances de fruis: les autres de coronnes ducales, les aucuns des brāches de palme, & autres des branches de myrthe & de veruene. mémes les lances gantellets, & autres armes appartenantes à vn Prince victorieux & guerrier: d'autant que ce sepulchre semble deuoir seruir tant au seigneur Duc, qu'à elle. Voila donques & assez appertement pour comprendre la description de ce peristile & portique, qui est comme vne ceinture, closture, & pourpris de sepulchre. Venons maintenant à la demonstration de plan & eluation de dedans. Quand vous étes arriué à cete cinquiesme (compté le premier degré) sixiéme & plushaute marche, qui est lare & plane de sepulchre, mémes le lieu & la place ou sont assises les colonnes: Si de cetemarche que à de largeur en tout trente & noeuf piez vuoos rabatez pour le proumenoir hors lesdites colonnes, & cinq pour celles de dedans, & cinq pour la largeur frāche du portique dicelles ceseront vint: Il reresteta dix & noef de vuide & espace au dedans pour seruir de place & lieu a comptempler toute la structure tant que par ce moien quand vous aurez abandonné le portique & laissant les colonnes & le peristile, cheminé dix & noeuf piez: Vous rencontrerez vn cors pareil asoi en toutes faces, de marbre noir, poli, hault de trous piez & aiant son are & parrerre de trois autres canelé, & oeuuré à la facon qui sensuit. C'est qu'ayant par le default de sa hauteur vn gros bozel sallissant d'vn pouce & demy, & par son dessous vn quarré & vn talon de pareilles proiecturers, i demeure canelé & strié entre ses deux petites moleures: & ce non pas d'vne caneleure cōtinuée, ains detrois piez en trois piez ou enuyron: & nya que cinq canaux en chacun endroit: les vns remplis d'vn bozel oufluste de marbre blanc, les autres tous vuydes & creux: puis lespace demeruant entre les endrois qui sont canelez, est entaillé d'vne marquetterie de marbre blanc: c'ect assauoir de pleusieurs triangles, enfermés & retenuz les vns les autres, aueques des noeus d'hercule (autrement dis cordelieres) des noeufs gordiens (dis noeufs sans fin) & noeus d'assurance: qui sont deux boucles l'vne dans lautre, lesquelles tant plus on les tire plus elles serrēt & asseurant la liaison: ledis noeus & triangles eniouchez les rinseaux de gland & de grandes M & E dorez: pur signifier Margaurite & Emanuel: qui sont les noms delle & de monseigneur le duc son mari: liez & asseurez d'vne si ferme constance que les liens en sont indissollubles :sur les coins & aux angles dudit cors, sont assises quatre Prouinces de marbre blanc statual: de sept piez de hault à les considerer stantes: & enuyrō de cinq, étant asizes l'vne est la FRANCE, l'autre L'ITALIE. L'ALEMAGNE. & L'ANGLETERRE. aiant leurs diademes, coiffeures, bandeaux, cabacetz, cuyrasses, manteaux, thyares & apparats selon que leur condition le requiert: & chacune à ses piez les animaux qui leurs sont familiers & consacrez: & mesmes sous leurs piez des latastres de bronze, dans lesquels leukrs noms sont escris en lettres noires, cōme à la France; GALLIAE INVICTISSIMAE S. & ainsi des autres selon leur merite. Mais pour arriuer par ce cors qui est haut comme auons dit de trous piez à celuy qui le surmonte sachez qu'en chacune face par son meilleu il est entrouuert de sept marches (l'autre cors y compris formées en hemicicle: au moien dequoi vous montez iusques a vn autre cors & second qui est de marbre bland, mixte, riolé piolé de venes noires & blautres, hault de quatre piez & auancé en son are & place d'autant semé por voie, de gros serpens de pronze renouëz ensemble auecques des fagotz de fleiches tortillées de lauande, grossis par dessus le macif, dans lequel ils sont enfoncez & mastiquez. & contre ce cors sont les prouinces appuiées. Or pour reuenir audessus de ce plynthe ou cours qui a quatre piez de hault & aultant de saillie, sachez que en chacun coin ou sont les prouinces appuiees, à reuenir & se rapprocher du meilleu enuyron quatre piez en forme de rampāt au dedans du cors coupé pour cet effet, est posé vn escalier large de trois piez, faisāt sept marches, au costé de quel (c'est assauoir dedans le cors) est vne porte de bronze, par laquelle auecques vn autre rampant, lon peut descendre dans la caue, qui est par le dessous de tout cet'edifice & dans laquelle au meilleu de l'eau qui y est côtinuelle tousiours dedās sont les cors morts couzus & enfermez dans ses sacs de cuir boully, tousiours flottans: & vangez par ce poien de pourriture à iamais: y tombant l'eau parinfinies flustes, canaux, & troux derobez à la veuë par les commis eures & lis des pierres & ouurages à mesure qu'il pleut: chose à la verité digne dadmiration & peu pratiquée ne entendue. Quand dōques vous étez paruenu au dessus de ce cors, aiant cheminé quatre piez, vous recontrez vn autre cors qui est en nombre le troizieme, de marbre blanc emaillé & distinct de goutes sanguines, aplani, & sans aucun ouurage, qui est eleué de quatre piez & sauance de quinze outre les marches qui sont pardessus luy & desquelles nous parlerons cy apres: pour arriuer donques au dessus de ce cors de marbre blanc & approcher des degrez, Il faut sauoir que au dela de ces angles & comme enuiron six piez il y à en chacun quartier vn escalier quarré de noeuf marches, aiant quatre piez de large & enclos dans le macif dudit cors, mais sur ce meme cors (audela desdits escaliers quatre piez qui sont dix a contger de l'angle) il y à en chacun quartier vne statue droite & siante qui est en chacune face deux, & entout le cors huit. Ces statues sont hautes de cinq piez faites de bronze dorées par les coiffures ornemēs enrichissemens & deffautz de leur accoutremes, guimples fronteaux equipages, & ioaux: elles representent les sept ars liberaux les mathematiques & disciplines, desorte que pour le huitieme l'Imprimerie ou Typice, tient ses matrices presses & burins en la main: honorant & eglant par son inuention (bien qu'elle soit moderne & recente) tout l'orgueil de l'antiquité superbe & glorieuses, Du parterre & assiete de ce cors ou plynthe, qui à quinze piez de poellier & de vuyde, vous remontez cinq marches de marbre blāc dun pié haut chacune par lesquelles vous arriuez à vng cors de marbre noir, vené de blanc & de verd, presque transparent hault de cinq piez: & large de dix: duquel les angles son recoupez en demy rond, & font cinq marches d'vn pié de hault: par lesquelles quand vous estes arriué à son dessus, vous tornoiez tout alentour d'vn triāgle equilateral de marbre collōbin, vené & raie de larmes dor & dargent, sans nombre: hault de cinq piez: contre les angles duquel sont appuiées & couchées les trois Graces faites de marbre blanc: ornées selon qu'il est requis: festonnées & ceintes de grandes echarpes & rameaus de guhis de chene doré, & à ledit triāgle dix & sept piez de lon en chacun costé: dans desquels parmi lesdites larmettes dor & dargent, est escrit en vne table dor DIGNA QVAE REGERET ORBEM. qui signifie quellestoit digne de gouuerner le mōde. Dans vne autre table dor sont escrits par les deux autres faces ces mots grez ΑΤΑΣ ΕΝ ΜΟΝΑΔΙ Qui signifient deux en vng. En quoy il ne fault oublier que le hault du triangle à vne moleure de bronze toute dorée qui le vironne tout autour comme si cestoit vne coronne icelle posée sus des modillons dorez parellement aiant les modillons demy pié de saillie & la mosleure huin pousses plus que les modillons. Dessus ce beau & excellent triangle, que denote vne perfection & constance inuincible: il y a vn globe de bronze aiāt sept piez de diametre, comparti, & remarqué de toutes ses bādes, lignes, cercles, colleures, planetes, poles, etoiles, zodiaque, signes & zones brief de tout ce que lon peult contrefaire pour representer cet'vniuers & les orbes & spheres de tout cet'admirable & merueilleux monde, Sus ce globe si sumpteueux est asize l'image venerable de ladite dame, & son effigie: faite de marbre éleu en partie vetue de son manteau ducal, & corōnée selon sa grandeur & hautesse: aiant l'vne des mains acoudée sur vne hermine: aminal dedié aux grandes princesés du sang roial de la Frāce: & ténant lieu aux armoiries de la Bretagne: de la quelle sa mere étoit duchesse. & tient en l'autre ven branche de lis lacée, d'vn col & teste de cigonne, antien ornement des sceptres roiaux: voila en somme toute la deescriptiō, & ce que ie vous puis representer de la sepulture, qui n'est sans ornemens proportions & inuentions biens memorables: Et toutesfois à c'ellefin que quelque habile & docte homme, ne pense que ie ne sache bien de default qui y est: ie ne veux obmettre à vous faire sauoir, Que le sepulchre estant d'vne structure equilaterale qui est à dire pareille en tous cens, & representant à la verité vn cours arondi & parfait: sans qu'il y ait (à bien parler) derriere, costé, ne deuant, comme semblable à soi entout & par tout: il y resteroit vne lourde faute & euidente: si la raison nesen baillot promtement: c'ect assauoir que leffigie & statue de medite dame montréroit le dos par l'vne des faces: chose grandement à reprendre: & en quoy les antiens ne faillirent iamais: aient les grans à inimitables personnages, obserué pour ce regard les niches à loger les statues, sil ne les mettoient aux acroteres des arcs triomphaux & sur les cornices, coronnes, & pointes des palais & bastimens, affin que le derriere nen fut veu que de celuy, qui cutieux louurage le recherchoit exprés: tellement que si par nécessité ils en ont, pour quelque regard, posé à toutes veuës, ils les ont accompaignées ou de rochiers par le derriere, ou d'animaux, ou de deopuilles & trophées & choses semblables: mais en cete endroit pour faire paroitre que sans auoir failli il y a apparence de faulte: il fault que vous sachiez que le place qui reste sur le globe, est pour y attendre (& le plustard qu'il plaira à Dieu) la statue de Monsiegneur le Duc son mari: & lors sera ladite omission desirée restablie, & sans suspition de faulte. Pour dōques conclure cete Ortograpie discours de ce tant beau & orné sepulchre vous voiez que ledit lobe aiant sept piez, le triangle dix & sept, le plus hault & prochain cors trente & sepᴛ le plusbas degré quarente & sept le second cors septante & sept, le troiseme octante & trois: le quatrieme octante & noeuf le cinqieme (qui est le plan & assiste du peristyle) cent soixante & sept piez: les quatre degrez qui restent, & le plus bas plynthe cent septente & noeuf: ladite mesure reuient au iuste & sa proportion premiere, qui est sept cent seize piez ent tout le tour: & pour la haulteur de dedans trente & cinq piez ou enuirō sans comprendre l'effigie. Pour c'elle du peristile (y compris les Trophées qui sont sur les acroteres des entrées) enuiron quarente & huit piez. Ce que ie di notamment & nay vouleu faillir a nombrer, pour deux passages qui si trouuent, l'vn dans Pline aux nombres du Mausolée, & l'autre en laissiette des colonnes de la maison de liban: Desquels nous auōs donné raison ailleurs. Chose que les sauans & doctes peu curieux n'ont recherchée, pour estre sans aucune consequence en la doctrine: bien que celuy de Pline soit ecoulé a Harmolas barbare & a tous les traducteurs & planistes cōme plusieurs autres en Vitruue que lon a plustost trahis que traduis.

INDEX

240